D0523421

VITAL
SIGNS
1998

OTHER NORTON/WORLDWATCH BOOKS

Lester R. Brown et al.

State of the World 1984

State of the World 1985

State of the World 1986

State of the World 1987

State of the World 1988

State of the World 1989

State of the World 1990

State of the World 1991

State of the World 1992

State of the World 1993

State of the World 1994

State of the World 1995

State of the World 1996

State of the World 1997

State of the World 1998

Vital Signs 1992

Vital Signs 1993

Vital Signs 1994

Vital Signs 1995

Vital Signs 1996

Vital Signs 1997

ENVIRONMENTAL ALERT SERIES

Lester R. Brown et al.
Saving the Planet

Alan Thein Durning
How Much is Enough?

Sandra Postel
Last Oasis

Lester R. Brown
Hal Kane
Full House

Christopher Flavin
Nicholas Lenssen
Power Surge

Lester R. Brown
Who Will Feed China?

Lester R. Brown
Tough Choices

Michael Renner
Fighting for Survival

VITAL SIGNS

1998

The Environmental Trends That Are Shaping Our Future

Lester R. Brown

Michael Renner

Christopher Flavin

Editor: Linda Starke

with

Janet N. Abramovitz
Seth Dunn
Hilary F. French
Gary Gardner
Brian Halweil
Nicholas Lenssen
Ashley T. Mattoon

Anne Platt McGinn
Jennifer D. Mitchell
Molly O'Meara
David M. Roodman
Payal Sampat
Michael Strauss
John Tuxill

W.W. Norton & Company
New York   London

Copyright © 1998 by Worldwatch Institute

All rights reserved
Printed in the United States of America
First Edition

VITAL SIGNS and WORLDWATCH INSTITUTE trademarks are registered in the U.S. Patent
and Trademark Office.

The views expressed are those of the authors and do not necessarily represent those of
the Worldwatch Institute; of its directors, officers, or staff; or of its funders.

The text of this book is composed in Garth Graphic
with the display set in Industria Alternate.

Composition by the Worldwatch Institute; manufacturing by the Haddon Craftsmen, Inc.
Book design by Charlotte Staub.

ISBN 0-393-31762-5 (pbk)

W.W. Norton & Company, Inc.
500 Fifth Avenue, New York, NY 10110
W.W. Norton & Company Ltd.
10 Coptic Street, London WC1A 1PU

1234567890

This book is printed on recycled paper.

WORLDWATCH INSTITUTE BOARD OF DIRECTORS

Andrew E. Rice, Chairman
UNITED STATES

Øystein Dahle, Vice Chairman
NORWAY

Lester R. Brown (Ex Officio)
UNITED STATES

Carlo M. Cipolla
ITALY

Edward S. Cornish
UNITED STATES

Herman Daly
UNITED STATES

Orville L. Freeman
UNITED STATES

Lynne Gallagher
UNITED STATES

Mahbub ul Haq
PAKISTAN

Hazel Henderson
UNITED STATES

Abd-El Rahman Khane
ALGERIA

Larry Minear
UNITED STATES

Izaak van Melle
THE NETHERLANDS

Wren Wirth
UNITED STATES

WORLDWATCH INSTITUTE STAFF

Janet N. Abramovitz
Ed Ayres
Richard C. Bell
Chris Bright
Lester R. Brown
Lori A. Brown
Mary Caron
Suzanne Clift
Elizabeth A. Doherty

Seth Dunn
Barbara Fallin
Christopher Flavin
Hilary F. French
Gary Gardner
Joseph Gravely
Brian Halweil
Millicent Johnson
Reah Janise Kauffman

Sharon Lapier
Ashley T. Mattoon
Anne Platt McGinn
Molly O'Meara
Michael Renner
David Malin Roodman
Curtis Runyan
Payal Sampat
Amy Warehime

OFFICERS

Lester R. Brown
PRESIDENT

Christopher Flavin
SENIOR VICE PRESIDENT,
RESEARCH

Richard C. Bell
VICE PRESIDENT, COMMUNICATIONS

Hilary F. French
VICE PRESIDENT, RESEARCH

Reah Janise Kauffman
VICE PRESIDENT, SPECIAL ACTIVITIES

Barbara Fallin
ASSISTANT TREASURER

Worldwatch Database Disk

The data from all graphs and tables contained in this book, as well as from those in all other Worldwatch publications of the past two years, are available on disk for use with IBM-compatible or Macintosh computers. This includes data from the State of the World *and* Vital Signs *series of books, Worldwatch Papers,* World Watch *magazine, and the Environmental Alert series of books. The data are formatted for use with spreadsheet software compatible with Lotus 1-2-3 version 2, including all Lotus spreadsheets, Quattro Pro, Excel, SuperCalc, and many others. For IBM-compatibles, a 3½-inch (high-density) disk is provided. Information on how to order the Worldwatch Database Disk can be found on the final page of this book.*

CONTENTS

Part One: KEY INDICATORS

Part Two: SPECIAL FEATURES

ACKNOWLEDGMENTS

The research and writing to produce *Vital Signs 1998* have been generously supported by the W. Alton Jones Foundation, the United Nations Environment Programme, and the Surdna Foundation.

But *Vital Signs* could not easily be assembled without the work done to put together the Institute's other publications—the annual *State of the World*, the bimonthly *World Watch* magazine, and the monographs published in the Worldwatch Paper series. These efforts rely on financial support from additional foundations and donors. We therefore also thank the Geraldine R. Dodge Foundation, the Foundation for Ecology and Development, the Ford Foundation, the William and Flora Hewlett Foundation, the John D. and Catherine T. MacArthur Foundation, the Charles Stewart Mott Foundation, the David and Lucille Packard Foundation, the Rasmussen Foundation, the Rockefeller Brothers Fund, Rockefeller Financial Services, the Summit Foundation, the Turner Foundation, the Wallace Genetic Foundation, the Wallace Global Fund, the Weeden Foundation, and the Winslow Foundation.

In addition, we would like to acknowledge those individuals who have provided support to Worldwatch Institute through our Friends of Worldwatch campaign. Special appreciation goes to our newly established Council of Sponsors: Toshishige Kurosawa, Kazuhiko Nishi, Roger and Vicki Sant, Robert Wallace, and Eckart Wintzen.

As in the previous editions of *Vital Signs*, independent editor Linda Starke played a crucial role in melding 54 individual manuscripts written by 17 different authors into a coherent set of indicators and features. Our in-house designer Elizabeth Doherty efficiently converted disparate file formats and graphs into the visually consistent series of texts, tables, and figures that our readers have come to expect. And we thank Lori Brown for making sure, as in years past, that all the tables and figures contained in the printed version of *Vital Signs* are properly incorporated into the Worldwatch Database Disk. Lori, together with Laura Malinowski, runs our library and keeps researchers amply supplied with everything from books and magazines to Web-derived materials.

In addition to current Worldwatch researchers, alumni Nick Lenssen, Jennifer Mitchell, and Mike Strauss contributed to the book from Colorado, Tennessee, and California, respectively. John Tuxill continues to pitch in from rural Panama. Seth Dunn, Brian Halweil, and Jennifer Mitchell not only prepared their own pieces, but also assisted with several others. Research intern Sophie Chou also helped with the book.

Beyond the research team, we are grateful to Vice President Reah Janise Kauffman, who assists in fundraising and serves as liaison with our domestic and foreign publishers, 20 of whom have published editions of *Vital Signs*. And without the bedrock of support from our administrative team of Barbara Fallin and Suzanne Clift, our communications team headed by Vice President Richard Bell and assisted by Mary Caron and Amy

Acknowledgments

Warehime, and our publications and sales support team of Millicent Johnson and Joseph Gravely, we could not publish, market, and disseminate *Vital Signs*.

Authors received feedback on drafts and critical inputs from a broad variety of outside experts. We would like to thank Markus Amann, Franz Baumann, Gerhard Berz, John Bloom, Nils Borg, Dirk Bryant, Chris Calwell, Mary Cesar, Janusz Cofala, John Culjak, Linda Doman, Lynne Gallagher, Catherine Godfrey, Chris Granda, Nigel Griffiths, James Hansen, Carl Haub, Mark Hereward, Jos Heyman, Paul Hunt, Frank Jamerson, Nicole Klingen, Murray Langesen, Birger Madsen, Laura Mannisto, Paul Maycock, Emily Miggins, Mika Ohbayashi, James Paul, Maurizio Perotti, John Pucher, Rob Quayle, William Quinby, Thomas Rabehl, Sunil Andrew Rajkumar, Richard Reynolds, Mark Rosegrant, Klaus Schlichte, Vladimir Sliviak, Margareta Sollenberg, David Sweanor, Arnella Trent, Rowena van der Merwe, Andreas Wagner, Rebecca Wetteman, and Timothy Whorf.

Finally, we want to once again express our gratitude to Nomi Victor and Andrew Marasia and their colleagues at W.W. Norton & Company for their unwavering support for *Vital Signs*—from the first edition in 1992 to the present, seventh, edition. Sadly, we end this year's acknowledgments by noting the passing of our closest collaborator and supporter at Norton: Iva Ashner. Over 14 years of working together, Iva was a true friend to Worldwatch. We will miss her.

Lester R. Brown
Michael Renner
Christopher Flavin

FOREWORD

We live, it is often said, in the "information age." Satellite television, fax machines, cellular telephones, and, of course, the Internet deliver instant, round-the-clock entertainment, news, and communications to even remote corners of the world. Such technology delivers text, sound, and still and moving images via far-flung computer networks at the click of a mouse.

Individuals and organizations can choose from an enormous, often overwhelming array of information. The new technologies make it almost trivially easy to send digitized scientific data and essential news around the globe, yet they convey misleading advertising, disjointed "factoids," and mindless entertainment just as easily. Indeed, much of what the information age has to offer caters to the trivial, the transient, or the fashionable.

The problem today is not the quantity of information, or the speed with which it is delivered, but the need to figure out which facts we need, and to separate knowledge from rumors. In our fast-changing world, accurate, relevant information is becoming ever more urgent for policymakers, businesspeople, international diplomats, community activists, and "ordinary" citizens alike. The premium is on interdisciplinary perspectives that transcend the confines of any particular academic specialty, international information that goes beyond the limited perspective of any single country or culture, insights on the interaction between human societies and natural systems, and "historical" information that is cognizant of the past but attentive to the needs of future generations.

With this seventh edition of *Vital Signs*, we again bring together an eclectic selection of disparate trends to offer a unique, multifaceted view of our rapidly changing world. In transportation, we have compiled the latest figures for world automobile production, but we report annual bicycle production as well—which is more than twice as high. In energy, we describe the 1.4-percent increase in oil consumption in 1997, but also note the 25-percent increase in wind power generation. In fishing, we point to the 1.9-percent increase in the fish catch in 1997, as well as the 11-percent increase in aquaculture production the preceding year.

Among the trends covered for the first time in *Vital Signs 1998* are frontier forests, plantation forestry, satellite launches, minerals exploration, small arms proliferation, and female education. By focusing on "minor" trends that other statistical reports leave out, we hope to identify some of the "leading edge" indicators that could be key to a more sustainable economic system in the next century. The production of highly efficient compact fluorescent light bulbs, for example, has soared eightfold in the past nine years; the 980 million bulbs now in use require the equivalent of 43 nuclear power plants less electricity than conventional incandescent bulbs.

In the future, renewable energy technologies and sustainable agriculture practices may overtake conventional technologies in the same way that the Internet is now coming to dominate the global telecommunications business. We note in this year's book that the number of Internet host computers grew by an impressive 36 percent in 1997, but global output of solar cells grew even faster—at 43 percent.

Still, despite these many small signs of success, the world has a long way to go to forge a sustainable society. This year's *Vital Signs* points out that global emissions of carbon, the leading contributor to global climate change, hit another new high, while nitrogen pollution also rose and frontier forests shrank as vast fires swept the Amazon Basin and large sections of Southeast Asia. By providing detailed, timely information on these trends and others, we help to mobilize policymakers and the public to reverse them.

To spread the word as broadly as possible, *Vital Signs* is now published in 21 languages, including Georgian and Spanish for the first time in the past year. The other languages include Arabic, Catalan, Chinese, Dutch, English, Estonian, Finnish, French, German, Indonesian, Italian, Japanese, Korean, Persian, Polish, Romanian, Thai, Turkish, and Vietnamese. Both *Vital Signs* and our database disk, which contains all the raw data from the book, are now widely used in university classrooms, corporate offices, and government agencies. In the future, we hope to make this information available on our Web site: < www.worldwatch.org >, and on a CD-ROM.

Thank you for reading *Vital Signs 1998*, and please let us know by e-mail or regular post how you use the book. Also, please tell us if you have ideas for new trends we should consider including in future editions.

Lester R. Brown
Michael Renner
Christopher Flavin
March 1998

Worldwatch Institute
1776 Massachusetts Ave., N.W.
Washington, DC 20036

VITAL
SIGNS
1998

OVERVIEW

New Records, New Stresses

Lester R. Brown

The world today is warmer, more crowded, more urban, economically richer, and environmentally poorer than ever before. This past year was one of near-record global economic growth—and of disturbing new signs of environmental stress.

In 1997, the Earth's average temperature was the highest since recordkeeping began in 1866. With each additional year of record or near-record temperature, the evidence of human-induced climate change becomes more convincing. In December 1997, government representatives gathered in Kyoto, Japan, to negotiate an agreement to reverse the rise in carbon emissions from human activities, with the hope of eventually checking the increase in temperature.

At the end of 1997, we shared the Earth with 80 million more people than a year earlier. Of this total, nearly 50 million people were added in Asia, the region that is already home to more than half of humanity. Each month, the world adds the equivalent of another Sweden. And it becomes more urban with each passing day: In 1800, only London had a million people. Now there are 326 cities that are at least that size. Sometime in the next decade, the number of people living in cities is expected to surpass those in the countryside.

Despite financial turmoil in Southeast Asia, the global economy expanded by 4.1 percent in 1997, marking the third consecutive year with growth of 4 percent or more. Economic output per person jumped by 2.6 percent. If the global economy continues to expand as projected, output per person worldwide will top $5,000 for the first time in 1998.

Signs of environmental stress continue to accumulate. Among the more disturbing in 1997 was the uncontrolled burning of Indonesia's rainforests, a conflagration that filled the air in the region with smoke for several months—smoke so intense at times in Indonesia and Malaysia that it caused acute respiratory stress, leaving millions physically sick. It led to the cancellation of 1,100 flights and a precipitous drop in earnings from tourism. The economic mismanagement in Indonesia that has led to bad debt, failing banks, and a falling currency has also weakened the rainforests to the point where they now burn out of control during droughts like the one induced by El Niño.

The Yellow River, the northernmost of China's two major rivers, was drained dry by withdrawals from upstream provinces for several months, failing to make it to the sea for the thirteenth consecutive year. The river ran dry for longer than ever before, and in 1997

Units of measure throughout this book are metric unless common usage dictates otherwise. Historical population data used in per capita calculations are from the Center for International Research at the U.S. Bureau of the Census. Historical data series in *Vital Signs* are updated each year, incorporating any revisions done by originating organizations.

failed to reach the sea for 226 days out of 365. Farmers in the lower reaches of the river, deprived of irrigation water, saw their grain output fall.

FOOD: SURPLUSES TO SCARCITY

In 1997, the world's farmers harvested a record 1,881 million tons of grain, narrowly eclipsing 1996's record harvest of 1,869 million tons. (See pages 28–29.) Although the harvest rose, it did not keep up with population growth, so per capita grain output dropped from 324 kilograms to 322 kilograms. The drop in per capita grain production worldwide of more than 6 percent since its all-time peak in 1984 is one indication that the half-century dominated by food surpluses may be coming to an end.

As recently as 1990, the world had two food reserves to call upon—carryover stocks of grain (the amount in the bin when a new harvest begins) and cropland idled under U.S. farm commodity programs that were designed to avoid price-depressing world grain surpluses. In 1995, the farm support programs were dismantled, letting the set-aside land be returned to production in 1996. The 11 million hectares of grainland held out in 1990, assuming a yield of 4 tons per hectare, represented a reserve of 44 million tons—nearly nine days of world consumption.

Even with this land back in production in 1996 and 1997, however, the world was not able to rebuild its depleted grain stocks. (See pages 38–39.) With carryover stocks of grain remaining below 60 days of world consumption, the world has little more than pipeline supplies. One poor harvest could lead to chaos in world grain markets.

Along with the scarcity of productive new land to bring under the plow and the diminishing response to the use of additional fertilizer in many countries, water scarcity is emerging as a serious constraint on efforts to expand world food production. For example, in North Africa and the Middle East—from Morocco in the west through Iran in the east—water shortages are making it impossi-

ble for farmers to keep up with the growth in demand. As countries in the region push against the limits of their water supplies, the growing demand by cities is typically satisfied by diverting irrigation water from farmers. Countries then are forced to import grain to offset the loss of irrigation water. Importing a ton of wheat is the same as importing a thousand tons of water. In 1997, the water required to produce the grain imported into this region was equal to the annual flow of the Nile River.

Under China's north central plain, which supplies nearly 40 percent of the country's grain harvest, the water table is falling by a reported 1.5 meters per year. At some point in the not too distant future, aquifer depletion in this region will lead to sharp cutbacks in irrigation water supplies. The bottom line is that if the world is facing a future of water scarcity, it is also facing a future of food scarcity.

AN APPETITE FOR PROTEIN

Perhaps the single most important distinguishing feature of dietary changes over the last half-century has been the growing appetite for animal protein. It is hunger for protein that spurred an increase in the world fish catch of nearly fivefold, boosting it from 19 million tons in 1950 to 93 million tons today. (See pages 34–35 and Figure 1.) This has pushed the oceans to their limits and in some cases beyond. Marine biologists at the U.N. Food and Agriculture Organization report that almost every oceanic fishery is now being fished at or beyond capacity.

As we reach the limits of the oceans to supply animal protein, many countries are turning to aquaculture, or fish farming. (See pages 36–37.) The disadvantage of fish farming is that fish in ponds or cages have to be fed—just like chickens in coops. Fish farmers are now competing with poultry and pork producers for grain and protein meal supplements, such as soybean meal.

Worldwide, the production of beef and mutton, like that of fish, depends heavily on

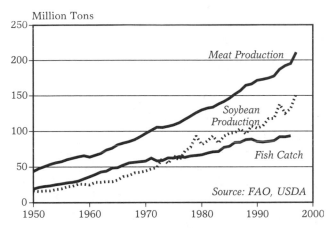

Figure 1: **World Protein Trends, 1950–97**

At 152 million tons, the world soybean harvest in 1997 was nine times larger than in 1950. (See pages 30–31.)

Although the soybean, the world's leading source of high-quality protein, originated in China, it has found its agronomic and economic niche in the United States, which produces half of the global harvest. Grown largely in rotation with corn, especially in the Corn Belt, the U.S. soybean harvest is now worth far more than the wheat harvest.

ENERGY REVOLUTION UNDER WAY

Although the changes in the world protein economy are dramatic, to say the least, even more far-reaching changes are in prospect in the world energy economy. Energy historians may remember 1997 as the year in which two of the world's largest oil companies announced they were making major investments in solar and wind energy. With the commitment of $1 billion and $500 million, respectively, by British Petroleum and Royal Dutch Shell to the development of wind,

a natural system—rangelands. And, like oceanic fisheries, rangelands are being pushed to the limits of their carrying capacity and beyond. Once rangelands are fully exploited and substantial growth in beef production can come only from feedlots, then the competition with pork and poultry for grain intensifies. Chickens, which require scarcely 2 kilograms of grain concentrate to produce a kilogram of live weight, have a decided advantage over cattle in the feedlot, which require nearly 7 kilograms of grain per kilogram of weight gain. As a consequence, world poultry production has now overtaken beef for the first time in history. (See pages 32–33 and Figure 2.)

Beef and pork production, which were running neck and neck from mid-century until 1978, have now separated: in 1997, pork production was easily a third higher than beef. Much of this surge in world pork production came in China, where half the world's pork is now produced and consumed.

One consequence of the growing demand for animal protein has been a dramatic growth in world soybean production over the last 50 years, since pork and poultry producers depend heavily on soybean meal as a supplement to grain in their feed rations.

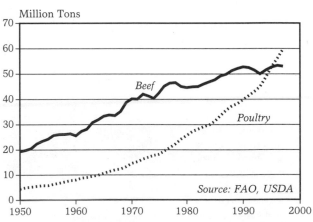

Figure 2: **World Poultry and Beef Production, 1950–97**

17

solar, and other renewable energy resources, these leading oil companies have, in effect, become energy companies. And they have indicated that they take the threat of global warming seriously.

From a commercial point of view, it is not too surprising that oil companies are beginning to look at renewable energy resources. Thus far during the 1990s, sales of coal and oil have grown just over 1 percent a year. (See pages 50–53 and Table 1.) The sale of natural gas, regarded by many as a transition fuel from the fossil fuel era to the solar/hydrogen age, has been growing at 2 percent a year since 1990. Wind power, meanwhile, has grown an amazing 26 percent a year. (See pages 58–59.) And sales of solar cells, averaging 15 percent annually from 1990 through 1996, jumped by a phenomenal 43 percent in 1997. (See pages 60–61.) At the end of the year, an estimated 400,000 homes, most of them in Third World villages, were getting their electricity from solar cell arrays.

Advancing technology is also fueling this growth in solar cell use. The use of a photovoltaic roofing material developed in Japan is now growing by leaps and bounds. The Japanese government plans to have in place 4,600 megawatts of rooftop generating capacity by 2010, an output comparable to the electricity generation of a country the size of Chile.

Corporations in the energy business that are interested in growth are starting to shift investments from oil, coal, and nuclear power, where growth is at a near standstill, to wind and solar, which have rather spectacular growth rates. Once thought of as fringe energy sources, wind and photovoltaic cells are seen increasingly as mainstays of the new energy economy now emerging. A wind resource survey by the U.S. Department of Energy, for example, concluded that North Dakota, South Dakota, and Texas had enough harnessable wind energy to meet all U.S. electricity needs. Today, the world gets roughly one fifth of its electricity from hydropower, but its potential is dwarfed by that of wind.

The energy revolution is not limited to new sources of energy. It also involves some dramatic gains in the efficiency of energy use. One of these involves the compact fluorescent light bulb, which provides the same amount of light as traditional incandescents, but with less than one fourth as much electricity. Sales of compact fluorescent bulbs have climbed from 45 million in 1988 to 356 million in 1997, an eightfold increase, with China now the leading manufacturer. (See pages 62–63.) The estimated 980 million compact fluorescent bulbs in use today lower electricity needs by the output of roughly 100 coal-fired power plants.

THE DESIRE FOR MOBILITY

Evidence of the human desire to become more mobile is reflected in sales of vehicles, such as bicycles, motorbikes, and automobiles. Although world production of bikes and cars was roughly the same in 1969, at just

TABLE 1. TRENDS IN ENERGY USE, BY SOURCE, 1990–97[1]

ENERGY SOURCE	ANNUAL RATE OF GROWTH (percent)
Wind power	25.7
Solar photovoltaics	16.8
Geothermal power[2]	3.0
Natural gas	2.1
Hydroelectric power[2]	1.6
Oil	1.4
Coal	1.2
Nuclear power	0.6

[1]Energy use measured in varying units: installed generating capacity (megawatts or gigawatts) for wind, geothermal, hydro, and nuclear power; million tons of oil equivalent for oil, natural gas, and coal; megawatts for shipments of solar photovoltaic cells. [2]1990–96 only. SOURCES: See pages 50–61.

over 20 million, the gap between the two has widened dramatically since then. (See pages 86–87, pages 90–91, and Figure 3.) Now more than 100 million bicycles come off the assembly lines each year, compared with fewer than 40 million automobiles. In 1997, car production increased more than 5 percent over 1996. Bicycle production, meanwhile, suffering from too much capacity and excessive inventories, dropped in 1996 (the latest year for which data are available) to 101 million from 109 million the year before.

The enormous differences in the sales volume of bicycles and automobiles reflects more than anything else the number of people reaching the level of affluence that lets them buy bicycles versus the much smaller number who can afford an automobile. In addition, those living in cities, particularly crowded Asian cities, have discovered that they can often be more mobile with a modest investment in a bike than with a far larger investment in an car.

Several countries in Europe systematically try to increase bicycle use. In Danish and Dutch cities, an estimated 20 percent and 30 percent respectively of all trips are taken by bicycle. Bikes have also been strongly encouraged in Germany, where use has increased by

50 percent over the last two decades.

In recent years, electric bicycles have begun to attract attention. Relying on a small battery, these provide electrical assistance on hills and in other situations that enable the average speed of the bicycle to increase. The technology is particularly attractive to older riders, to those who have to contend with hilly terrain, or to those who have a particularly long daily commute.

WORLD GETTING WARMER

In 1997, carbon emissions, carbon dioxide (CO_2) concentrations in the atmosphere, and the Earth's average temperature all climbed to record highs. Carbon emissions in 1997 totaled 6.3 billion tons, up 1.5 percent from the 6.2 billion tons of 1996. (See pages 66–67.) Atmospheric concentrations of CO_2 climbed to 364 parts per million—the highest in 160,000 years. (See Figure 4.) The Intergovernmental Panel on Climate Change, a body of some 1,500 of the world's leading meteorologists and other scientists, estimates that annual carbon emissions will have to drop below 2 billion tons by 2050 if atmospheric concentrations of CO_2 are to stabilize.

With the record temperature of 1997, the 14 warmest years since recordkeeping began in 1866 have all occurred since 1979. (See pages 68–69 and Figure 5.) And the 5 warmest have come during the 1990s. Although this strong warming trend over the last two decades does not provide absolute proof of CO_2-induced climate change, it is yet another piece of evidence that global warming is indeed under way.

Additional evidence can be found in melting icecaps in the Andes, shrinking glaciers in the European Alps, and the shrinkage in the sea ice around Antarctica. The combination of ice melting and the expansion of water from warm-

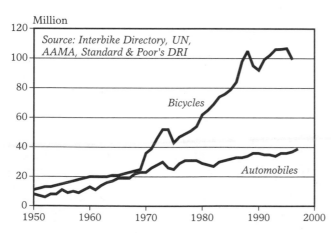

Figure 3: World Bicycle and Automobile Production, 1950–97

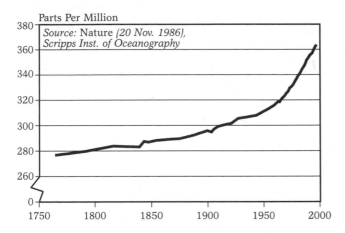

Figure 4: Atmospheric Concentrations of Carbon Dioxide, 1764–1997

ing has raised average sea level between 10 and 25 centimeters over the last century.

ALTERING NATURAL SYSTEMS

By far the most visible human alteration of the planet has been the destruction of forests. Almost half the forests that once covered vast expanses of the Earth are already gone. Between 1980 and 1995, the world lost at least 200 million hectares of forest—an area three times as large as Texas. In recent years, the world has experienced an estimated net loss of 16 million hectares a year. (See pages 124–25.)

The amount of nitrogen fixed in forms that plants can use through fertilizer manufacturing, the burning of fossil fuels, and the extensive planting of leguminous crops such as soybeans now exceeds the amount fixed by nature. (See pages 132–33.) Synthesized nitrogen fertilizer, the use of which has increased ninefold since 1950, is the major form of nitrogen fixation as a result of human activities. Wherever it leads to excessive nutrient runoff, as it does in the Midwest and the lower Mississippi Valley, it often leads to vast algal blooms that then decay, absorbing the free oxygen in the water and depriving fish of oxygen. The hypoxic region, or "dead zone," now formed through this process each year in the Gulf of Mexico is roughly the size of New Jersey.

Closely associated with the burning of fossil fuels is the emission of sulfur dioxide and nitrous oxides, which combine with moisture in the atmosphere to form acid rain. Although emissions of these two pollutants have been sharply reduced in North America and Western Europe, they are still climbing rapidly in Asia. (See pages 134–35.) Acid deposition in parts of China is now far higher than the levels reached in Japan in 1975 before that nation established stringent emission limits. Acids can eliminate fish in freshwater lakes, rendering them lifeless.

Another economic activity that is particularly disruptive of the environment is mining. In recent years, mineral exploration has expanded dramatically in developing coun-

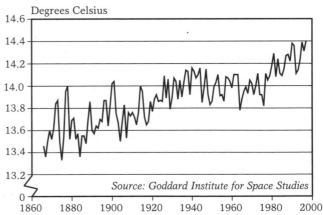

Figure 5: Average Temperature at the Earth's Surface, 1866–1997

tries as mines have been depleted in industrial nations. (See pages 148–49.) Gold mining is especially disruptive. The 2,400 tons of gold produced in 1997 generated 725 million tons of waste—one ton of waste for every eight people on the planet. In addition to the physical disruption that gold mining brings, the resulting waste includes large quantities of cyanide solution and mercury, which are used to separate gold from the ore.

One of the consequences of the many alterations in the environment just described is an accelerating loss of species. The most recent study of the state of life on Earth by the World Conservation Union–IUCN estimates that 11 percent of all bird species are threatened with extinction. (See pages 128–29.) For fish, the figure is far higher—34 percent. In the U.S. Colorado River basin, 29 of 50 native fish species are either endangered or already extinct. Among the 233 species of primates, of which humans are one, half are now threatened with extinction. The surviving populations of some primate species are measured in the hundreds.

CHANGING SOCIAL CONDITIONS

As noted earlier, at the end of 1997 we shared the planet with 80 million more people than at the beginning of the year. (See pages 102–03.) Close to 60 percent of these people were added in Asia, in countries that are already densely populated. If recent urbanization trends continue, in a few years—for the first time in human history—more people will live in cities than in the countryside. (See pages 108–09.)

Educational levels are rising worldwide. Among the more prominent gains in recent years has been the increase in female education in developing countries. (See pages 154–55.) Between 1990 and 1995, female enrollment in some 47 developing countries surveyed by the U.S. Agency for International Development increased from 226 million to 254 million. As a result, nearly 70 percent of girls of primary-school age worldwide were in school in 1995. Notwithstanding this progress,

a third of all children in the developing world fail to complete even four years of education.

In industrial countries, the big difference between men and women in educational achievement traditionally has been in graduate degrees in professional schools. But now this, too, is changing. Law and business school enrollments are approaching gender parity. In medical schools in the United States and Canada, more than 40 percent of students are female. For veterinary schools, it is nearly 70 percent. In engineering and architecture schools, however, men still greatly outnumber women.

Of the social trends that affect human health most directly, the spread of HIV is among the most destructive. In 1997, nearly 6 million people were newly infected with the virus that causes AIDS, bringing the total infected worldwide to 42 million. (See pages 106–07.) Although a majority of HIV infections are found in Africa, the number of new infections is growing fastest in Asia. Some countries, such as Uganda and Thailand, have made impressive progress in checking the spread of HIV. In sheer numbers, the principal threats today are in India and China: prostitutes in Bombay, India, and intravenous drug users in parts of China have infection rates over 50 percent. If the virus cannot be contained in these early centers of infection, it could spread rapidly in these huge populations, infecting record numbers. With 2.3 million fatalities in 1997, this new disease now claims more than twice as many lives as malaria.

One threat to health that affects far more people than AIDS is cigarette smoking. Roughly half of those who smoke will eventually be killed by the effects of this habit, either through heart disease, stroke, or lung cancer or through one of the many other life-threatening illnesses associated with smoking.

In 1997, the world produced some 5.8 trillion cigarettes, roughly 1,000 for each of its 5.8 billion men, women, and children. (See pages 110–11.) The one encouraging sign is that production is not expanding as fast as population. As a result, the number of cigarettes manufactured per person has fallen 4 percent from the all-time high reached in 1990. China is by far the largest manufacturer of cigarettes, followed by the United States.

While cigarette smoking has been declining in industrial countries, it has been expanding rapidly in developing ones. If recent smoking trends continue, tobacco-related deaths, now estimated at 3 million annually, could reach 10 million in 2020, with 70 percent of them being in the developing world. Raising taxes on cigarettes in many countries has helped reduce smoking and the soaring health care costs associated with this deadly habit. (See pages 146–47.) In some countries, including Norway, the United Kingdom, and Denmark, the tax per pack of cigarettes now exceeds $4. This compares with a cigarette tax in the United States of 66¢ per pack.

One developing country that is making progress in reducing cigarette smoking is the Philippines, where a combination of an aggressive educational effort and a stiff new tax on cigarettes lowered cigarette production by 16 percent. In some countries, higher cigarette taxes have achieved dramatic results. For example, in New Zealand an increase in the tax per pack of nearly $2 between 1980 and 1991 reduced the cigarettes smoked per person from 4,100 a year to just over 1,500. And in Belgium, a 46-percent increase in cigarette prices between 1985 and 1995 appears to have cut cigarette consumption by one fourth. A number of national governments, as well as California and Massachusetts in the United States, use the cigarette tax proceeds to fund educational programs to discourage smoking.

A WIRED WORLD

Although more than a century has passed since Alexander Graham Bell invented the telephone, most people in the world do not yet have ready access to this modern mode of communication. The good news is that the number of new telephone hookups is increasing at 7 percent a year, bringing the total number of hookups to 740 million in 1996.

(See pages 96–97.) Since 1960, the telephone network has expanded eightfold.

The number of telephones per 100 people varies widely from country to country. The United States, for example, has a telephone density of 60 phones per 100 people, while China has 4. Most of the growth in phone installations is now coming in developing countries, where the number of telephones is increasing by 19 percent a year.

Even more exciting in terms of facilitating communication among people is the worldwide boom in cellular phones, the number of which has increased by more than half each year since 1991. By 1996, there were 135 million cellular phone subscribers worldwide.

Although this technology was first adopted in industrial countries, it is moving even more rapidly in developing ones. In those that have not yet invested in a vast network of telephone lines strung along poles, the cellular phone—linked either by relay towers or, within the next year or two, by a network of satellites—will conserve millions of tons of copper and wood. It enables developing countries to literally leapfrog into the future, avoiding investment in traditional equipment and networks.

Increasing even more rapidly than the number of telephones is the number of computers linked together electronically. In 1997, there were more than 30 million host computers on the Internet. (See pages 98–99.) The number of Internet users was far greater, since one host computer could plug several computers into the global network. The number of personal computers now linked together is estimated at more than 100 million.

Of the 100 million or so people who are online, more than half are in the United States. Most of the rest are in Australia, Europe, Canada, and Japan. Thus far, developing countries have only 8 percent of the Internet hookups. But like the telephone network, the Internet is now expanding rapidly in poorer countries. For example, Internet access has grown fivefold in Brazil and Russia in the last two years alone. Hookups are also increasing rapidly in China and India, where the numbers in 2000 are projected at 4 million and 1.5 million, respectively.

One technology facilitating the explosion in electronic communications is satellites. The number of satellites launched annually has exceeded 100 in all but a few years since 1965, typically ranging between 100 and 150. (See pages 94–95.) Thirty years ago, just over half the satellites launched were for military purposes—reconnaissance, surveillance, and other military uses. With the end of the cold war, this shifted dramatically. In 1997, only 8 percent of satellites launched were for military uses, while 69 percent were for communications. Over the next decade, some 1,700 additional communications satellites—10 times the number now in orbit—are scheduled for launch. This new generation of satellites, mostly for low orbit, is expected to revolutionize global communications.

DEMILITARIZATION CONTINUES

After peaking in 1984 at $1,140 billion (in 1995 dollars), global military expenditures dropped to $701 billion in 1996, a decline of 39 percent. (See pages 114–15.) The United States still accounts for one third of the total. But at $243 billion in 1997, U.S. military outlays were down from some $370 billion in the late 1980s. The most precipitous drop has occurred in Eastern Europe and the former Soviet republics, where expenditures have fallen from $247 billion in 1985 to just $21 billion in 1995.

The number of armed conflicts is also declining. In 1992, the number exceeded 50, but by 1997 it had dropped to 24. (See pages 116–17.) In contrast to earlier historical periods, nearly all these armed conflicts were taking place within rather than between nations. They involved government forces, paramilitary forces, insurgent and guerilla bands, and drug warlords, among others. Unfortunately, civilians are more often the victims of these conflicts than in earlier eras—rising from 67 percent of the victims in World War II to 90 percent in the 1990s. The heaviest fighting in 1996 was in Afghanistan, Algeria, Sri Lanka,

Sudan, and Turkey, typically involving ethnic, tribal, or religious conflicts.

This decline in armed conflicts, particularly in countries such as Croatia and Angola, also reduced the U.N. peacekeeping presence. After peaking at $3.3 billion in 1994, U.N. peacekeeping expenditures dropped to an estimated $1.3 billion in 1997. (See pages 118–19.)

ENVIRONMENTAL CHANGE: THE FISCAL FACTOR

As analysts have focused on the magnitude of changes needed to convert the existing fossil-fuel-based, automobile-centered, throwaway economy into one that is environmentally sustainable, it is clear that an increasingly popular instrument for doing this is fiscal policy. At present, most governments tax income and savings heavily. But working and saving are constructive activities and should be encouraged. Activities that should be discouraged include carbon emissions, sulfur emissions, the generation of hazardous waste, the use of virgin raw materials (as opposed to recycled ones), and the use of pesticides.

Six European countries have begun this tax shifting process. (See pages 140–41.) Sweden, Denmark, Spain, the Netherlands, the United Kingdom, and Finland have all begun reducing taxes on personal income and wages while raising taxes on such things as carbon emissions, vehicle ownership, and landfilling.

The other side of this coin is that governments have long subsidized environmentally destructive activities, with the most important activity being the use of fossil fuels. One reason fossil fuel use and carbon emissions have declined so precipitously in the former Soviet republics and Eastern Europe is that subsidies have been sharply reduced during the 1990s. In 1991, subsidies for fossil fuel use in the former Soviet Union and Eastern Europe exceeded $130 billion. By 1995, this had dropped to $40 billion. (See pages 142–43.)

Substantial cuts in fossil fuel subsidies have also occurred in China, from $26 billion to $11 billion thus far during the 1990s.

These cuts in China have led to higher coal prices and more-efficient energy use. The United Kingdom was able to cut its carbon emissions during this decade in part because it largely eliminated the subsidies to coal mines, many of which were too inefficient to compete on their own.

Although the world is still in the early stages of restructuring fiscal policies to achieve environmental goals, this approach does promise to accelerate the shift to an environmentally sustainable economy. One advantage of tax policy over regulation is that it enables policymakers to steer the economy in the right direction while exploiting the inherent efficiency of the market.

Part **ONE**

Key Indicators

Food

Trends

Grain Harvest Up Slightly   Lester R. Brown

At 1,881 million tons, the 1997 world grain harvest was up slightly from the previous record of 1,869 million tons in 1996.[1] (See Figure 1.) Yet production per person dropped from 324 kilograms in 1996 to 322 kilograms, a decline of nearly 1 percent.[2] (See Figure 2.) More important, the 1997 per capita figure was 6 percent below the all-time high of 342 kilograms in 1984.[3]

With good harvests in the major producing countries, wheat was the big gainer in 1997. (See Figure 3.) Record or near-record harvests in China, India, the United States, and the European Union pushed world wheat production to 609 million tons, passing 600 million tons for the first time.[4] This was up from 583 million tons in 1996, a gain of more than 4 percent.[5]

Although it may surprise many people, the world's leading wheat producer today is China. With a record 124-million-ton harvest, China is now getting close to doubling the U.S. wheat harvest of 69 million tons.[6] Indeed, in some recent years, India also has eclipsed the United States, moving into the number two slot.[7]

The 1997 rice harvest barely held on to the gain of the year before, edging up to 382 million tons from 378 million tons.[8] Gains in the rice harvests in Myanmar (formerly Burma), India, and Thailand were largely offset by slight declines in Indonesia and Japan.[9] Not surprisingly, the world's two leading rice producers are China and India. With harvests of 139 million tons and 82 million tons, respectively, these two population giants accounted for nearly 60 percent of the world rice harvest.[10]

Production of corn, the third major grain, totaled 579 million tons in 1997, down from the all-time high of 592 million tons the year before.[11] Most of the reduction in the world corn crop came in China, the number two producer, where heat and drought dropped the harvest from 127 million tons to 105 million tons, a decline of 17 percent.[12]

The U.S. corn crop, essentially unchanged at 238 million tons, accounts for a staggering 41 percent of the world corn crop and more than one eighth of the overall grain harvest.[13] This is far and away the largest harvest of a single grain by any country. Corn, the only grain crop originating in the New World, also has the highest worldwide yield per hectare of any grain.[14]

The big news on the grain front is the apparent loss of momentum in the growth of the world harvest during the 1990s. Even though the 11 million hectares of cropland that were idled under U.S. farm commodity programs in 1990 (1.6 percent of the world grainland total) have been returned to production, the world grain harvest has grown barely 1 percent a year since 1990.[15]

The backlog of unused agricultural technology that farmers can use to raise yields appears to be shrinking. For some farmers, such as U.S. wheat growers and Japanese rice growers, there are simply not many unused technologies available to raise yields. Even farmers in some developing countries, such as wheat growers in Mexico and rice growers in South Korea, are having difficulty sustaining the rise in yields.[16]

Spreading water scarcity is also slowing growth in the harvest. The fastest-growing grain import market during the 1990s is North Africa and the Middle East.[17] In this region, which stretches from Morocco through Iran, demand is driven by record population growth rates and by oil-generated gains in incomes. On the supply side, efforts to expand production in the region are being hampered by water scarcity. In 1997, the water required to produce the grain imported into this region was roughly equal to the annual flow of the Nile.[18]

The bottom line is that the world's farmers are now struggling to keep up with the growth in demand. Despite unprecedented advances in technology in fields such as computers, telecommunications, and space exploration, the ancient struggle to make it to the next harvest is emerging as a major preoccupation of governments in many developing countries.

WORLD GRAIN PRODUCTION, 1950–97

YEAR	TOTAL (mill. tons)	PER CAPITA (kilograms)
1950	631	247
1955	759	273
1960	824	271
1965	905	270
1966	989	289
1967	1,014	291
1968	1,053	296
1969	1,063	293
1970	1,079	291
1971	1,177	311
1972	1,141	295
1973	1,253	318
1974	1,204	300
1975	1,237	303
1976	1,342	323
1977	1,319	312
1978	1,445	336
1979	1,410	322
1980	1,430	321
1981	1,482	327
1982	1,533	333
1983	1,469	313
1984	1,632	342
1985	1,647	339
1986	1,665	337
1987	1,598	318
1988	1,549	304
1989	1,670	322
1990	1,768	335
1991	1,708	319
1992	1,790	329
1993	1,714	310
1994	1,763	314
1995	1,711	301
1996	1,869	324
1997 (prel)	1,881	322

SOURCES: USDA, *Production, Supply, and Distribution,* electronic database, February 1998; USDA, "World Grain Database," unpublished printout, 1991; USDA, FAS, *Grain: World Markets and Trade,* December 1997.

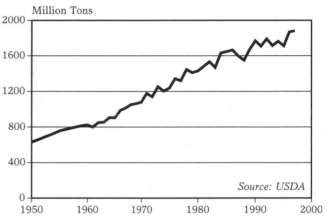

Figure 1: World Grain Production, 1950–97

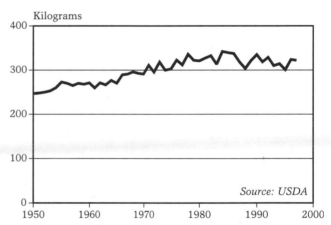

Figure 2: World Grain Production Per Person, 1950–97

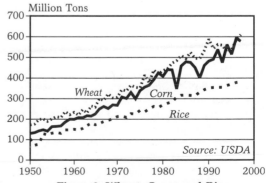

Figure 3: Wheat, Corn, and Rice Production, 1950–97

Soybean Production Jumps   Lester R. Brown

World soybean production in 1997 jumped to a record 152 million tons, up 15 percent from 1996 and 10 percent above the previous record, set in 1994.[1] (See Figure 1.) In per capita terms, the 26.0 kilograms produced in 1997 also set a new record, up from the previous high of 24.6 kilograms in 1994.[2] (See Figure 2.) During the half-century since 1950, world soybean production per person has increased from 6.5 kilograms to 26.0 kilograms, nearly a fourfold gain.[3]

Soybeans dominate the world oilseed economy. In 1997, the soybean harvest accounted for 54 percent of global oilseed production.[4] (The crops making up most of the remaining 46 percent were cottonseed, peanuts, sunflower seed, rapeseed, copra, and palm kernels.)[5]

The U.S. harvest of 74 million tons in 1997 accounted for 49 percent of the global harvest.[6] Brazil, at 30 million tons and 20 percent, was in second place.[7] Argentina, with just over 16 million tons, accounted for more than 9 percent.[8] And China, where the soybean was apparently domesticated, was fourth in output, with 11 percent.[9] Thus just four countries accounted for nearly 90 percent of the world soybean harvest, which means that production is concentrated in fewer hands than for any other major crop.[10]

Of the world harvest of 152 million tons of soybeans, an estimated 124 million tons will be crushed, yielding an estimated 98 million tons of meal and 22 million tons of oil. Much of the remainder will be used for food and for seed.[11]

One reason for the extraordinarily dynamic character of the world oilseed economy in recent years has been the unprecedented rise in affluence in China. As China's consumption of pork, poultry, and eggs has climbed, the demand for oilseed meal to upgrade the quality of grain-based feed has soared. So, too, has its demand for the vegetable oils used for cooking.

China's imports of soybeans in crop year 1997/98 are estimated at 3 million tons, a phenomenal increase from 130,000 tons just four years earlier.[12] During the same period, imports of soybean meal have climbed from 40,000 to 4.6 million tons and those of soy-

bean oil have risen from 640,000 tons to 1.8 million tons, roughly tripling.[13]

As China's livestock and poultry economy expands at a breakneck pace, its dependence on soybean meal is rising commensurately. The combination of imported soybean meal and the meal content of the imported soybeans totals 6.5 million tons in 1997/98, accounting for 56 percent of China's estimated soybean meal consumption of 12.1 million tons.[14]

China is unique among major soybean producers in that it consumes large quantities of soybeans as food in the form of tofu, soy sauce, and other soy products. An estimated 8.5 million tons, roughly two thirds of its 1997 harvest of 13.8 million tons, will be consumed directly as food.[15]

In the United States, the soybean harvest has grown by leaps and bounds over the last half-century in response to the growing world need for protein meal supplements in grain-based livestock and poultry feeds. The area planted to soybeans there is roughly the same as that planted to corn and wheat.[16] The value of the U.S. soybean crop is well above that of wheat, making it the number two crop in the United States after corn.[17]

Much of the U.S. soybean crop is grown in the midwestern region of the country, generally in a two-year rotation with corn.[18] The soybean, a nitrogen-fixing crop, is ideal for rotation with corn, a crop with a strong nitrogen appetite. The U.S. heartland that is typically referred to as the Corn Belt is today in reality the Corn/Soybean Belt.

Worldwide, a major share of the growth in the soybean harvest has come from expanding the area planted, since yield per hectare is rising rather slowly.[19] (See Figure 3.) With little new land left to plow in the world, part of the increase in the soybean harvest comes by shifting land from grain. Indeed, in the major producing countries the competition between soybeans and grain for land and water resources is intensifying. If the world economy continues its steady expansion, the battle between these crops will likely grow more fierce, perhaps driving up the prices of both soybeans and grain.

WORLD SOYBEAN PRODUCTION, 1950–97

YEAR	TOTAL (mill. tons)	PER CAPITA (kilograms)
1950	17	6.5
1955	19	7.0
1960	25	8.2
1965	32	9.5
1966	36	10.7
1967	38	10.8
1968	42	11.7
1969	42	11.7
1970	44	11.9
1971	47	12.5
1972	49	12.7
1973	62	15.9
1974	55	13.6
1975	66	16.1
1976	59	14.3
1977	72	17.1
1978	78	18.0
1979	94	21.4
1980	81	18.2
1981	86	19.0
1982	94	20.3
1983	83	17.7
1984	93	19.5
1985	97	20.0
1986	98	19.9
1987	104	20.6
1988	96	18.8
1989	107	20.7
1990	104	19.7
1991	107	20.0
1992	117	21.6
1993	118	21.3
1994	138	24.6
1995	125	22.0
1996	132	22.9
1997 (prel)	152	26.0

SOURCES: USDA, *Production, Supply, and Distribution*, electronic database, February 1998; USDA, FAS, *Oilseeds: World Markets and Trade*, December 1997.

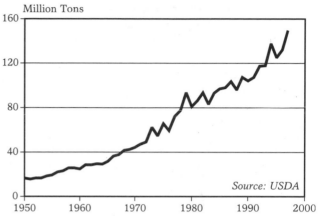

Figure 1: World Soybean Production, 1950–97

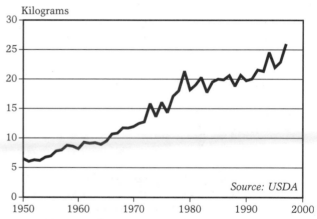

Figure 2: World Soybean Production Per Person, 1950–97

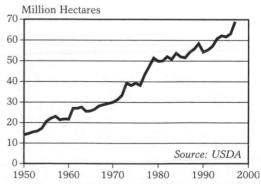

Figure 3: World Soybean Area, 1950–97

World Meat Production Climbs

Lester R. Brown

In 1997, world meat production reached 211 million tons, up from 206 million tons in 1996.[1] (See Figure 1.) This gain of 2.4 percent, spurred by a big jump in poultry, was one of the largest on record, and it raised the amount of meat produced per person from 35.7 kilograms to 36.1 kilograms—an all-time high.[2] (See Figure 2.) Output gains were concentrated in China, the United States, and the European Union.

World pork production in 1997 further widened the margin over beef, once the leading red meat.[3] (See Figure 3.) Pork also maintained a wide lead over poultry, which had surpassed production of beef in 1996.[4] Mutton, including both sheep and goats, is a distant fourth in the global meat hierarchy.[5]

Growth in pork consumption, which totaled 85.4 million tons in 1997, slowed to less than 1 percent, compared with an expansion of more than 4 percent in 1996, largely because of higher feedgrain prices.[6] China, the leading producer at 42.5 million tons, accounts for half of world pork production and consumption.[7] No country has ever dominated production and consumption of a single meat as China now does that of pork.

World poultry production rose to 60 million tons in 1997, up from 56.7 million tons in 1996, a gain of 6 percent.[8] This robust increase matched the 6-percent rise during the preceding year. In each of the last several years, poultry has been the world's fastest-growing source of meat, reflecting its lower price in most countries.

The United States and China dominate poultry consumption, accounting for close to half of the total eaten.[9] The next three countries, all with much lower use, are Brazil, Russia, and Japan.[10] In per capita terms, the United States is far and away the leader among major countries, at 47 kilograms of poultry each year.[11]

The decrease in world beef output in 1997 was negligible, declining to 53.1 million tons from 53.4 million tons in 1996.[12] In contrast to pork, the use of beef is much more widely dispersed around the world. Nearly one fifth of the world's beef and veal is consumed in the United States.[13] Brazil and China, using 6 million tons and 5.8 million tons, together account for another fifth.[14] Russia comes next, with 2.5 million tons, followed by France, Japan, and Italy.[15]

Most of the world's beef comes from rangelands, but now that these are rather fully exploited, major further gains can come only in feedlots. At this point, the relatively inefficient conversion ratio of grain to live weight of 7 kilograms of grain per kilogram of beef puts it at a disadvantage with both pork, roughly 4 to 1, and poultry, just over 2 to 1.[16]

World mutton production at 10.9 million tons was up from 10.5 million tons in 1997.[17] Although overall consumption of this meat per capita is rather low, the use of mutton does dominate in some smaller countries, such as Kazakhstan and Saudi Arabia. In some others, including Australia, New Zealand, and Ireland, it rivals beef as the principal source of meat.

Between 1988 and 1997, international trade in meat doubled, growing much faster than production.[18] U.S. meat exports went from less than a million tons in 1988 to roughly 4 million tons in 1997, enabling this country to eclipse the European Union, once the leading meat exporter.[19] Most of the growth in world meat trade over this nine-year span, from 7 million tons to 12 million tons, came from rapidly expanding exports of poultry.[20] Trade in meat is highly concentrated, with the United States and the European Union accounting for half of all exports, and Japan and Russia taking half of all imports.[21]

The U.S. Department of Agriculture reports that the most dynamic part of the world meat economy between 1988 and 1997 was China. At 67 million tons of production in 1997, it accounted for nearly one third of the world total.[22] This country has long led the world in pork production, but with poultry production climbing from 5.7 million tons in 1993 to 12.5 million tons in 1997, China promises to soon overtake the United States, which produced 15 million tons of poultry in 1997.[23]

WORLD MEAT PRODUCTION, 1950–97

YEAR	TOTAL (mill. tons)	PER CAPITA (kilograms)
1950	44	17.2
1955	58	20.7
1960	64	21.0
1965	81	24.2
1966	84	24.4
1967	86	24.5
1968	88	24.8
1969	92	25.4
1970	97	26.2
1971	101	26.7
1972	106	27.4
1973	105	26.8
1974	107	26.6
1975	109	26.6
1976	112	26.9
1977	117	27.6
1978	121	28.2
1979	126	28.8
1980	130	29.2
1981	132	29.2
1982	134	29.0
1983	138	29.4
1984	142	29.7
1985	146	30.1
1986	152	30.8
1987	157	31.3
1988	164	32.2
1989	166	32.0
1990	171	32.5
1991	173	32.2
1992	175	32.1
1993	177	32.1
1994	187	33.3
1995	197	34.7
1996	206	35.7
1997 (prel)	211	36.1

SOURCES: FAO, *1948–1985 World Crop and Livestock Statistics* (Rome: 1987); FAO, *FAO Production Yearbooks 1988–1991* (Rome: 1990–1993); USDA, FAS, *Livestock and Poultry: World Markets and Trade*, October 1997.

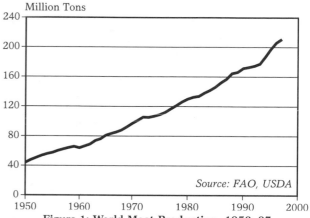
Figure 1: World Meat Production, 1950–97

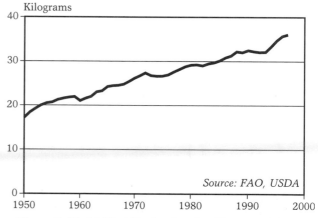
Figure 2: World Meat Production Per Person, 1950–97

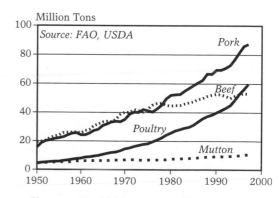
Figure 3: World Meat Production, by Type, 1950–97

Fish Catch Hits a New High — Michael Strauss

The world fish catch climbed to a record 93 million tons in 1996, the latest year for which data are available—a 1.9-percent increase in the catch of 1995.[1] (See Figure 1.) With more fish available, the catch worldwide rose slightly, to 16.0 kilograms per person.[2] (See Figure 2.)

A large share of the increase in tonnage can be attributed to extraordinary growth in the Indonesian and Mexican catch in 1996, which together account for 450,000 additional tons of fish.[3] Significantly, this increase in the sheer tonnage of fish caught—the first since 1993—masks a portentous trend: fishers worldwide are catching more species of fish that would never before have been worth their while. Low-value species accounted for 73 percent of overall world fisheries growth in the 1980s, a trend that shows no signs of abating.[4]

Chronic overfishing continues to threaten the productivity and viability of ocean ecosystems worldwide. According to the Food and Agriculture Organization (FAO), 11 of the world's 15 major fishing grounds are seriously depleted.[5] FAO projects that by the end of this decade there will no longer be an increase in capture fisheries output on average. Nonetheless, FAO estimates that roughly 10 million additional consumable tons of fish could be caught sustainably in the long run if stocks were managed properly and if unwanted bycatch (which may account for 32 percent by mass of all fish caught) were effectively reduced.[6]

Driving overfishing in recent years is a flourishing international trade in fish. A very labor-intensive activity, both capture fishing and aquaculture increasingly happen in the developing world, where wages are lower. Fully 75 percent of fish caught in the world are from developing countries or nations in transition, with a large share coming from China, Chile, Peru, India, and Thailand.[7]

Nearly half of all fish caught today are traded internationally, with the bulk flowing from developing to wealthy nations.[8] Consumers in the industrial world account for 85 percent of world fish imports by value.[9]

While leases of fishing rights—generally by developing nations to industrial ones—proliferated in the 1980s and 1990s, a 1985 U.S. government study found that African signatories to such fishing agreements were left with only "overfishing, undernourishment, and undercompensation."[10]

The matter of assignment of fishing resource rights is emerging as a novel area of international security as violence over fishing rights has become endemic. The high-profile row between the United States and Canada over salmon rights in 1997 was but one of more than 100 fishery disputes between nations, according to U.N. estimates.[11] The Philippine navy confronted Chinese fishers, and the coast guards of Iceland and Denmark also clashed over fish, to name a few instances.[12]

In 1997, the unusually strong warming in the South American Pacific known as El Niño was expected to reduce fish exports from Peru by 40 percent.[13] Peru and Chile have traditionally captured and exported a large share of the world's fish destined to be turned into oils and fish meal, so El Niño should carry with it an appreciable dip in fish catch in 1997.

Despite the mounting urgency of the overfishing crisis, crucial efforts to limit and manage catch internationally have foundered. The U.N. fishing stocks agreement signed in New York in 1995 set promising new standards internationally for the conservation of marine fish.[14] But by the end of 1997 only 15 nations had ratified the treaty—15 short of the number required for it to become binding international law.[15] Among those ratifying the treaty are only 4 of the 20 major fishing nations: the United States, Russia, Norway, and Iceland.[16] Achieving FAO's estimated 10-million-ton potential increase in long-term fishery production while safeguarding the world's aquatic ecosystems will require, at the very least, expanded international cooperation.

WORLD FISH CATCH, 1950–96

YEAR	TOTAL (mill. tons)	PER CAPITA (kilograms)
1950	19	7.5
1955	26	9.5
1960	36	12.0
1965	49	14.7
1966	53	15.4
1967	56	16.0
1968	56	15.9
1969	57	15.8
1970	58	15.7
1971	62	16.5
1972	58	15.1
1973	59	15.0
1974	63	15.6
1975	62	15.3
1976	65	15.5
1977	63	15.0
1978	65	15.2
1979	66	15.1
1980	67	15.0
1981	69	15.3
1982	71	15.4
1983	72	15.3
1984	77	16.1
1985	79	16.2
1986	84	17.0
1987	84	16.8
1988	88	17.2
1989	89	17.1
1990	85	16.2
1991	85	15.8
1992	85	15.6
1993	86	15.5
1994	91	16.2
1995	92	15.9
1996	93	16.0

SOURCES: FAO, *Yearbook of Fishery Statistics: Catches and Landings* (Rome: various years); 1990–96 data from FAO, Rome, letters to Worldwatch, 5 and 11 November 1997.

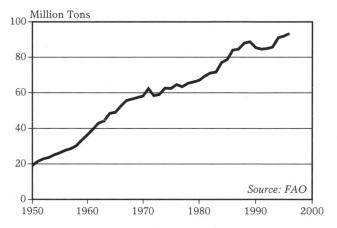

Figure 1: World Fish Catch, 1950–96

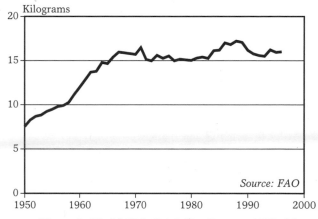

Figure 2: World Fish Catch Per Person, 1950–96

Aquaculture Growing Rapidly — Anne Platt McGinn

Fish farming—known as aquaculture—is one of the fastest-growing sectors in world food production.[1] From 6.9 million tons in 1984, farmed fish production more than tripled, reaching 23.1 million tons in 1996.[2] (See Figure 1.) In terms of value, aquaculture represented a $36.2-billion industry in 1995, the latest year for which data are available, up from $9.5 billion in 1984.[3]

Between 1990 and 1995, world aquaculture production expanded at an average annual rate of 11 percent.[4] Fish farming is expected to provide a growing share of animal protein because fish process grain more efficiently than other animals do.[5] Two kilograms of grain are needed to raise 1 kilogram of fish or chicken, compared with 4 kilograms of grain for each kilogram of pork and 7 kilograms of grain for 1 kilogram of beef.[6]

Worldwide, one out of every five fish eaten today was raised on a farm.[7] By 2000, this is expected to be one in four.[8] An estimated 30 percent of shrimp, 40 percent of salmon and mollusks (oysters, clams, scallops, and mussels), and 65 percent of freshwater fish consumed today have lived in captivity for most of their lives.[9]

China is the world's leading producer, accounting for 61 percent of total farmed fish.[10] Between 1990 and 1995, China's aquaculture output increased by 120 percent, from 5.8 million to 12.8 million tons.[11] (See Figure 2.) India, Indonesia, Japan, and Thailand together accounted for another 17 percent of world production in 1995 (3.5 million tons).[12] In contrast, all industrial countries combined cultivated 2.9 million tons of fish—14 percent of world production that year.[13]

An estimated 85 percent of farmed fish worldwide are noncarnivorous, freshwater species—such as carps, tilapias, and milkfish—and mollusks, which eat low on the food chain.[14] The remainder are primarily carnivorous species such as salmon, catfish, and shrimp, which need a minimum of 2 kilograms of fish meal for each kilogram of farmed fish.[15] Cultivating these products exacerbates pressures on wild fish stocks and results in a net loss of protein.

Giant tiger prawns, a species of shrimp, were valued at $3.5 billion in 1995, making this the most valuable aquaculture commodity, even though only 500,000 tons were cultivated.[16] Driven by high profits and export markets, shrimp farming now spans 50 countries and is expanding rapidly.[17]

Between 1990 and 1995, the number of shrimp farms in Southeast Asia tripled.[18] This development is not without problems, however. Shrimp ponds in Taiwan were abandoned in the late 1980s after several years of intensive production triggered diseases and environmental damage.[19] In response to repeated environmental degradation, global activists formed the Industrial Shrimp Action Network in October 1997 to call for an end to unsustainable shrimp farming.[20]

Worldwide, 65 percent of aquaculture occurs in inland areas, although farming in coastal and marine areas poses a growing threat to local ecosystems and water quality. In the Philippines, for instance, shrimp ponds account for half of the country's mangrove losses.[21] High demand for fresh water has depleted drinking supplies and limits future growth in many areas.[22]

Intensive fish farms produce high volumes of biological waste, primarily from uneaten food and waste material. Other problems include disease outbreaks, chemical pollution, and escapes of genetically modified fish, which can dilute the gene pool of wild fish and displace them altogether.[23]

Recirculating water systems, although expensive to build, offer fish farmers significant water savings and higher production.[24] Israeli farmers have designed a system that reuses the water to raise tilapia, trout, and salmon, and then channels the nutrient-rich discharge to agricultural land.[25]

If aquaculture is to remain an important source of food and income, production needs to shift toward more sustainable practices, such as reducing water use and pollution, preserving coastal ecosystems, and cultivating less resource-intensive species, such as carp and tilapia.

WORLD AQUACULTURE PRODUCTION, 1984–96

YEAR	TOTAL (mill. tons)
1984	6.9
1985	7.7
1986	8.8
1987	10.1
1988	11.2
1989	11.7
1990	12.4
1991	13.0
1992	14.4
1993	16.4
1994	18.4
1995	20.9
1996 (prel)	23.1

SOURCES: FAO, *Aquaculture Production Statistics, 1984–93* and *1986–95* (Rome: 1995 and 1997); Maurizio Perotti, Fisheries Department, FAO, letter to author, 11 November 1997.

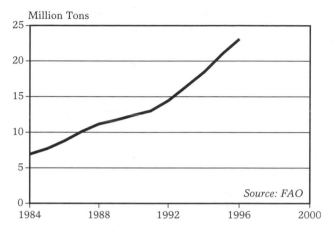

Figure 1: World Aquaculture Production, 1984–96

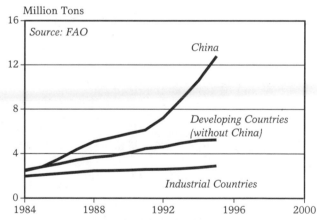

Figure 2: Aquaculture Production, by Region, 1984–95

Grain Stocks Remain Low   Lester R. Brown

World carryover stocks of grain in 1998 are estimated at 57 days of consumption, just one day more than in 1997, and the third lowest level on record.[1] (See Figures 1 and 2.) Carryover stocks of grain, the amount in the bin when a new harvest begins, are a measure of the margin of food security as the world moves from one harvest to the next. When stocks drop below 60 days of consumption, they amount to little more than pipeline supplies.

The decline in world food security is actually even greater than that indicated by the fall in carryover stocks. Over most of the last half-century, the world has in effect had two grain reserves: carryover stocks plus the cropland idled under U.S. farm commodity programs (which were designed to avoid price-depressing surpluses).

As recently as 1990, 11 million hectares of grainland were being held out of production in the United States under these commodity programs.[2] If we assume an average harvest of four tons per hectare, this idled cropland represented a reserve of 44 million tons—nearly nine days of world consumption, and a reserve that could be tapped with a simple directive from the U.S. Secretary of Agriculture. But by 1996, all the commodity programs had been abolished and the previously set-aside land was back in production.[3] Yet even with this additional land in use in 1996 and 1997, the world was not able to rebuild depleted stocks.

There are two reasons for the drop in carryover stocks of grain and the loss of cropland idled under commodity programs. One is that the growth in world grain production has slowed during the 1990s. Two, the growth in world demand for grain is perhaps stronger than ever. The rate of population growth has been slowly falling, but the world still adds 80 million people each year.[4] In addition, rising affluence is also generating demand for more grain.

Some commentators note that a doubling of population growth will require a doubling of grain production. But this assumes that the world's poor will remain poor, when in fact many of them are becoming more affluent. As a result, they are moving up the food chain—diversifying their diets and consuming more pork, poultry, beef, eggs, and milk. In short, they want to live like the affluent consumers of Western Europe, North America, and Japan.

In China, for example, where population growth has slowed to 1 percent a year, the rise in affluence now dominates the growth in the demand for grain.[5] After the economic reforms in 1978, China's use of grain for feed has climbed from less than 20 million tons to more than 100 million.[6] During the 1990s, easily two thirds of the demand growth for grain in China has been for feed, mostly to produce pork, poultry, and eggs.[7]

One of the central questions now facing humanity is, What is the prospect for rebuilding depleted grain stocks? Without any idled U.S. cropland, the world needs at least 70 days of carryover stocks as a cushion against one poor grain harvest. Even this might not be sufficient to prevent acute scarcity and dramatic price rises in the event of exceptionally poor weather and a sharply reduced harvest. In a world that consumes some 5 million tons of grain per day, rebuilding stocks from 57 days to 70 days will require a world grain harvest that exceeds consumption by 65 million tons.[8] To do this, the 1997 harvest (1,881 million tons) would need to expand by 26 million tons in 1998 just to cover population growth and by an additional 65 million tons to rebuild stocks to a more secure level—a total of 91 million tons.[9] Based on the experience of the last few years, this does not seem likely to happen in 1998.

If the world experiences a poor harvest in 1998, at a time when carryover stocks are depleted, chaos in world grain markets could soon follow. Indeed, in the spring of 1996 world prices of wheat, corn, and barley were twice those of a year earlier because carryover stocks of grain had dropped to 52 days of world consumption, the lowest level in history.[10] Fortunately, the prospect of a bumper grain harvest checked the rise in grain prices. But if it had instead been a poor harvest, grain prices could have soared far higher.

WORLD GRAIN CARRYOVER STOCKS, 1961–98[1]

YEAR	STOCKS (mill. tons)	(days use)
1961	203	90
1962	182	81
1963	190	82
1964	193	83
1965	194	78
1966	159	62
1967	189	72
1968	213	79
1969	244	87
1970	228	77
1971	193	63
1972	217	69
1973	180	56
1974	191	56
1975	199	61
1976	219	66
1977	279	79
1978	277	77
1979	326	85
1980	315	81
1981	288	72
1982	307	77
1983	356	88
1984	305	73
1985	366	85
1986	434	100
1987	466	104
1988	405	89
1989	314	70
1990	296	64
1991	339	72
1992	324	69
1993	363	76
1994	317	66
1995	304	62
1996	251	52
1997	282	56
1998 (prel)	293	57

[1] Data are for year when new harvest begins
SOURCES: USDA, ERS *Production, Supply, and Distribution*, electronic database, February 1998; USDA, FAS, *Grain: World Markets and Trade*, December 1997.

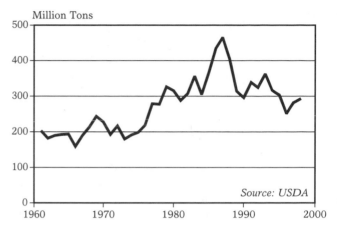

Figure 1: World Grain Carryover Stocks, 1961–98

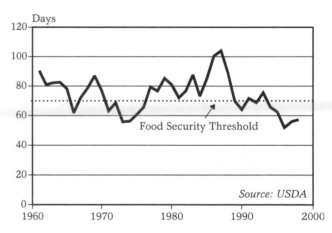

Figure 2: World Grain Carryover Stocks as Days of Consumption, 1961–98

Agricultural Resource
Trends

Grain Yield Rises   Brian Halweil

World grain yield per hectare inched up to 2.70 tons in 1997, edging out the record of 2.66 tons set in 1996.[1] (See Figure 1.) This marginal increase continues a slowdown in the growth in yield that has driven grain production since mid-century.

Of the three major cereals, wheat set a new yield record in 1997, rice yield held steady, and corn had a downturn.[2] (See Figures 2 and 3.) The 5-percent increase in wheat yield and 2-percent decline in corn yield were both weather-related.[3] Near-perfect growing conditions prevailed in wheat-producing areas, while drought and heat combined to hurt the U.S. and Chinese corn harvest.

Raising yield is central to increasing grain production. Farmers have traditionally satisfied growth in demand by plowing new land, but opportunities for expansion are now limited. World grain area per person is only half what it was in 1950.[4] Urbanization and land degradation continue to eliminate grainland at an alarming pace, putting more pressure on yield to shoulder the soaring demand for grain.[5]

While world grain yield grew at an annual rate of 2.1 percent from 1950 to 1990, during the 1990s it has increased scarcely 1 percent a year.[6] Annual yield growth from 1990 to 1997 for rice, wheat, and corn stood at 1.1, 1.2, and 1.6 percent, respectively.[7] Slowdowns in yield growth confront industrial and developing nations alike, for all nations are drawing on the same set of yield-maximizing technologies and are therefore encountering similar barriers to additional yield increases.[8]

Breeders have boosted the yield potential of cereals substantially in past decades, but are beginning to approach various biological limits to further growth. For example, wheat breeding has raised the share of photosynthetic product that goes to grain—as opposed to roots, stem, and leaves—from 20 percent to some 50–55 percent.[9] This has been a major source of yield gains, yet crop physiologists estimate the theoretical limit to be around 60 percent.[10] Current breeding limitations are intrinsic to plant design and the process of photosynthesis.

Biotechnology has been touted as a possible source of new yield increases, but it has yet to produce a grain with a yield greater than for varieties already available. At best, biotechnology will likely lead to incremental yield gains from reduced losses to drought, disease, pests, and other crop stresses.[11]

The much-awaited "super rice" developed at the International Rice Research Institute in the Philippines holds promise for raising yield potential in this major grain. Available in the next few years, it is expected to boost tropical and subtropical rice yields by 20–25 percent.[12] Yet this pales in comparison to the doubling or tripling accomplished by the first high-yielding rice varieties.

Fertilizer has worked in synergy with crop breeding to raise grain yield, but it may have largely exhausted its contribution in many countries. Diminishing returns to increased applications in the United States, Western Europe, and Japan indicate that fertilizer does not guarantee unlimited yield gains.[13]

While there remains a gap in fertilizer applications between industrial and developing countries, the principal constraint to greater use is lack of water rather than lack of financing. Indeed, in Egypt, where grainland is irrigated with Nile River water and well fertilized, grain yields are over three times those of affluent Australia, where water shortages handicap fertilizer efficacy.[14] China and India, with much of their grainland irrigated, have already raised fertilizer inputs substantially, but only India has room for further significant increase.[15]

Irrigation has been another key to increased grain yield worldwide, expanding by 2.3 percent a year from 1950 to 1995.[16] Yet growth in irrigated land is expected to slow to just 0.3 percent a year in coming decades.[17] At the same time, waterlogging and salinization cripple yields on a growing share of irrigated lands.[18] As per capita freshwater supplies plummet in many nations, formidable forces constrain future irrigation projects, and thus any accompanying gains in yield.[19]

WORLD GRAIN YIELD PER HECTARE, 1950–97

YEAR	YIELD (tons per hectare)
1950	1.06
1955	1.17
1960	1.29
1965	1.39
1966	1.51
1967	1.52
1968	1.57
1969	1.58
1970	1.63
1971	1.75
1972	1.73
1973	1.82
1974	1.74
1975	1.75
1976	1.87
1977	1.85
1978	2.03
1979	1.98
1980	1.98
1981	2.02
1982	2.14
1983	2.08
1984	2.30
1985	2.30
1986	2.35
1987	2.33
1988	2.25
1989	2.41
1990	2.55
1991	2.47
1992	2.58
1993	2.50
1994	2.57
1995	2.51
1996	2.66
1997 (prel)	2.70

SOURCES: USDA, *Production, Supply, and Distribution*, electronic database, Washington, DC, February 1998; USDA, "World Gain Database," unpublished printout, Washington, DC, 1991.

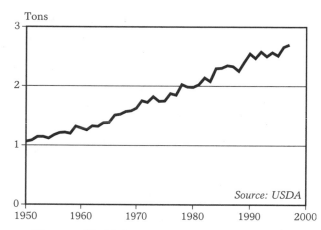

Figure 1: World Grain Yield Per Hectare, 1950–97

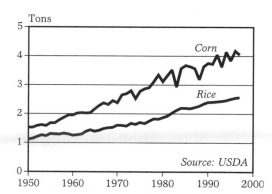

Figure 2: Corn and Rice Yield Per Hectare, 1950–97

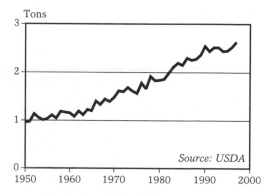

Figure 3: Wheat Yield Per Hectare, 1950–97

Fertilizer Use Up   Lester R. Brown

World fertilizer use in 1997 totaled 131 million tons, up 1.6 percent from the 129 million tons used in 1996.[1] (See Figure 1.) This third consecutive annual gain in fertilizer use was concentrated in India, Brazil, and the United States.[2] In per capita terms, fertilizer use was 22.4 kilograms, virtually unchanged from 1996.[3]

Three countries—China, the United States, and India—account for more than half of world fertilizer use.[4] China, using 33 million tons in 1997, applied more fertilizer to its cropland than any other country.[5] (See Figure 2.) The United States used 20 million tons, and India, 14 million tons.[6] (See Figure 3.) The U.S. figure is down slightly from the all-time high of 21.5 million tons in 1981.[7] The adoption of precision farming techniques, which include a more precise matching of the application of fertilizer to crop needs, has contributed to the slight decline in U.S. fertilizer use over the last two decades.

In most European countries, fertilizer use has also reached the saturation point. In addition, there is widespread public concern about the health effects of rising levels of nitrates in underground water supplies due to fertilizer runoff.[8] In part because of this, the European Fertilizer Manufacturers Association is projecting a slight decline in fertilizer use in Western Europe over the next decade.[9]

The region of the world that may have the largest potential for increasing fertilizer use is the Indian subcontinent, home to 1.3 billion people.[10] It also has perhaps the steadiest growth in fertilizer use. In each of the big three countries there—India, Bangladesh, and Pakistan—fertilizer use has gone up almost every year for the last several years.[11]

Another region with a large unrealized potential is South America, including, importantly, Brazil and Argentina. Growth in fertilizer use in this region has been particularly strong because of strong economic growth in both Brazil and Argentina.[12] Economic reforms in the latter have helped to nearly double fertilizer use there over the last four years.[13]

The principal reason for the slower growth or stabilization of fertilizer use in many countries is that the amount being used is approaching the physiological capacity of crops to absorb nutrients. Once this limit is reached, further rises in grain prices will not increase the amount of fertilizer that can be used economically.

Another emerging constraint is the lack of growth in irrigation. After expanding at more than 2 percent a year from 1950 to 1980, the growth in world irrigated area slowed to scarcely 1 percent a year in the 1980s and probably to even less during the 1990s.[14] Some analysts, including David Seckler, head of the International Irrigation Management Institute in Sri Lanka, believe that the world irrigated area is no longer increasing—that losses due to aquifer depletion, to the diversion of irrigation water to nonfarm uses, and to abandonment because of waterlogging and salinity are offsetting gains from new irrigation projects.[15]

The precipitous drop in world fertilizer use from the all-time high of 146 million tons in 1989 was due almost entirely to the drop in usage in the former Soviet Union—from 25 million tons in 1989 to 5 million tons in 1995.[16] Initially this fall was due to the abandonment of heavy fertilizer subsidies as a part of economic reforms. After 1990, however, the breakup of the Soviet Union into its constituent republics and the associated economic disruption and semi-collapse of economies also played an important role.

World fertilizer use will undoubtedly increase further in the years ahead, but growth is likely to be slow, gradual, and concentrated in a shrinking list of countries where there is still a strong yield response to the use of additional fertilizer.

WORLD FERTILIZER USE, 1950–97

YEAR	TOTAL (mill. tons)	PER PERSON (kilograms)
1950	14	5.5
1955	18	6.5
1960	27	8.9
1965	40	12.0
1966	45	13.2
1967	51	14.6
1968	56	15.7
1969	60	16.5
1970	66	17.8
1971	69	18.2
1972	73	18.9
1973	79	20.1
1974	85	21.2
1975	82	20.1
1976	90	21.6
1977	95	22.5
1978	100	23.2
1979	111	25.4
1980	112	25.1
1981	117	25.8
1982	115	24.9
1983	115	24.5
1984	126	26.4
1985	131	27.0
1986	129	26.2
1987	132	26.3
1988	140	27.4
1989	146	28.1
1990	143	27.1
1991	138	25.7
1992	134	24.6
1993	126	22.8
1994	121	21.6
1995	122	21.5
1996	129	22.3
1997 (prel)	131	22.4

SOURCES: FAO, *Fertilizer Yearbook* (Rome: various years); International Fertilizer Industry Association, Annual Conference, 18–21 November 1997.

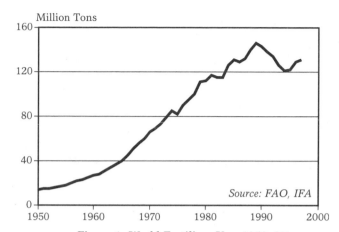

Figure 1: World Fertilizer Use, 1950–97

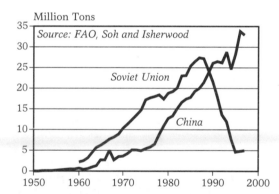

Figure 2: Fertilizer Use in China and the Soviet Union, 1950–97

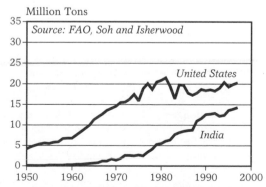

Figure 3: Fertilizer Use in the United States and India, 1950–97

Irrigated Area Up Slightly   Gary Gardner

Global irrigated area expanded by less than half a percent in 1995, the last year for which comprehensive data are available.[1] The increase of 1.4 million hectares brought the world total to 255.4 million hectares. (See Figure 1.) Although year-to-year changes sometimes reflect statistical adjustments rather than actual changes on the ground, the trend this decade is clearly one of sluggish growth. The world now has fewer than 45 hectares of irrigated land per thousand people, the smallest area per capita since 1969.[2] (See Figure 2.)

The greatest growth occurred in developing countries. Latin America saw an increase of 1.2 percent between 1994 and 1995, some four times more than the global figure, while Africa and Asia expanded their area slightly faster than the world rate.[3] Industrial countries, in contrast, posted a loss in irrigated area of 0.3 percent.[4] Countries in transition ended a four-year contraction caused by their shift away from managed economies, achieving a 0.3-percent expansion in irrigated area.[5]

Irrigated land is key to agricultural productivity, supplying some 36 percent of the world's food from only 16 percent of its cropland.[6] Developing countries are especially dependent on irrigated area: 60 percent of their rice and 40 percent of their wheat comes from irrigated land.[7] Because of irrigation's importance for meeting global food needs, the slowdown in expansion has worrisome implications for growth in the global food supply.[8]

In addition to sluggish expansion, some of the world's irrigated land continues to be watered unsustainably. In China, nearly all basins depend on overpumping of aquifers, with groundwater levels plunging more than a meter per year in parts of north China.[9] And in three coastal provinces—Hebei, Shandong, and Liaoning—seawater has invaded aquifers as water tables have fallen.[10]

In India, 12 districts of Punjab and 3 in Haryana report falling water tables, while 2 districts in Gujarat and Tamil Nadu have seen aquifers permanently depleted.[11] The proliferation of tubewells in India—growing from 360,000 in the late 1960s to some 6 million in 1997—is partly responsible for the overdrafting.[12] In the Punjab, for example, some 840,000 wells are functioning, 40 percent more than the estimated safe number.[13] Chronic overpumping for irrigation also continues on the southern Great Plains of the United States, on the Arabian Peninsula, and in North Africa, all of which rely on aquifers that are essentially nonrenewable.

At the same time, households, industry, and the environment compete with farming for water, and these needs will likely increase, especially where economic growth is rapid. In China, the share of water claimed by homes and factories is expected to jump from 13 percent in 1995 to 35 percent in 2020.[14] For Southeast Asia, these nonagricultural shares will climb from 25 percent to 47 percent of total water use in the same period.[15] Where water is already scarce, this increasing demand could spell trouble for agriculture. Irrigation's share of total water use in India, for example, is projected to fall from 83 percent in 1990 to 73 percent in 2025, even as population increases by 66 percent.[16]

Expansion of irrigated area could conceivably be helped by an increase in irrigation efficiency; in some situations, as much as 60–75 percent of the water applied to crops is wasted.[17] Use of sprinkler or drip irrigation systems rather than traditional flood irrigation can greatly reduce water wastage on the farm. But because water lost on one farm often becomes available to another downstream, basin-level efficiencies are often greater than those on the farm.[18] Thus raising water efficiency on the farm does not necessarily increase the amount of water available throughout the basin.[19]

Irrigation is projected to grow much more slowly in the next century. A U.N.-sponsored assessment of global water use projects growth of less than half a percent annually between 2000 and 2025, and even slower growth in the second quarter of the next century.[20] This will place great pressure on scientists and farmers to find new ways to increase food production.

WORLD IRRIGATED AREA, 1961–95

YEAR	TOTAL (mill. hectares)	PER CAPITA (hectares per thousand population)
1961	139	45.1
1962	141	45.1
1963	144	45.0
1964	147	44.8
1965	150	44.8
1966	153	44.8
1967	156	44.7
1968	159	44.8
1969	164	45.0
1970	167	45.1
1971	171	45.1
1972	174	45.1
1973	180	45.6
1974	183	45.6
1975	189	46.1
1976	194	46.6
1977	198	46.8
1978	204	47.3
1979	207	47.3
1980	209	47.0
1981	213	47.0
1982	215	46.5
1983	216	46.0
1984	221	46.3
1985	224	46.1
1986	225	45.7
1987	227	45.2
1988	230	45.0
1989	236	45.4
1990	241	45.7
1991	245	45.7
1992	248	45.6
1993	252	45.5
1994	254	45.2
1995	255	44.9

SOURCES: FAO, *FAOSTAT Statistics Database*, Rome; USDA, *Agricultural Resources and Environmental Indicators* (Washington, DC: 1996–97).

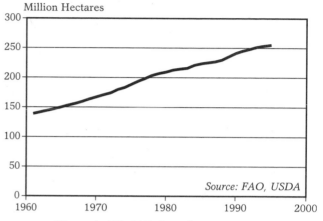

Figure 1: World Irrigated Area, 1961–95

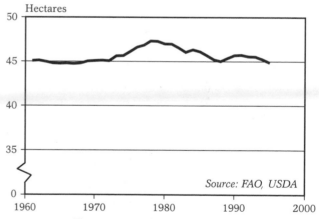

Figure 2: World Irrigated Area Per Thousand People, 1961–95

Energy Trends

Oil and Gas Use Reach New Highs   Christopher Flavin

Propelled by strong economic growth, particularly in Asia and the Americas, world use of oil and natural gas set new records in 1997.[1] (See Figure 1.) Oil use grew faster, at 1.4 percent, while gas use increased by only 0.5 percent due to mild weather and high prices in the dominant European and North American markets.[2] Overall, oil accounts for about 35 percent of the world's commercial energy supply, while natural gas accounts for 23 percent.[3]

Growing use of oil—up 14 percent since 1990—is propelled mainly by transportation, including increased dependence on cars and trucks in developing countries.[4] Since the 1990s began, oil use has increased 25 percent in Brazil, 40 percent in Indonesia, and 60 percent in China.[5] The Asian economic crisis is likely to slow this growth in 1998, but the potential for resuming a rapid growth rate in later years remains strong: Los Angeles alone has more cars today than all of China.[6]

Even in the United States, which has dominated the world oil market since the century began, infatuation with sport utility vehicles in the 1990s—which together with small trucks now account for half of the car market—continues to drive oil consumption up.[7] The United States, with less than 5 percent of the world's population, consumed 25 percent of the oil used in 1997—half of it imported from other nations.[8]

The use of natural gas grew surprisingly slowly in 1997, due to mild winter weather in northern countries, including the United States, following unusually cold weather the year before. Gas consumption actually fell 1.5 percent in Europe—though some individual countries saw large increases, including Spain at 33 percent.[9] Central and East European countries saw a sharper 5-percent decline as consumer subsidies were reduced once again.[10]

All signs point to a resumption of steady growth in gas use in the coming years and decades, however, due to the abundance and environmental advantages of this relatively clean-burning fuel.[11] Major exploration, development, and pipeline projects are under way around the world. New developments in fuel cells and hybrid electric cars will likely allow gas to replace oil as a transportation fuel in the decades ahead.[12]

Despite the growth in demand in 1997, world oil supplies were more than ample to meet it, and prices fell to less than $18 per barrel, from an average of $20 per barrel the year before.[13] Russian oil production rebounded slightly, to just under 6 million barrels a day in 1997—the first annual increase there since 1987, when production was almost double what it is today.[14] Production also rose modestly in Mexico and Venezuela, but declined slightly in the United Kingdom and the United States.[15]

The largest increases in oil production in 1997 came from the Persian Gulf, where output rose by 1 million barrels a day to nearly 19 million—the highest level since the fall of the Shah of Iran in 1979.[16] (See Figure 2.) With two thirds of the world's proven oil reserves, these countries remain positioned to dominate oil markets well into the next century.[17]

Developments in 1997 made clear that the Caspian Sea and surrounding areas of Central Asia will be the next great "prize" for the oil industry in the early twenty-first century, with what could turn out to be more than 100 billion barrels of reserves—similar in scale to Iran's or Iraq's.[18] Powerful companies from Europe, Russia, the United States, and China are planning to pour some $60 billion into the region, and are vying for access to tanker and pipeline routes across politically contentious terrain in countries such as Afghanistan, Iran, and Russia.[19]

Oil resources in Central Asia and the Middle East appear sufficient to fuel rising world oil demand for at least another decade, though supplies could be disrupted in the event of a major political or military crisis in that part of the world. Beyond that, the outlook is cloudy: Geologists Colin Campbell and Jean Laherrere noted in March 1998 that the world is having trouble locating major new oil supplies—and that global oil production in likely to peak within the next decade. After that, "the world could see radical increases in oil prices."[20]

WORLD OIL AND NATURAL GAS USE, 1950–97

YEAR	OIL	NATURAL GAS
		(mill. tons of oil equivalent)
1950	451	190
1955	663	296
1960	913	453
1965	1,313	676
1966	1,437	736
1967	1,523	791
1968	1,661	866
1969	1,807	948
1970	2,327	1,022
1971	2,458	1,100
1972	2,467	1,164
1973	2,854	1,192
1974	2,821	1,217
1975	2,791	1,212
1976	2,977	1,266
1977	3,075	1,293
1978	3,190	1,363
1979	3,226	1,464
1980	3,145	1,443
1981	3,010	1,458
1982	2,933	1,445
1983	2,888	1,480
1984	2,940	1,600
1985	2,933	1,683
1986	3,015	1,713
1987	3,068	1,798
1988	3,160	1,888
1989	3,203	1,965
1990	3,203	1,973
1991	3,225	2,010
1992	3,225	2,025
1993	3,220	2,088
1994	3,278	2,088
1995	3,325	2,145
1996	3,405	2,246
1997 (prel)	3,487	2,257

SOURCE: Worldwatch estimates based on UN, DOE, BP, EC, PlanEcon, and *Journal of Commerce.*

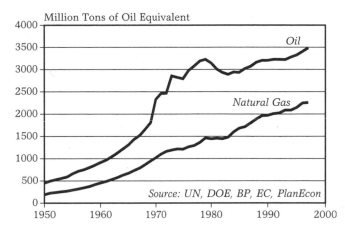

Figure 1: World Oil and Natural Gas Use, 1950–97

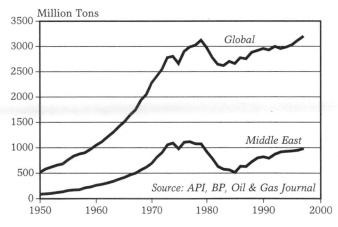

Figure 2: Oil Production, Global and Middle East, 1950–97

Coal Use Continues Rebound Seth Dunn

Global consumption of coal increased 1 percent in 1997, reaching a new high for the fourth consecutive year.[1] Use of this fuel stands at 2,532 million tons of oil equivalent, having grown 236 percent since 1950.[2] Though growth during the 1990s has totaled only 8.7 percent—the slowest among fossil fuels—coal use still accounts for 27 percent of overall energy use.[3]

Coal use grew an estimated 1.7 percent in 1997 in China, which with a 30-percent share of overall use is the world's leading consumer.[4] (See Figure 2.) Coal in China—used for cooking, space heating, and power generation—accounts for nearly three quarters of the country's total energy, and usage has risen 27 percent since 1990.[5] The Chinese government currently plans to build some 500 power plants, many of them coal-fired, between now and 2010.[6]

Use of coal grew slightly more—2.5 percent—in the United States, the second-leading consumer, with 23 percent of the world total.[7] Coal supplies 55 percent of U.S. electricity and 24 percent of the overall energy supply, and usage has increased 29 percent since 1990.[8]

Consumption has risen most quickly in a handful of Asian countries, where energy and power demands are large and growing. According to the International Energy Agency, more than 40 percent of the projected growth in world electricity demand by 2010 will come from East and Southeast Asia, where coal is currently the dominant fuel for power generation.[9] In India, where coal supplies 57 percent of energy and 70 percent of electricity, coal use expanded 36 percent between 1990 and 1996.[10] Coal use grew 88 percent between 1990 and 1996 in Indonesia, which is already the third largest coal exporter; the government predicts nearly a 10-fold increase in coal use for electricity by 2009.[11]

In Europe, with 17 percent of world coal use, consumption fell an estimated 3.7 percent in 1997, extending a 22-percent decline between 1990 and 1996.[12] Several countries have already or will soon shut down their pits, and as of April 1998 British power gener-

ators will no longer be required to buy coal at above market prices.[13] In Germany, where coal costs four times as much to produce as the world average, the government decided in March 1997 to begin cutting its generous subsidies, sparking demonstrations.[14]

Coal use dropped 4.9 percent in 1997 in the former Eastern bloc, where the industry has become a major economic burden.[15] In July 1997, the Ukrainian government announced it could not even afford to close 40 money-losing mines.[16] Poland's mining industry lost $730 million in 1996, while producing one quarter as much coal per miner as in the United Kingdom.[17] Russia has halted production from 90 coal pits and abolished its state-owned company, expecting to shut 130 of its 200 mines by 2000.[18]

Russia, China, and India are beneficiaries of a $1-billion World Bank initiative to restructure their state-owned coal industries by shutting down inefficient mines and improving more productive ones.[19] But the program's impact is unclear—in 1997, $100 million of a $500-million loan to Russia "disappeared."[20] And according to the Institute for Policy Studies, the World Bank has since 1992 financed 20 new coal-fired power plants and 26 coal mines in China, India, Poland, Russia, and several other countries.[21]

Coal remains entrenched in areas of the world where low energy prices and limited attention to cleaner and more economical alternatives sustain misperceptions of the fuel's low cost and relative abundance.[22] But pressures to restrain its use are intensifying. In some industrial countries, coal is increasingly being displaced by natural gas and other cleaner fuels as a power generation source—a shift that may be encouraged by electric utility restructuring.[23] And the case for phasing out support for coal use is strengthening elsewhere, whether the impetus is costly subsidies, carbon emissions—coal is the most carbon-intensive fossil fuel—or a broad array of other social and environmental ills, from rural land loss to urban air pollution to acid rain.

WORLD COAL CONSUMPTION, 1950–97

YEAR	USE (mill. tons of oil equivalent)
1950	1,074
1955	1,270
1960	1,544
1965	1,579
1966	1,605
1967	1,524
1968	1,600
1969	1,648
1970	1,515
1971	1,677
1972	1,684
1973	1,554
1974	1,772
1975	1,577
1976	1,657
1977	1,718
1978	1,736
1979	1,807
1980	1,836
1981	1,861
1982	1,882
1983	1,938
1984	2,012
1985	2,127
1986	2,196
1987	2,253
1988	2,319
1989	2,371
1990	2,330
1991	2,228
1992	2,259
1993	2,214
1994	2,355
1995	2,451
1996	2,507
1997 (prel)	2,532

SOURCE: Worldwatch estimates based on UN, DOE, BP, EC, PlanEcon, and *Journal of Commerce.*

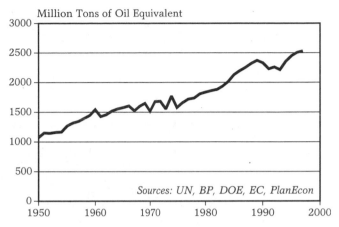

Figure 1: World Coal Consumption, 1950–97

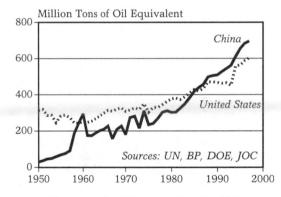

Figure 2: Coal Consumption in China and the United States, 1950–97

Nuclear Power Steady
Nicholas Lenssen

Between 1996 and 1997, total installed nuclear generating capacity increased by just two tenths of 1 percent, bringing the total to a new high of 343,261 megawatts.[1] (See Figure 1.) Since 1990, global nuclear capacity has increased by less than 5 percent.[2] It now appears as if the world's installed capacity of nuclear power is at or near its peak—since the capacity of reactors being closed each year is roughly equal to that of the new reactors being completed.

Five new reactors were connected to the electricity grid in 1997, while five units were permanently closed.[3] This brings to 92 the number of reactors that have been retired after an average service life of less than 18 years, representing a generating capacity of 27,366 megawatts.[4] (See Figure 2.) The total number of operating reactors dropped by four in the past year, to 431.[5]

Construction started on four reactors in 1997, two in North Korea and two in China, bringing the global total of reactors under active construction to 33—a combined 25,009 megawatts.[6] The small number of reactor orders makes this the lowest number in 30 years. (See Figure 3.) The Korean reactors were promised in 1994 by the United States, Japan, and South Korea in exchange for North Korea's promise to drop its suspected nuclear weapons program.[7] China now has six reactors under construction, tied with South Korea for the most in the world.[8]

In the industrial regions of North America, Western Europe, and Japan, nuclear power has reached a standstill. Three U.S. reactors were permanently closed in 1997 due to high maintenance costs, and another two dozen or so are likely to close in the near future as restructuring of the electric power industry exposes their high costs.[9] Canada "laid up" four reactors in 1997, ostensibly for extensive repairs, but it is unlikely that these (or three others due to be shut in 1998) will ever operate again due to technical problems and high costs.[10]

In Western Europe, only one reactor remains under construction—in France.[11] It will be completed in 1998, and there are no firm plans to build new reactors in the region. Meanwhile, two reactors were permanently closed in Europe in 1997: one each in the Netherlands and France.[12] Sweden has pledged to close its first reactor in 1998.[13]

Japan opened its last reactor of the century in 1997.[14] The country has only one unit under construction. Though the government has plans for more, the country remains deeply divided on nuclear power because of concern about safety and the use of plutonium in civilian reactors.[15]

The former Eastern Bloc fares no better. In Russia, no reactors were under construction at the end of 1997, despite the fact that roughly a dozen partially built Soviet-era reactors are sitting idle due to a lack of funding.[16] Shortages of money have also held up pay to nuclear workers in both Russia and Ukraine.[17] Two Czech reactors at Temelin scheduled to open originally in the early 1990s will likely not come online until 2000—if they are finished at all—and at an increasing high price.[18]

The last hope for nuclear vendors is in the developing regions of Asia, an area that has two thirds of the reactors still being built.[19] But the region's recent financial crises have cast a dark cloud over an already less-than-bullish market.[20]

Indonesia, for instance, had long been planning to order a reactor for operation by 2003, but in early 1997 the government announced that the earliest it would now need nuclear power would be 2020 or 2030.[21] Efforts to sell reactors to Thailand and Viet Nam have also dissolved.[22]

The last remaining market of any size is China, which plans to have 50,000 megawatts operating by 2020.[23] As it develops economically and politically, however, the country is likely to face economic and social obstacles that have frustrated nuclear planners elsewhere.

Finally, Turkey still seems set on joining the nuclear club. In 1997 the government received bids from foreign vendors to build two reactors, and expects to sign with one company in June 1998.[24] Financing remains a problem, though, and the project also faces some domestic opposition.

WORLD NET INSTALLED
ELECTRICAL GENERATING CAPACITY
OF NUCLEAR POWER PLANTS,
1960–97

YEAR	CAPACITY (gigawatts)
1960	1
1961	1
1962	2
1963	2
1964	3
1965	5
1966	6
1967	8
1968	9
1969	13
1970	16
1971	24
1972	32
1973	45
1974	61
1975	71
1976	85
1977	99
1978	114
1979	121
1980	135
1981	155
1982	170
1983	189
1984	219
1985	250
1986	276
1987	297
1988	310
1989	320
1990	328
1991	325
1992	327
1993	336
1994	338
1995	340
1996	343
1997 (prel)	343

SOURCE: Worldwatch Institute database,
compiled from the IAEA and press reports.

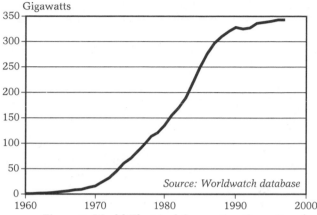

Figure 1: World Electrical Generating Capacity of
Nuclear Power Plants, 1960–97

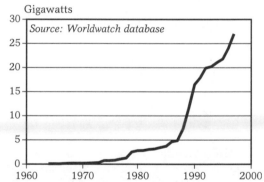

Figure 2: Cumulative Generating Capacity
of Closed Nuclear Power Plants, 1964–97

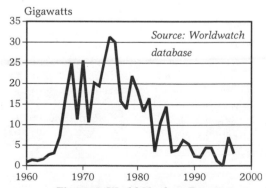

Figure 3: World Nuclear Reactor
Construction Starts, 1960–97

Hydroelectric Power Up Slightly

Seth Dunn

Worldwide installed capacity of hydroelectric power—electricity generated from the gravitational energy of falling water—rose 0.8 percent to an estimated 714,600 megawatts in 1996, the latest year for which data are available.[1] (See Figure 1.) Hydropower use has risen nearly 15-fold since 1950—averaging an annual addition of 15,000 megawatts during the last four decades, though the 1996 addition of 5,671 megawatts was the lowest since 1974 and made hydropower the year's slowest-growing energy source.[2] It remains, however, the renewable energy source most relied on to generate electricity, accounting for 23 percent of use.[3]

The United States and Canada are the world's leading hydroelectricity generators, together accounting for a quarter of global supply.[4] (See Figure 2.) But environmental considerations, particularly the effect of dams on migratory fish populations, are hampering hydropower's viability. In 1997 the U.S. government refused for the first time to relicense a hydroelectric dam—required of all power-producing plants—in Maine, and ordered the dismantling of dams in Washington State to restore declining populations of migratory fish.[5] With some 550 U.S. dams due for relicensing over the next 15 years, the pressure is building to remove other projects endangering river systems, including the long-controversial Glen Canyon Dam.[6]

The human resettlement impacts of large dams—which have already displaced an estimated 30 million people worldwide—are driving resistance in the developing world, where most future projects are planned.[7] Greater public scrutiny and criticism during the 1990s have forced the World Bank, traditionally the main funder of large dams, to cancel support for massive projects in India and Nepal.[8] A 1996 Bank internal review of large dams financed between 1960 and 1995 concluded that only 14 out of 50 met "acceptable social and environmental standards."[9]

In response to these problems, in April 1997 the Bank agreed to create an independent commission to review the viability of large dam projects, and to work with the World Conservation Union to establish international guidelines for dam construction and operation.[10] Later that summer, however, the Bank began supporting Southeast Asia's largest dam, a 680-megawatt plant in Laos that will displace 4,500 people.[11] And in August 1997 the International Finance Corporation, the Bank's private-sector lending arm, was accused of censuring an independent review criticizing the social and environmental impacts of a dam being built along Chile's Bío-Bío River.[12]

The fate of large dam projects in developing countries is increasingly being determined by private investors.[13] European and Japanese multinationals, with the help of export agencies, are supporting the 18,200-megawatt Three Gorges Dam on China's Yangtze River.[14] Diversion of the Yangtze was completed in November 1997 to allow construction of the dam, which would be the largest hydroelectric project ever built and is expected to displace some 1.9 million people.[15] At the same time, the Malaysian government's failure to attract investors for its controversial Bakun Dam—canceled in 1990 and revived in 1993—has forced a delay in construction.[16] The proposed 2,400-megawatt dam would flood an estimated 70,000 hectares of tropical forest and displace more than 9,000 people.[17]

As large dams come increasingly under siege, some experts are pointing to a potentially greater role for "microhydro" projects that develop river tributaries in a more benign fashion. These smaller plants, some of which are known as "run-of-river" as they do not require the damming of river systems, have a worldwide potential estimated at some 20,000 megawatts.[18] China is already estimated to have 16,000 megawatts of small-hydro capacity installed.[19]

At present, an estimated additional 50,000 megawatts of large hydropower projects are planned worldwide, mostly in developing countries.[20] But the long-term potential of hydroelectricity is likely to be constrained by its high up-front costs and greater attention to its social and ecological effects.[21]

WORLD HYDROELECTRIC GENERATING CAPACITY, 1950–96

YEAR	CAPACITY (megawatts)
1950	44,956
1955	67,857
1960	157,080
1965	214,023
1966	223,997
1967	236,088
1968	251,249
1969	266,900
1970	290,607
1971	295,564
1972	305,339
1973	335,561
1974	339,271
1975	371,495
1976	383,667
1977	396,426
1978	423,601
1979	443,836
1980	466,938
1981	483,938
1982	505,041
1983	517,899
1984	540,244
1985	560,956
1986	575,665
1987	596,262
1988	618,186
1989	631,374
1990	641,731
1991	656,094
1992	670,829
1993	685,907
1994	697,839
1995	708,931
1996 (prel)	714,602

SOURCES: Worldwatch estimates based on UN, BP.

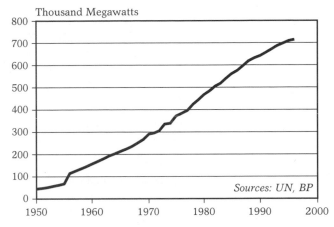

Figure 1: World Hydroelectric Generating Capacity, 1950–96

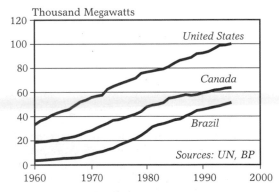

Figure 2: Hydroelectric Generating Capacity in the United States, Canada, and Brazil 1960–95

Wind Power Sets Records Christopher Flavin

Global wind power generating capacity rose 25 percent in 1997, reaching 7,630 megawatts by year's end, according to preliminary estimates by BTM Consult, a Danish wind consulting firm.[1] (See Figure 1.) Some 1,560 megawatts of wind turbines were added in 1997—a new record, and a big increase from the 1,290 megawatts added in 1996.[2] (See Figure 2.)

Wind power's impressive growth continues to be led by four countries with strong policies to promote use of this increasingly economical energy source. Germany's wind industry rebounded in 1997, with a record 530 megawatts added, taking installed capacity past 2,000 megawatts—the first country to reach that milestone.[3] (See Figure 3.) A large protest in Bonn opposed plans to cut government support for wind power.[4] Still, the Parliament considered capping at 5 percent the amount of wind power that electric utilities are required to purchase at the premium price—which could slow the pace of development.[5]

The second largest wind power market in 1997 was Denmark, where 285 megawatts were added, taking total capacity above 1,100 megawatts.[6] The wind now provides 7 percent of Denmark's electricity, higher than in any other country.[7] In some townships, the wind capacity exceeds local demand for electricity, so the excess is sent to nearby towns.[8] The popularity of wind power in Denmark was demonstrated by an opinion poll showing that Vestas, the largest wind turbine manufacturer, was the country's second most "environmentally friendly" corporation—just behind Lego Toys.[9]

Spain's wind market surged to number three in 1997, adding 272 megawatts, more than double the amount in 1996.[10] Of Spain's 552 megawatts of installed capacity, more than two thirds were added in the last two years.[11] Unlike Denmark and Germany, which install most of their turbines alone or in small clusters, Spain has focused on large wind farms—including a 72-megawatt installation announced in late 1997.[12]

India's wind power industry kept struggling in 1997, with just 120 megawatts added, due to political uncertainties and efforts to scale back overly generous wind energy tax incentives.[13] India still has the developing world's largest wind power installations, however, at 950 megawatts.[14]

China's wind power industry continued to make headway in 1997, with 67 megawatts added—the most ever.[15] Several European companies have developed active wind power joint ventures in China, where the wind resource is huge.[16] The government is now providing a number of incentives for wind energy development, but no firm legal underpinning for wind power development has yet been established.[17] One intriguing project is General Motors' plan to operate the world's first "zero emission" transportation system—a fleet of wind-powered electric cars and trucks on the island of Nan'ao in the South China Sea.[18]

The next three largest wind power markets in 1997 were the United Kingdom, with 55 new megawatts; the Netherlands, at 44 megawatts; and Ireland, at 42 megawatts.[19] Project delays held the United States to 11 megawatts installed in 1997, but the American Wind Energy Association identified 800 megawatts of projects that could be completed in the next few years.[20]

The most intriguing development in 1997 was the move of several large companies into the wind energy business. Enron Corp added the German wind energy company Tacke to its earlier acquisition of the U.S. wind leader, Zond Corporation.[21] Tomen, a Japanese trading company, announced plans to invest $1.2 billion in European wind projects.[22] In November, Royal Dutch Shell said it would invest $500 million in renewables, and also joined the European Wind Energy Association.[23] It may find the burgeoning offshore market attractive, given its experience in building and operating North Sea oil rigs.

As the wind energy market expands, wind turbine costs continue to fall. An analysis by British economist David Milborrow indicates that generating costs for new wind turbines in Germany are competitive with new coal-fired power plants—a technology with nearly a century of engineering experience behind it.[24]

WORLD WIND ENERGY GENERATING CAPACITY, 1980–97

YEAR	CAPACITY (megawatts)
1980	10
1981	25
1982	90
1983	210
1984	600
1985	1,020
1986	1,270
1987	1,450
1988	1,580
1989	1,730
1990	1,930
1991	2,170
1992	2,510
1993	2,990
1994	3,680
1995	4,820
1996	6,115
1997 (prel)	7,630

NET ANNUAL ADDITIONS TO WORLD WIND GENERATING CAPACITY, 1980–97

YEAR	CAPACITY (megawatts)
1980	5
1981	15
1982	65
1983	120
1984	390
1985	420
1986	250
1987	180
1988	130
1989	150
1990	200
1991	240
1992	340
1993	480
1994	720
1995	1,294
1996	1,290
1997 (prel)	1,566

SOURCES: Birger Madsen, BTM Consult, Denmark, 10 January 1998; BTM Consult, *International Wind Energy Development: World Market Update 1996* (Ringkobing, Denmark: March 1997).

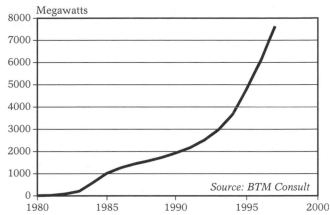

Figure 1: World Wind Energy Generating Capacity, 1980–97

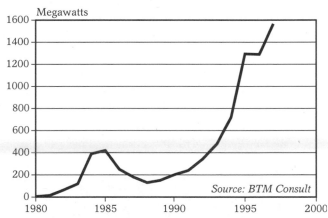

Figure 2: Net Annual Additions to World Wind Energy Generating Capacity, 1980–97

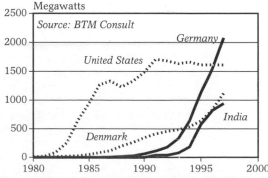

Figure 3: Wind Generating Capacity in the United States, Germany, Denmark, and India, 1980–97

Solar Cell Shipments Hit New High   Molly O'Meara

Global shipments of photovoltaic (PV) cells surpassed 126 megawatts in 1997, up 43 percent from 1996.[1] (See Figure 1.) This was the largest increase in 14 years and the fourth straight year of double-digit growth for PV cells, the wafer-thin semiconductors that turn sunlight into electricity.[2] Cumulative output reached more than 800 megawatts.[3]

This jump in PV shipments was spurred primarily by demand from Japan, where government support for solar homes, through subsidies and tax incentives, is strong.[4] In 1997, solar systems were installed in 9,400 homes; the goal for 1998 is 13,800 homes.[5] These efforts prompted shipments from Japanese companies to soar 65 percent, to 35 megawatts, in 1997.[6] The Ministry of Trade and Industry plans to reduce the level of direct subsidy gradually to zero in 2001, when increased production will have made solar systems competitive without the subsidy.[7] By 2000, the government expects to see solar cells installed on more than 70,000 homes.[8]

The cost of producing PV cells continued to drop in 1997, as manufacturers increased their capacity to make less costly thin-film silicon.[9] But demand was so strong that wholesale factory prices for PV cells actually edged above $4 per watt, reversing a downward trend of two decades.[10] (See Figure 2.)

In part to meet demand from the burgeoning Japanese market, U.S. companies increased shipments by 36 percent, to 53 megawatts, in 1997.[11] Solar electricity remains a niche market in the United States, although it is gaining a foothold in some areas, as electric utilities become more competitive and consumers voice a preference for "green power."[12] For example, the Sacramento Municipal Utility District in California has installed 5.7 megawatts' worth of electrical grid-linked solar panels on more than 420 homes and buildings, and above several parking lots.[13] To further encourage the domestic market, President Clinton announced in June 1997 a campaign to install solar systems in 1 million U.S. buildings by 2010.[14] The details of the U.S. rooftop program have yet to materialize, however, and the effort will likely lag behind that of Japan.

European output of PVs jumped 56 percent, to 29.3 megawatts, in 1997.[15] Production in Germany, at under 3 megawatts, was behind that in the United States, Japan, France, Italy, and India. German PV shipments have declined in recent years as federal subsidies have dwindled and major manufacturers have relocated to the United States.[16] In an effort to reverse this trend, Germany's Research and Technology Minister announced new financial support in 1997 for two major solar projects that will boost Germany's production capacity beyond 40 megawatts by 1999.[17] One of these will be a 25-megawatt solar cell production plant, the world's largest, built by Pilkington Solar International and Shell.[18]

Solar cells are already the most economical power source for many of the 2 billion people in developing countries who lack access to electricity.[19] Shipments of PVs to the developing world have increased with the announcement of new financing initiatives that reduce the up-front cost of solar electricity for rural villagers.[20] For instance, the Solar Electric Light Company operates subsidiaries in India and Viet Nam, supports joint ventures in China and Sri Lanka, and has lined up several million dollars for consumer finance.[21] Soluz, Inc., offers monthly solar electric service in the Dominican Republic and Honduras and by late 1997 was serving more than 1,000 customers at rates comparable to the monthly cost of kerosene.[22] A new company, Sunlight Power International, plans to provide solar service on three continents, in part through strategic investments in Soluz.[23]

Although the Asian financial crisis could well slow PV demand in the short term, the industry's characteristic strong growth is expected to prevail over the long term.[24] Even large oil companies announced new commitments to solar in 1997. For instance, British Petroleum revealed plans to increase sales of solar products 10-fold over the next decade, and Shell said it will invest more than $500 million in solar and other renewables over the next five years.[25]

WORLD PHOTOVOLTAIC SHIPMENTS, 1971–97

YEAR	SHIPMENTS (megawatts)
1971	0.1
1975	1.8
1976	2.0
1977	2.2
1978	2.5
1979	4.0
1980	6.5
1981	7.8
1982	9.1
1983	17.2
1984	21.5
1985	22.8
1986	26.0
1987	29.2
1988	33.8
1989	40.2
1990	46.5
1991	55.4
1992	57.9
1993	60.1
1994	69.4
1995	78.6
1996	88.6
1997 (prel)	126.7

SOURCE: Paul Maycock, *PV News.*

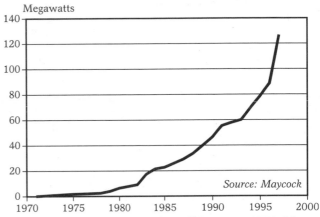

Figure 1: World Photovoltaic Shipments, 1971–97

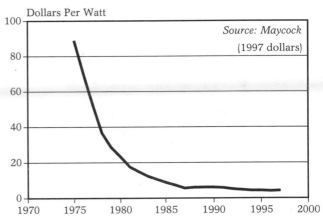

Figure 2: Average Factory Price for Photovoltaic Modules, 1975–97

Sales of Compact Fluorescents Surge Molly O'Meara

Worldwide sales of energy-efficient compact fluorescent lamps (CFLs) rose 24 percent in 1997, to 356 million.[1] (See Figure 1.) Since 1988, sales have increased eightfold.[2] The 980 million CFLs used today would require 14,700 megawatts of electricity, versus 58,800 megawatts for the same light from old-fashioned incandescents. The difference in electricity requirements is the equivalent of about 100 average-sized coal-fired power plants.[3]

Electricity savings translate into averted pollution: the 228 million CFLs in use in North America at the beginning of 1998 will avoid 2.5 million tons of carbon emissions in the course of one year and 55,000 tons of sulfur dioxide.[4]

Compact fluorescents were outsold 28 to 1 by incandescent bulbs in 1997, a market that continues to grow by 3–5 percent a year worldwide.[5] But because CFLs last 10 times as long as traditional bulbs, they accounted for fully 26 percent of the combined lighting capacity sold.[6] CFLs may cost 8–20 times as much upfront as incandescents, but they yield savings in electricity costs that make them ultimately less expensive.[7] For example, in the United States, buying a CFL instead of a standard bulb will save the buyer nearly $40 over the lifetime of the lamp.[8]

In the late 1990s, CFLs are spreading to new markets. Western Europe and North America accounted for just half of world CFL sales in 1997, down from 70 percent five years earlier.[9] In the same five years, CFL sales in Eastern Europe soared from nothing to 10 million, and sales in developing nations of Asia and Latin America rocketed from less than one sixth of total sales to one third.[10]

The strongest growth is in China, where CFL sales in 1997 increased 147 percent to reach 37 million—one tenth of the world total.[11] (See Figure 2.) A government-sponsored Green Lights program aims to further boost the number of high-efficiency lights sold domestically.[12] China, with annual production of roughly 100 million bulbs, is the world's largest maker of CFLs.[13] The number of companies producing CFLs in China doubled between 1995 and 1997.[14]

As production capacity swells, prices for CFLs are falling. In 1997, retail prices from Philips, a major manufacturer, were half those of 1996.[15] And the Swedish retail giant IKEA, which has furniture stores in 28 countries, began selling Chinese-made CFLs for as low as $5 in Europe.[16]

In Poland, the International Finance Corporation, the private-sector arm of the World Bank, has used Global Environment Facility funds to subsidize CFL manufacturers and thereby reduce the cost of these bulbs to consumers.[17] The program resulted in a threefold increase in the number of CFLs produced and a 50-percent drop in retail price between 1995 and 1997.[18] Several countries in Eastern Europe and South America have expressed interest in replicating the program.[19]

The market for energy-efficient lighting is becoming more diverse as new alternatives, such as metal halide bulbs that can be one third more efficient than CFLs, begin to enter the residential market.[20] Metal halides, whose bright white light is commonly shed in large, outdoor sports arenas, are now available in smaller sizes and in warmer colors closer to those of incandescents.[21]

A boom in inefficient halogen floor lamps in North America and parts of Europe, however, is negating electricity savings.[22] Since the early 1990s, low prices and bright lights have made these lamps popular among college students, apartment dwellers, and others who live or work in rooms that lack built-in, high-quality lighting.[23] The 40 million halogen lamps in use in the United States are consuming more electricity than CFLs are saving.[24]

In addition, high-wattage halogens may reach fire-starting temperatures in excess of 400 degrees Celsius.[25] (CFLs rarely get hotter than 60 degrees.) In 1997, spurred by safety concerns and the extension of an energy-efficiency labeling program to residential light fixtures, at least seven U.S. manufacturers introduced alternatives that look like the popular halogen model but use more-efficient CFLs or metal halides.[26]

WORLD SALES OF COMPACT
FLUORESCENT BULBS, 1988–97

YEAR	SALES (million)
1988	45
1989	59
1990	83
1991	112
1992	138
1993	179
1994	206
1995	244
1996	286
1997	356

SOURCES: Evan Mills, Lawrence Berkeley
Laboratory, letter to Worldwatch,
3 February 1993; Nils Borg, *IAEEL
Newsletter*, March–April 1998.

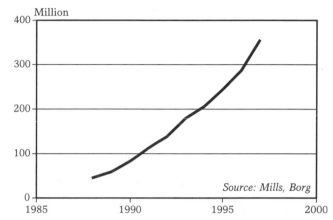

**Figure 1: World Sales of Compact Fluorescent Bulbs,
1988–97**

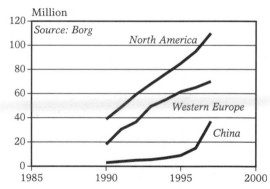

**Figure 2: Regional Sales of Compact
Fluorescent Bulbs, 1990–97**

Atmospheric
Trends

Carbon Emissions Resume Rise Seth Dunn

Annual global emissions of carbon from the burning of fossil fuels rose 107 million tons in 1997 to a new high of 6.3 billion tons.[1] (See Figure 1.) The 1.5-percent increase was due to continued emissions growth in the industrial and developing worlds, and a drop of emissions in the former Eastern bloc.[2] (See Figure 2.) World carbon emissions have risen nearly fourfold since 1950.[3]

Western industrial countries account for approximately 55 percent of the carbon emitted since 1950, and for 45 percent of current emissions.[4] The world's leading emitter is the United States, with 23 percent of the total.[5] U.S. carbon output expanded 8.8 percent between 1990 and 1996, with a 3.5-percent increase in 1996 alone.[6] Emissions from Japan grew 12.5 percent over this six years, and Australia's increased 9.6 percent.[7]

The European Union was only 1 percent above 1990 levels by 1996, however, thanks largely to reductions of 7.6, 2.0, and 1.1 percent in Germany, the United Kingdom, and France.[8] These cuts resulted, respectively, from energy reforms and the shutdown of energy-intensive industries, coal subsidy removal, and reduced reliance on fossil-fuel-based electricity.

In Eastern Europe and the former Soviet Union, which account for 21 percent of historical emissions since 1950 and 15 percent of today's output, emissions have plateaued after dropping dramatically earlier in the decade.[9] Emissions from Russia, the world's third highest, are nearly 33 percent below 1990 levels; those in the Ukraine are almost 56 percent under this mark.[10] Although emissions from these countries are expected to rebound as economies continue their recovery, they are unlikely to return to 1990 levels.

Emissions are growing fastest in the developing world—responsible for 24 percent of emissions since 1950 and a 40-percent share today.[11] China, the world's second leading emitter with a 14-percent share, has seen a 29-percent rise in carbon output since 1990.[12] India has registered a 38-percent increase, and Indonesia, 47 percent.[13] On a per capita basis, however, developing-country emissions are well below those of the industrial world: the average American accounts for 21 times as much carbon as the typical Indian.[14] And the volume of industrial-country output is far greater: the increase in U.S. emissions alone between 1990 and 1996 exceeded the combined total annual output of Brazil and Indonesia.[15]

When released to the atmosphere, carbon reacts with oxygen to form carbon dioxide (CO_2), the greenhouse gas responsible for 64 percent of ongoing human-induced changes in climate.[16] Atmospheric concentrations of CO_2 reached 363.6 parts per million (ppm) in 1997, their highest point in 160,000 years.[17] According to the Intergovernmental Panel on Climate Change (IPCC), a doubling of preindustrial concentrations to 550 ppm would increase global average surface temperatures 1–3.5 degrees Celsius over the next century.[18] This would cause a wide array of dislocations to human and natural systems.[19]

The IPCC estimates that annual carbon emissions must be reduced to below 2 billion tons by 2050 to stabilize concentrations at 350 ppm—a level scientists believe would keep temperature within the maximum rates of change during the last 200,000 years.[20] Movement toward this accelerated decarbonization was made in Kyoto, Japan, in December 1997, when 171 nations agreed to a legally binding protocol to the U.N. climate treaty committing western industrial and former Eastern bloc nations to cut their collective greenhouse gas emissions 5.2 percent below 1990 levels between 2008 and 2012.[21]

Meeting the Kyoto target would actually require only a 2.9-percent cut from current levels, as emissions from this group of countries are already 2.3 percent below the 1990 mark.[22] Countries will also be permitted to trade emissions, allowing western industrial nations to purchase from former Eastern bloc countries the right to emit as much as 300 million tons of carbon annually in order to meet their goals.[23] Rules for trading and new developing-country commitments will be discussed at the next climate conference, being held in Buenos Aires in November 1998.[24]

WORLD CARBON EMISSIONS FROM FOSSIL FUEL BURNING, 1950–97

YEAR	EMISSIONS (mill. tons of carbon)
1950	1,609
1955	2,009
1960	2,520
1965	3,068
1966	3,222
1967	3,334
1968	3,501
1969	3,715
1970	3,986
1971	4,143
1972	4,306
1973	4,538
1974	4,545
1975	4,518
1976	4,777
1977	4,910
1978	4,950
1979	5,229
1980	5,159
1981	4,988
1982	4,948
1983	4,935
1984	5,103
1985	5,273
1986	5,459
1987	5,580
1988	5,795
1989	5,897
1990	5,952
1991	6,017
1992	5,915
1993	5,876
1994	6,011
1995	6,219
1996 (est)	6,212
1997 (prel)	6,305

SOURCES: Worldwatch estimates based on ORNL, BP, DOE, EC, PlanEcon, and *Journal of Commerce*.

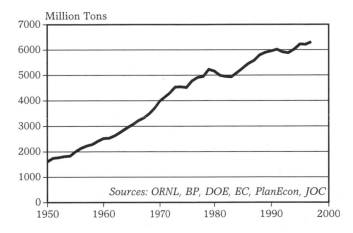

Sources: ORNL, BP, DOE, EC, PlanEcon, JOC

Figure 1: World Carbon Emissions from Fossil Fuel Burning, 1950–97

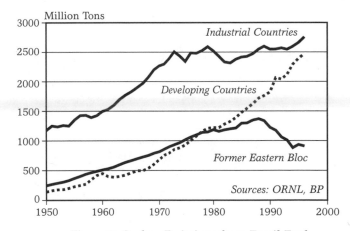

Sources: ORNL, BP

Figure 2: Carbon Emissions from Fossil Fuel Burning, by Economic Region, 1950–96

Global Temperature Reaches Record High   Molly O'Meara

Spurred by a strong El Niño in the tropical Pacific, the air temperature at the Earth's surface in 1997 averaged 14.40 degrees Celsius, just barely surpassing the record high set in 1995, according to NASA's Goddard Institute of Space Studies in New York.[1] (See Figure 1, which uses a lower base number than earlier *Vital Signs*.)[2] Long-term surface temperature data sets maintained by the Climatic Research Unit of the University of East Anglia in England and the U.S. National Oceanic and Atmospheric Administration (NOAA) also show 1997 as the hottest year on record.[3] (The data sets are based on slightly different combinations of worldwide land and sea measurements.)

The 1990s—the hottest decade since recordkeeping began in 1866—appear to be part of a twentieth-century warming trend.[4] Ice core records from Antarctica show that temperatures this century are higher than any since at least 1400 AD.[5] With warmer temperatures, the timing of the seasons appears to have shifted in northern latitudes in the past half-century, with spring now occurring earlier and fall later.[6]

Lonnie Thompson of Ohio State University has found that ice caps in the Andes are melting more quickly since the 1970s; glaciers atop the European Alps have lost half their volume since 1850, according to Wilfried Haeberli, director of the World Glacier Monitoring Service.[7] Satellite radar shows that North Greenland's ice cap is thinning by about 2.5 centimeters a year.[8] And at the South Pole, analysis of whaling records suggests that a quarter of the sea ice around Antarctica has disappeared, with a 15-year period of dramatic loss starting in the late 1950s.[9] Average sea level worldwide has risen 10–25 centimeters in the last century as water has expanded and ice has melted.[10]

Announcing the record-breaking warmth of 1997, NOAA Senior Scientist Tom Karl linked the sustained trend toward increasingly warmer global temperatures to heat-trapping "greenhouse gases" released by human activities, such as the burning of fossil fuels.[11] Indeed, this is the consensus of the world's top climate scientists, assembled by the United Nations in the Intergovernmental Panel on Climate Change.[12] The magnitude, timing, and geographic pattern of observed temperature changes over the past century match closely those simulated by computer models.[13]

The El Niño that influenced temperatures in 1997 characteristically began with a warming of the ocean off the coast of Peru, bringing heavy precipitation to the eastern Pacific while stranding the western Pacific in a drought.[14] By the fall of 1997, sea surface temperatures in the equatorial Pacific were warmer than those recorded at the same time in 1982, during the last strong El Niño.[15] This warming contributed to a record high global average sea surface temperature in 1997.[16] (See Figure 2.) Although the link between El Niño and human-induced climate change is not well understood, El Niños have occurred more often since 1977, with an unusually prolonged event from 1990 to 1995.[17]

If average temperatures continue to rise as projected, the consequences are likely to include a greater incidence of floods and droughts, diminished food production, and an expanded range for disease vectors.[18] In concert with other problems that stem from a growing human population, warmer temperatures could push ecosystems past tolerable thresholds.[19] These unhealthy synergisms may already be spurring events such as the worldwide decline of amphibians, the large-scale growth of toxic algae in the oceans, and the death of coral reefs.[20]

One of the gravest threats is the effect of higher temperatures on the North Atlantic "conveyor belt": an infusion of fresh water from melting ice caps could lessen the subtle differences in water temperature and salinity that drive the oceanic conveyor.[21] Without the heat that the conveyor brings to the North Atlantic, Europe might be plunged into a mini-ice age—an ironic side effect of global warming.[22]

GLOBAL AVERAGE TEMPERATURE, 1950–97

YEAR	TEMPERATURE[1] (degrees Celsius)
1950	13.86
1955	13.92
1960	13.98
1965	13.88
1966	13.95
1967	13.99
1968	13.93
1969	14.05
1970	14.02
1971	13.92
1972	14.00
1973	14.11
1974	13.92
1975	13.92
1976	13.82
1977	14.11
1978	14.05
1979	14.09
1980	14.18
1981	14.29
1982	14.08
1983	14.24
1984	14.11
1985	14.09
1986	14.15
1987	14.27
1988	14.28
1989	14.22
1990	14.38
1991	14.36
1992	14.11
1993	14.14
1994	14.23
1995	14.39
1996	14.31
1997 (prel)	14.40

[1]Base number is 1 degree Celsius lower than in earlier *Vital Signs*.
SOURCE: Surface Air Temperature Analyses, Goddard Institute for Space Studies, New York, 14 January 1998.

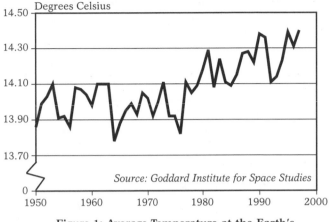

Figure 1: Average Temperature at the Earth's Surface, 1950–97

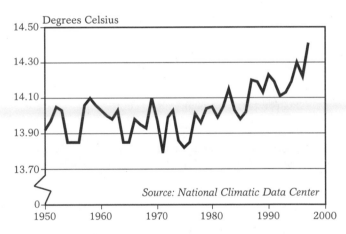

Figure 2: Global Average Sea Surface Temperature, 1950–97

CFC Production Continues to Plummet   Molly O'Meara

Global production of chlorofluorocarbons (CFCs), compounds that deplete Earth's protective ozone shield, decreased by 50 percent in 1996, the most recent year for which data are available.[1] Falling for the ninth straight year, CFC output in 1996 dropped to 88 percent below the 1988 peak. (See Figure 1.)

A landmark treaty, the 1987 Montreal Protocol, spurred this rapid decline.[2] The Protocol and its amendments have banned CFC production in industrial countries since 1996, except for a small volume produced either for export to developing countries or for essential domestic uses, such as asthma inhalers.[3] The top two CFC producers in 1996 were China and India, which are bound by the protocol's 1999 stabilization target and 2010 phaseout deadline for developing countries (see Figure 2); the third highest producer was Russia, which failed to meet the 1996 deadline.[4]

Chlorine from CFCs destroys ozone in the stratosphere, 10–50 kilometers above Earth's surface. The effect is most pronounced over Antarctica, where an ozone hole first observed in 1985 recurs during the Southern Hemisphere spring, when temperatures and winds maximize ozone depletion.[5] Although CFC production has already plummeted, these compounds take years to reach the stratosphere, and some last for decades or centuries once there. Thus maximum ozone loss is expected right around now, as the concentration of CFCs in the stratosphere peaks between 1997 and 1999.[6]

In 1997, the 22 million-square-kilometer Antarctic ozone hole, more than twice the size of Europe, nearly matched the 1995 record.[7] A springtime ozone hole over the Arctic, observed for the first time in 1995, is a new source of concern.[8] And record ozone losses have also occurred over the populous and agriculturally abundant mid to high latitudes of both hemispheres.[9]

Ozone loss leaves Earth vulnerable to ultraviolet rays that damage humans, crops, natural ecosystems, and even plastics.[10] The Montreal Protocol will save the world some 19.1 million cases of nonmelanoma skin cancer through 2060 and at least $459 billion in damages to fisheries, agriculture, and plastic building materials, according to a recent study by Environment Canada, a government agency.[11] The costs of complying with the protocol, calculated to be $235 billion, are less than first estimated because many of the industries that relied on CFCs have saved money by redesigning manufacturing processes or using simpler, cheaper substances.[12] For example, the replacement of CFCs in aerosol cans with compressed air or hydrocarbons saves U.S. consumers an estimated $165 million a year.[13]

Despite the steep drop in CFC production, the decline is somewhat slower than expected.[14] Projections of ozone recovery made in 1994 assumed that CFC production would have fallen to 50,000 tons by 1996—but actual production was three times as much.[15] To help speed the move away from CFCs, the Multilateral Fund—a joint initiative of the World Bank and U.N. agencies—has allocated more than $695 million to projects in 111 developing countries that convert processes or product lines to ozone-benign technologies.[16]

The black market is thwarting the transition away from CFCs.[17] An estimated 40,000 tons of CFCs, more than a quarter of total production, were smuggled into industrial countries in 1996.[18] Today's inflated production levels, sustained by the black market, will affect future levels, as production between 1995 and 1997 forms the baseline for the 1999 freeze and subsequent phaseout in developing countries.[19] As Russia is believed to be a major source of illicit CFCs, the World Bank is urging industrial countries to help fund the conversion of Russian CFC manufacturing plants to ozone-friendly alternatives.[20]

Although CFCs are on the decline, other ozone-depleting compounds are not. Remaining challenges include phasing out the pesticide methyl bromide and moving away from hydrochlorofluorocarbons, an interim substitute for CFCs.[21]

WORLD CFC PRODUCTION, 1950–96

YEAR	TOTAL[1] (thousand tons)
1950	42
1955	86
1960	150
1965	330
1966	390
1967	440
1968	510
1969	580
1970	640
1971	690
1972	790
1973	900
1974	970
1975	860
1976	920
1977	880
1978	880
1979	850
1980	880
1981	890
1982	870
1983	950
1984	1,050
1985	1,090
1986	1,130
1987	1,250
1988	1,260
1989	1,150
1990	820
1991	720
1992	630
1993	520
1994	388
1995	300
1996 (prel)	141

[1] Includes the major CFCs: CFC-11, CFC-12, CFC-113, CFC-114, and CFC-115.
SOURCES: 1950 and 1955, Worldwatch estimates based on Chemical Manufacturers Association; 1960–95 from DuPont, Wilmington, DE, private communication; 1996, Worldwatch estimate based on UNEP.

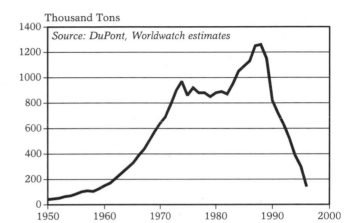

Thousand Tons
Source: DuPont, Worldwatch estimates

Figure 1: World Production of Chlorofluorocarbons, 1950–96

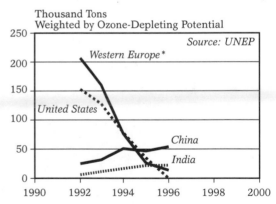

Thousand Tons
Weighted by Ozone-Depleting Potential
Source: UNEP
Western Europe*
United States
China
India

Figure 2: Production of Chlorofluorocarbons, Selected Countries, 1992–96

*France, Germany, Italy, Netherlands, Spain, United Kingdom

Economic Trends

World Economy Continues Rapid Expansion   Lester R. Brown

Despite the financial turmoil in East Asia that began in the last half of 1997, the world economy expanded from $28.0 trillion in 1996 to $29.1 trillion in 1997, a gain of 4.1 percent.[1] (See Figure 1.) This marked the third consecutive year of growth at 4 percent or more.

With world population expanding at 1.4 percent in 1997, income per person rose from $4,821 to $4,977, a gain of 2.6 percent.[2] (See Figure 2.) Given this advance, income per person worldwide should surpass $5,000 in 1998—2.6 times the level in 1950.

Advanced industrial economies expanded at 3 percent in 1997, while developing countries grew at roughly 6 percent.[3] And the countries in transition from centrally planned to market economies—those in Eastern Europe and the former Soviet Union—expanded at 2 percent.[4] For the transition economies, this was their fastest rate of collective growth in several years.

The United States and Canada led the major industrial countries in 1997, with growth in their economies of 3.7 percent each.[5] The United Kingdom's 3.3 percent topped the major industrial countries of Europe by a wide margin.[6] Germany and France came in at just over 2 percent, while Italy barely made 1 percent.[7]

Growth in the transition economies was led by Georgia, which turned in a second year of 10-percent growth, the fastest of any transition economy since the breakup of the former Soviet Union.[8] The Kyrgyz Republic in Central Asia expanded at nearly 7 percent, maintaining its rapid growth.[9] The countries registering between 5 and 6 percent growth were Armenia, Azerbaijan, Croatia, Estonia, Macedonia, and Poland.[10]

Among developing regions, Asia again was first, expanding by 7.6 percent, marking the first time in five years that growth in this region was below 8 percent.[11] Within Asia, China continued to set the pace with an expansion of more than 9 percent, though Viet Nam also managed a second consecutive year of 9-percent growth.[12]

Thailand fell from the ranks of the fast-growth economies as financial disorder took a heavy toll. Indonesia, Malaysia, and South Korea are also losing momentum as their economies are weakened by bad loans and an associated fall in confidence and currency values. Between May and December of 1997, the International Monetary Fund (IMF) lowered its 1997 estimated growth for Thailand from 6.8 percent to 0.6 percent, for Indonesia from 8.0 to 5.0, for Malaysia from 8.0 to 7.6, and for the Philippines from 6.3 to 4.3 percent.[13]

The Indian subcontinent, led by India with growth of 6.6 percent, racked up an overall growth of roughly 6 percent in 1997.[14] The net effect was a rise in incomes for the region's 1.3 billion people of nearly 4 percent.[15] While India's growth over the last three years has averaged nearly 7 percent, it does not put the nation on quite the same steep growth trajectory as China.[16] In Bangladesh, growth has hovered around 5 percent a year in each of the last five years, slightly faster than in Pakistan during the same period.[17]

Latin America grew at 4.1 percent in 1997, roughly half the rate of Asia.[18] Within this region, Argentina set the pace among the big three economies, with a 7.5-percent expansion.[19] Mexico and Brazil followed at 4.5 and 3.5 percent, respectively.[20] Among the four Andean countries, growth ranged from a low of 2.8 percent in Colombia to a high of 5.5 percent in Chile.[21]

Africa's economy, slowing from the 5 percent pace of 1996, expanded by 3.7 percent in 1997, slightly faster than population growth.[22] Uganda again set the pace with another 7-percent expansion.[23] Countries growing 5 to 6 percent were Cameroon, Côte d'Ivoire, Sudan, and Tunisia.[24]

In December 1997, when it issued a special interim report in response to the turmoil in East Asia, the IMF lowered its estimate for worldwide economic growth in 1997 from 4.2 percent to 4.1 percent. For 1998, it lowered its projections to 3.5 percent, much slower than the 4.3 percent estimated in its regular semiannual assessment that came out in October.[25]

GROSS WORLD PRODUCT, 1950–97

YEAR	TOTAL (trill. 1995 dollars)	PER CAPITA (1995 dollars)
1950	4.9	1,925
1955	6.3	2,282
1960	7.9	2,599
1965	10.2	3,058
1966	10.7	3,147
1967	11.1	3,196
1968	11.8	3,313
1969	12.6	3,459
1970	13.1	3,529
1971	13.6	3,593
1972	14.2	3,690
1973	15.2	3,848
1974	15.3	3,808
1975	15.4	3,771
1976	16.2	3,893
1977	16.8	3,979
1978	17.5	4,063
1979	18.1	4,141
1980	18.3	4,100
1981	18.5	4,088
1982	18.6	4,045
1983	19.2	4,086
1984	19.9	4,181
1985	20.7	4,272
1986	21.2	4,306
1987	22.0	4,387
1988	23.1	4,516
1989	23.8	4,591
1990	24.3	4,613
1991	24.2	4,517
1992	24.6	4,524
1993	25.2	4,559
1994	26.0	4,633
1995	26.9	4,736
1996	28.0	4,821
1997 (prel)	29.1	4,977

SOURCES: GWP data for 1950 and 1955 from Herbert R. Block, *The Planetary Product in 1980: A Creative Pause?* (Washington, DC: U.S. Department of State, 1981); World Bank and International Monetary Fund tables.

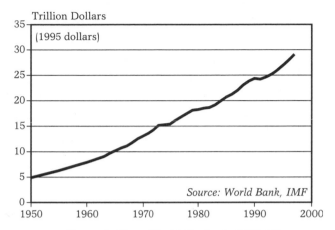

Figure 1: Gross World Product, 1950–97

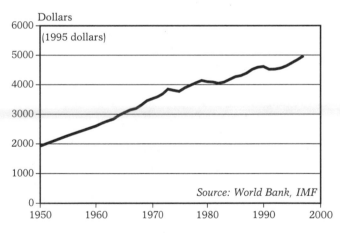

Figure 2: Gross World Product Per Person, 1950–97

Trade Remains Strong   Michael Strauss

In 1997, global trade grew 4.4 percent in value, to $5.9 trillion (1995 dollars).[1] Despite turmoil in the Asian currency markets in the fall, preliminary estimates indicate strong overall trade growth for the year. The increase is consistent with the rapid expansion of exports worldwide throughout the 1990s. (See Figures 1 and 2.) By value, trade has grown at twice the pace of world economic output this decade.[2]

Leading the way in 1997 were developing nations, whose exports grew at 6.1 percent.[3] Their exports also diversified; the proportion that included minerals and agricultural items (primary products) declined precipitously from 80 percent in 1980 to 40 percent in 1996.[4] In the same period, manufactured goods as a proportion of developing nations' exports grew from 20 to 60 percent.[5]

Trade trends are still dominated by the United States, Japan, and the European Union, but the World Bank projects that in the future they will be set by the "big five" developing nations—China, India, Indonesia, Brazil, and Russia.[6] These five countries account for more than 50 percent of world population, but only 9 percent of world exports.[7] This share will explode to 25–40 percent by 2020, according to the World Bank.[8] And the Bank predicts that half of all export growth in the industrial world from now until 2020 will come from expanded trade with currently developing countries.[9]

Exports within regions remain a major source of the overall growth in trade as well. Several regional trade regimes expanded their memberships and mandates in 1997. Chile saw modest increases in trade and foreign investment as the newest member of Mercosur (the South American customs union, which also includes Brazil, Argentina, Paraguay, and Uruguay).[10] A much larger Free Trade Area of the Americas is under discussion that would unite 35 Pan-American economies in a free-trade zone sometime in the next decade.[11]

In late November, Vancouver hosted the Asia Pacific Economic Co-operation summit, where the 18-member organization—after considering a strategy of trade protection for the crisis-stricken nations of the region—chose to back the International Monetary Fund's reform plan, including the removal of tariffs on 15 traded sectors.[12]

In June, the United States International Trade Commission released an assessment of the North American Free Trade Agreement (NAFTA).[13] While an overall evaluation of NAFTA after three years would be premature, it is clear that trade between the United States, Canada, and Mexico has increased much faster than U.S. trade with the rest of the world.[14] By the end of 1997, an estimated $1 billion in trade crossed the U.S.-Canadian border on any given day.[15]

One of the latest sectors to see reduced barriers to trade is services. More than 100 of the 132 members of the World Trade Organization (WTO) agreed to reduced trade restrictions for banking and insurance in December 1997.[16] Two other specialized trade initiatives concluded in 1997 lowered barriers in telecommunications and information technology.[17]

China began in 1997 what may be a protracted process of entry into the WTO.[18] The country already ranks eleventh in the world for the value of its trade, yet it maintains a relatively closed trade policy.[19] The deep devaluation of its neighbors' currencies makes it more difficult for China's exports to compete in world markets.

The tension between trade matters and national sovereignty came into high relief in late 1997 when the U.S. Congress denied President Clinton's request for "fast track" authority in negotiating further trade deals.[20] In addition, the Helms-Burton Act in the United States drew increasing criticism from the European Union, Canada, and the United Nations for punishing multinational corporations that trade with Cuba by restricting their access to the U.S. market.[21]

Meanwhile, negotiations aimed at integrating concern about the environment into the international trading system moved forward slowly in the WTO and other forums.

WORLD EXPORTS, 1950–97

YEAR	EXPORTS (bill. 1995 dollars)
1950	380
1955	519
1960	675
1965	926
1966	990
1967	1,081
1968	1,232
1969	1,374
1970	1,520
1971	1,608
1972	1,756
1973	1,979
1974	2,108
1975	2,000
1976	2,227
1977	2,310
1978	2,428
1979	2,622
1980	2,643
1981	2,646
1982	2,549
1983	2,619
1984	2,853
1985	2,958
1986	2,989
1987	3,174
1988	3,417
1989	3,673
1990	3,889
1991	4,056
1992	4,258
1993	4,467
1994	4,933
1995	5,365
1996	5,614
1997 (prel)	5,859

SOURCE: Worldwatch calculations based on IMF data and deflators.

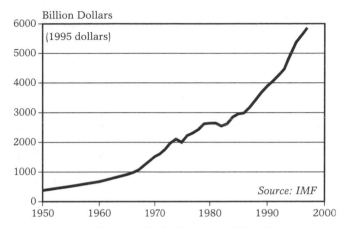

Figure 1: World Exports, 1950–97

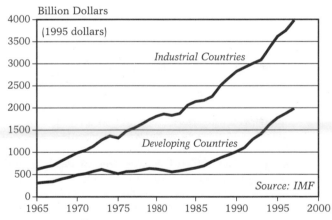

Figure 2: Exports from Industrial and Developing Countries, 1965–97

Paper Production Remains High Ashley T. Mattoon

According to preliminary figures from the U.N. Food and Agriculture Organization (FAO), world production of paper and paperboard rose from approximately 282 million tons in 1995 to 286 million tons in 1996.[1] (See Figure 1.) Since 1961, paper production has increased more than three and a half times and global average per capita use has increased from approximately 25 kilograms to 50 kilograms.[2] FAO predicts that by 2010 world production will reach nearly 396 million tons.[3]

Since 1970, export volumes of paper and paperboard products have tripled.[4] Today, nearly 25 percent of global production is traded internationally, accounting for roughly 44 percent of the value of world forest products exports.[5]

The United States is by far the largest producer and consumer of paper. With less than 5 percent of the world's population, this one country is responsible for close to 30 percent of the world's paper and paperboard production, and more than 31 percent of the use.[6] The second and third largest producers are Japan and China, accounting for approximately 11 percent and 9 percent of global production.[7]

The United States, Western Europe, and Japan, which represent a combined total of less than 15 percent of the world's population, consume 66 percent of the world's paper and paperboard.[8] Yet the share used by developing countries is increasing. In 1980, these nations consumed approximately 15 percent of global paper production, and by 1993 this share rose to nearly 25 percent.[9]

Disparities in per capita consumption between industrial and developing countries are even more dramatic. (See Figure 2.) In 1995, average per capita use in developing countries stood at approximately 18 kilograms, compared with 158 kilograms in industrial countries.[10] A 1996 report from the International Institute for Environment and Development projects that by 2010, these figures will rise to 26 and 241 kilograms per person, respectively.[11]

In recent years, Southeast Asia has been home to the world's fastest-growing paper market, increasing at approximately 10 percent a year (compared with 2–3 percent in Europe).[12] Up until the recent economic crisis in the region, Southeast Asia was expected to account for more than half of the global growth in paper demand over the next five years.[13] As a result of the weakened Asian markets, global demand for paper and paperboard is projected to fall to 2 percent in 1998, down from overall growth of 5.5 percent in 1997.[14]

In 1994, virgin wood fiber (in the form of pulpwood logs and wood chip residues from sawmills) accounted for approximately 57 percent of the total fiber used in making paper. Nonwood fibers (such as straw, bagasse, and kenaf) accounted for 7 percent, and recovered paper for the remaining 36 percent.[15] In 1970, by comparison, the contribution of wood pulp to total fiber used in paper production was 73 percent, and the share of recovered paper was 23 percent.[16]

Relative to recovered paper, the share of nonwood fibers in total fiber supply for paper production has remained relatively small over the last 30 years. But the contribution of these materials to paper production varies dramatically around the world. In industrial countries, nonwood fibers represent less than 1 percent of all fiber used to make paper, while in developing countries it is more than 50 percent.[17] In China, 60–65 percent of the total paper fiber supply is from such sources (primarily straw).[18] In recent years, however, the Chinese pulp and paper industry has begun to move toward using more wood fiber. By 2010, the share of wood fiber in pulp for paper (not including recovered paper) there is expected to increase to 22 percent, up from 14 percent in 1995.[19]

The wood fiber used in paper production represents approximately 40 percent of the world's industrial wood harvest.[20] While roughly 25 percent of the industrial wood harvest flows directly to pulp mills, up to another 15 percent comes from manufacturing residues or off-site chipping operations.[21] These primary and secondary wood pulp flows made the U.S. paper industry the largest industrial consumer of wood in the world in the early 1990s, which is likely still true today.[22]

WORLD PAPER AND PAPERBOARD PRODUCTION, 1961–96

YEAR	PRODUCTION (million tons)	PER CAPITA (kilograms)
1961	77	25
1962	81	26
1963	86	27
1964	92	28
1965	98	29
1966	105	31
1967	106	30
1968	114	32
1969	123	34
1970	126	34
1971	128	34
1972	138	36
1973	148	38
1974	150	37
1975	131	32
1976	147	35
1977	152	36
1978	160	37
1979	169	39
1980	170	38
1981	171	38
1982	167	36
1983	177	38
1984	190	40
1985	193	40
1986	203	41
1987	215	43
1988	228	45
1989	233	45
1990	240	46
1991	243	45
1992	245	45
1993	253	46
1994	281	50
1995	282	50
1996 (prel)	286	50

SOURCES: FAO, *FAOSTAT Statistics Database*; U.S. Bureau of the Census.

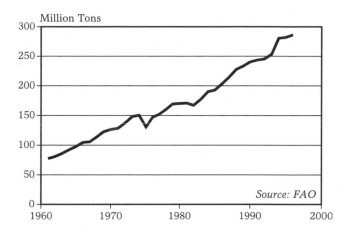

Figure 1: World Paper Production, 1961–96

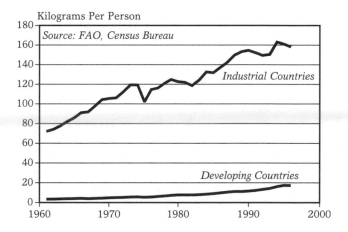

Figure 2: Per Capita Consumption of Paper and Paperboard, Industrial and Developing Countries, 1961–96

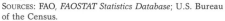

Weather Damages Ease Christopher Flavin

Economic damages from weather-related disasters fell to an estimated $30 billion in 1997, down sharply from the record $60 billion in losses in 1996, according to figures assembled by the Munich Reinsurance Company in Germany.[1] (See Figure 1.) Insured losses were also cut in half—to just $4.5 billion.[2] (See Figure 2.)

The 1997 disaster pattern was heavily shaped by the strong El Niño conditions that appeared in the tropical Pacific late in the year and dramatically affected weather trends in countries as widely separated as Australia, Brazil, Indonesia, and the United States.[3]

One result of El Niño was an unusually placid Atlantic Hurricane season, which spared the Gulf and Atlantic coasts of the United States—regions that are heavily built up and well insured, and therefore often figure heavily in annual storm losses.[4] The tropical Pacific, on the other hand, had an active typhoon season that included the devastating Typhoon Winnie that hit northeast Asia in August, causing $2.7 billion in losses and killing 311 people.[5] Later in 1997, Hurricane Pauline killed more than 200 people in the area near Acapulco, Mexico.[6]

In the western Pacific, on the other hand, El Niño caused severe droughts, including in Australia—where scores of wildfires resulted, destroying hundreds of homes.[7] Indonesia suffered its worst drought in 50 years, which devastated the country's rice harvest.[8] Fires in Indonesia's Bornean and Sumatran tropical forests were deliberately set in August and lasted through the end of the year, generating headlines worldwide.[9] Tropical forests do not normally burn, but widespread disruption of the area's forests by logging and palm oil companies have allowed them to dry out, and opened the way for 1997's devastating fires.[10]

The extensive smoke from these fires covered an area the size of the continental United States with a hazy smog, which left millions of people with respiratory problems and led to the cancellation of 1,100 airline flights.[11] According to an estimate by the World Wide Fund for Nature, losses from this prolonged disaster were $20 billion.[12] Most of

these losses were indirect, however, and are not included in the global figure of $30 billion assembled by Munich Re.

El Niño also exacerbated the seasonal conflagration that now rages in the Amazon each fall. Although they received far less attention than the southeast Asian fires, the Amazonian blazes appear to have been even more extensive, accelerating the considerable loss of forests in the Amazon Basin.[13]

The weather-related disasters that caused the most human suffering in 1997 were El Niño–related floods in eastern Africa in the fall that killed 1,600 people and displaced another 230,000 in Ethiopia, Kenya, and Somalia.[14] Lack of transportation infrastructure and effective government relief programs, let alone significant private insurance, allowed the burden to fall directly on the backs of the poor victims.

Severe July flooding in Central Europe pushed rivers such as the Oder to record levels. Economic losses were estimated at $5.3 billion.[15] The northern plains and west coast of the United States were also hit by separate, severe floods in 1997, causing $1 billion and $2 billion in damages respectively.[16]

According to Munich Re's analysts, despite the decline in losses in 1997, the overall rate of loss in the 1990s is three times that in the 1960s, even after adjusting for inflation.[17] Although it is impossible to link this increase definitively to human-induced climate change, Munich Re believes that climate change could greatly increase such losses in future decades.[18] The links between El Niño and climate change are uncertain, but some scientists now suggest that global temperature increases may be disrupting the natural El Niño cycles, causing them to be more frequent and severe.[19]

Concern about the possibility of increased damages from climate change led more than 70 insurers to urge the climate negotiators meeting in Kyoto in December 1997 to limit greenhouse gas emissions—and thereby reduce the risk of escalating losses in future decades.[20]

ECONOMIC LOSSES FROM WEATHER-RELATED NATURAL DISASTERS WORLDWIDE, 1980–97

YEAR	OVERALL LOSSES (bill. dollars)
1980	1.5
1981	7.8
1982	2.1
1983	6.2
1984	2.3
1985	5.0
1986	6.7
1987	9.6
1988	3.2
1989	9.7
1990	15.0
1991	27.0
1992	36.0
1993	22.5
1994	22.5
1995	38.5
1996	60.0
1997 (prel)	30.0

YEAR	INSURED LOSSES (bill. dollars)
1980	0.1
1981	0.4
1982	1.0
1983	2.9
1984	1.0
1985	2.0
1986	0.2
1987	4.3
1988	0.8
1989	4.5
1990	10.0
1991	8.0
1992	22.5
1993	5.5
1994	1.8
1995	9.0
1996	9.0
1997 (prel)	4.5

SOURCE: Gerhard A. Berz, Münchener Rückversicherungs-Gesellschaft, press release (Munich, Germany: 29 December 1997).

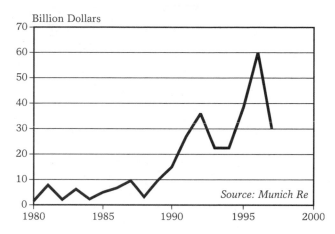

Figure 1: Economic Losses from Weather-Related Natural Disasters Worldwide, 1980–97

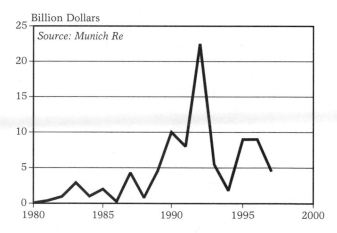

Figure 2: Insured Losses from Weather-Related Disasters Worldwide, 1980–97

The regular budget for the United Nations, which funds the headquarters in New York, U.N. offices in Geneva, Vienna, and Nairobi, and the operations of five regional commissions, stood at $1.1 billion in 1997—about the same as the year before.[1] (See Figure 1.) This is equivalent to just 4 percent of New York City's municipal budget.[2]

Total U.N. expenditures amounted to $10.4 billion in 1995—the most recent year for which comprehensive data are available.[3] This includes the organization's regular budget as well as assessed and voluntary contributions to its agencies and other organs, but excludes peacekeeping expenses.[4] Financial resources at the disposal of the U.N. system have stagnated since 1992 (all data are expressed in current dollars); taking inflation into account, they have declined.[5]

Under pressure from the United States and other large contributors, the U.N. General Assembly has since 1987 adopted "zero–real growth budgets" for the organization's regular budget—that is, funding can expand only to accommodate inflation or adverse exchange rate fluctuations.[6] For 1996–97, however, a "zero–nominal growth budget" was adopted for the first time—meaning that no adjustments could be made even for these factors.[7]

U.N. specialized agencies are funded through mandatory and voluntary contributions. (See Figure 2.) Among the largest are the World Health Organization ($774 million in total funds in 1995), the Food and Agriculture Organization ($579 million), the International Labour Organization ($350 million), and the International Atomic Energy Agency ($330 million).[8] Assessed contributions to these and other agencies climbed from $229 million in 1971 to $2.05 billion in 1997.[9] The largest amount of funds enters the U.N. system via voluntary contributions, however, and these grew from $815 million in 1971 to a peak $7.5 billion in 1994 before dropping to $7.4 billion in 1995.[10]

Several U.N. organs are financed entirely through such voluntary payments. The U.N. Development Programme is by far the largest, attracting almost $2.2 billion in 1996, up from $1.5 billion in 1992.[11] Yet funding for its core programs—those that focus on sustainable human development and poverty eradication—fell at the same time, from $1.1 billion to $844 million.[12] The World Food Programme (WFP), UNICEF, and the U.N. High Commissioner for Refugees (UNHCR) all have annual budgets of more than $1 billion.[13] But as food aid has plunged in recent years, WFP's operating budget has fallen from $1.7 billion in 1992 to $1.2 billion in 1995.[14] In line with fewer refugees to care for, UNHCR expenditures declined to $1.2 billion in 1997 from a peak of $1.4 billion in 1996.[15] Contributions to the U.N. Environment Programme, having fallen short of funding targets for several years, stood at a relatively meager $109 million in 1997.[16]

Arrears on the U.N.'s regular budget have soared since the mid-1980s, reaching a high of $564 million in 1995 and $474 million in 1997.[17] (See Figure 3.) As a result, the United Nations has been in a perpetual financial crisis.

U.S. debts ballooned from zero in 1980 to $414 million in 1995, falling only slightly to $373 million in 1997, when Washington accounted for 79 percent of all members' arrears.[18] (The United States owes an additional $254 million to various U.N. specialized agencies.)[19] Since the mid-1980s, the U.S. Congress has withheld portions of the money due each year and imposed a variety of conditions before arrears will be paid.[20] An effort to pay off old debts was derailed in late 1997.[21]

As a quid pro quo for settling its debts, the United States seeks to have its share of the U.N. budget reduced from 25 to 20 percent by the year 2000. Resenting the U.S. failure to pay legally owed debts, the other members turned the tables—making payment of arrears a condition for lowering the U.S. assessment.[22] With recent changes in the scale of assessments, by 2000 the biggest contributors after the United States will be Japan (20.5 percent), Germany (9.63 percent), and France (6.49 percent).[23] None of these other nations were in arrears on the regular budget at the end of 1997.[24]

UNITED NATIONS REGULAR BUDGET, 1971–97

YEAR	AMOUNT (mill. dollars)
1971	172
1972	184
1973	205
1974	265
1975	265
1976	337
1977	337
1978	458
1979	458
1980	532
1981	532
1982	631
1983	631
1984	682
1985	682
1986	725
1987	725
1988	752
1989	765
1990	838
1991	999
1992	1,008
1993	1,031
1994	1,088
1995	1,088
1996	1,120
1997	1,120

SOURCES: U.N. General Assembly, "Budgetary and Financial Situation of Organizations of the United Nations System" (New York: 18 October 1996); Global Policy Forum, "Assessed Payments to the Regular Budget and Specialized Agencies: 1971–1995."

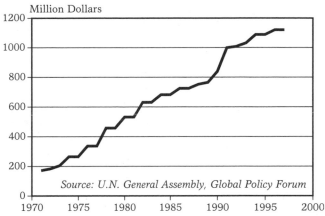

Figure 1: United Nations Regular Budget, 1971–97

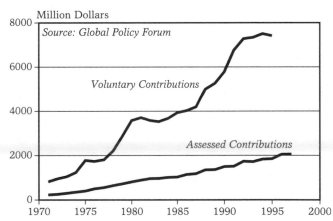

Figure 2: Budgets of U.N. Agencies and Organs, 1971–97

Figure 3: Arrears on Regular U.N. Budget, 1971–97

Transportation Trends

Automobile Production Sets Record   Seth Dunn

Worldwide annual production of passenger cars grew 5.4 percent in 1997, to 39 million—an all-time high.[1] (See Figure 1.) This pushed the global auto fleet up 2.4 percent, to 501 million.[2] (See Figure 2.) The world's car population has increased more than ninefold since 1950, while the number of people per car has dropped at least fourfold.[3] (See Figure 3.) But sales have lagged production recently, leading to a worldwide glut that analysts expect to continue for the near future.[4]

In the United States, which accounts for 23 percent of world production, output rose 2 percent and sales less than 1 percent, although these data mask the growing popularity of sport utility vehicles—gas-guzzlers that qualify as light trucks.[5] Even so, U.S. car numbers have grown six times faster than the U.S. population since 1950.[6] Production in Japan, with a 20-percent share of the global total, rose 6 percent while sales there dropped 7 percent.[7]

Western and Eastern Europe account for 34 percent of global carmaking.[8] Production and sales rose just 5 and 6 percent last year in the west, but increased 16 and 14 percent in Eastern Europe.[9] Nine companies have made plans for production in Turkey, where output leapt 16 percent and sales 25 percent last year.[10] In Russia, production grew 8 percent and sales 11 percent.[11]

Eastern Europe, Latin America, and Asia are the expected locales for three quarters of the car factories to be built during the next three years.[12] Production and sales were up 19 and 13 percent in Latin America in 1997, the fastest-growing region.[13] Lured by attractive government incentives, car manufacturers from the United States, Europe, and Asia are planning some $17 billion in investments before 2000 in Brazil, which saw output and sales jump 14 and 13 percent in 1997 and which will soon become the world's fourth-leading carmaker.[14] Some $3.9 billion in automotive industry investments are meanwhile planned in Argentina, where production grew 44 percent but sales only 16 percent.[15]

In Asia, where 31 percent of global car production now occurs, overcapacity contributed to and was in turn exacerbated by the region's financial crisis in late 1997.[16] South Korean car production rose 2 percent while sales dropped 7 percent, forcing the nation's second largest carmaker into bankruptcy—although the conglomerate Samsung opened a new plant with plans to produce 80,000 cars in 1998.[17] In Thailand, where foreign carmakers have invested $1.7 billion, output and sales fell 33 and 36 percent, causing Toyota to shut down two plants.[18] Indonesia and Malaysia, which are developing homegrown auto industries, saw production rise 26 and 10 percent but sales only 10 and 5 percent.[19]

Production also outpaced sales in India and China, the two largest potential markets. In India, production and sales grew just 6 and 5 percent in 1997 after government joint ventures with foreign companies spurred a 91-percent expansion between 1993 and 1996.[20] In China, output grew 10 percent but sales only 8 percent, causing the government to reconsider ambitious plans for the sector shortly after approving a $1-billion venture with General Motors to build 100,000 midsize cars annually.[21]

General Motors has become particularly active overseas, investing $2.2 billion in four new car plants in Argentina, Poland, China, and Thailand—all countries that actively encourage domestic production.[22] By early 1999 it plans to have nine new assembly plants overall—with a combined annual production capacity of nearly 720,000 cars—running in Latin America, Eastern Europe, and Asia.[23]

In late 1997 and early 1998 several automakers unveiled fuel-efficient, low-pollution vehicles—including Toyota's Prius, with a fuel economy twice the current average.[24] Such cars are considered the industry's contribution to mitigating climate change, as auto emissions are among the fastest-growing contributors.[25] Ironically, though, some of these firms exclude more basic controls on vehicles in new markets: General Motors plans no catalytic converters for its cars in China.[26]

WORLD AUTOMOBILE PRODUCTION AND FLEET, 1950–97

YEAR	PRODUCTION (million)	FLEET (million)
1950	8	53
1955	11	73
1960	13	98
1965	19	140
1966	19	148
1967	19	158
1968	22	170
1969	23	181
1970	23	194
1971	26	207
1972	28	220
1973	30	236
1974	26	249
1975	25	260
1976	29	269
1977	31	285
1978	31	297
1979	31	308
1980	29	320
1981	28	331
1982	27	340
1983	30	352
1984	31	365
1985	32	374
1986	33	386
1987	33	394
1988	34	413
1989	36	424
1990	36	445
1991	35	456
1992	35	470
1993	34	469
1994	36	480
1995	36	477
1996	37	489
1997 (prel)	39	501

SOURCES: American Automobile Manufacturers Association; Standard & Poor's DRI.

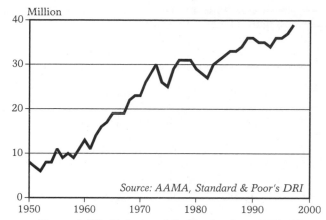

Figure 1: World Automobile Production, 1950–97

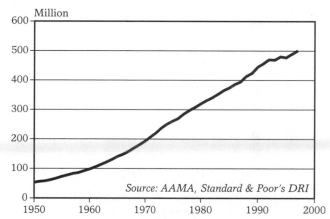

Figure 2: World Automobile Fleet, 1950–97

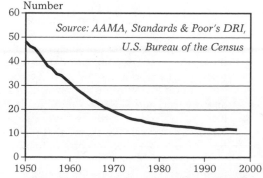

Figure 3: People Per Automobile, 1950–97

Motorbike Production Accelerating   Gary Gardner

Global production of motorbikes topped 19 million in 1995, the last year for which comprehensive data are available.[1] (See Figure 1.) The total, which includes production of motorcycles, mopeds, and all other motorized two- and three-wheelers except electric bicycles, represents nearly a 15-percent increase over 1994.[2] The surge is part of an explosion in motorbike popularity this decade, when global output has grown by more than 50 percent.[3]

Asia is the hub of motorbike production, accounting for nearly 90 percent of global output and for most of the surge in production this decade.[4] China alone produces more than 40 percent of the world's motorbikes.[5] (See Figure 2.) While production decreased in the 1990s in Africa, and grew modestly in Europe and the Americas, Asian output more than doubled between 1990 and 1995.[6]

Asia also accounts for most motorbike use. These vehicles are an attractive alternative to bicycles in developing countries for those in the expanding working class who cannot afford a car. Indeed, motorbike ownership in Asia is growing faster than auto ownership. In New Delhi, for example, where buses tend to be slow and subways are nonexistent, the number of two-wheeled motorized vehicles has jumped fivefold since 1980 to 1.7 million, compared with an auto fleet of a half-million.[7] And the Chinese cities of Guangzhou and Shantou saw motorbike increases of 35–40 percent a year between 1980 and 1993.[8]

Despite the popularity of motorbikes, several factors threaten growth in their production and use. Motorbikes are typically the noisiest vehicles on the road, with decibel levels roughly an order of magnitude above those of a car.[9] They are also dangerous: in the United Kingdom, a motorcyclist is 22 times more likely to die in transit than someone in a car, and 333 times more likely than a bus rider.[10] And motorbikes are heavy polluters. The two-stroke engine that powers many motorbikes emits more unburned hydrocarbons and carbon monoxide per kilometer than almost any other engine.[11] In Asia, motorcycles are second only to trucks and buses in emissions of particulates, which are exceptionally hazardous to human health.[12]

For these reasons, some governments have begun to rein in motorbikes. Taiwan has decreed that 2 percent of scooters must be emission-free by the year 2000.[13] And regulations taking effect in India in 1998 will require large reductions in emissions from two- and three-wheelers.[14] Some Chinese cities have gone further by placing restrictions on the number of motorbikes allowed. Guangzhou, for example, stopped issuing motorcycle licenses in 1992.[15] Shanghai followed suit for mopeds in 1997, in an effort to reduce their number by 80 percent over three years.[16]

The future of motorbike use will depend in part on economic and demographic trends. Countries such as Italy and the Netherlands saw rapid growth in motorbikes in the 1950s and 1960s, a trend that slowed markedly as cars became affordable. In Taiwan, by contrast, the use of motorbikes grew in a rapid and sustained way over several decades even after substantial income gains, in part because crowded cities left little room for massive expansion of the automobile fleet. Because many prospering cities in Asia are also crowded, if restrictions on motorbike ownership are not adopted, the surge in motorbike use might be expected to continue for many years.

Market growth will also depend on how well the problems of motorbikes are overcome. Emissions levels can be reduced by using fuel injection or by substituting four-stroke engines for the two-stroke design, changes that would cost $60–80 per bike.[17] Computer controls and catalytic converters can also lower pollution levels in motorbike engines.[18] And electric motorbikes, which eliminate noise and atmospheric pollution, are now found in some Asian cities.[19] Indeed, the Taiwanese government has targeted electric motorbikes as one of six industries that will spur Taiwanese development into the next century.[20] If these technologies prove to be viable and affordable, the future of motorbikes may be bright.

WORLD MOTORBIKE PRODUCTION, 1982–95

YEAR	PRODUCTION (million)
1982	15
1983	12
1984	11
1985	13
1986	11
1987	11
1988	13
1989	13
1990	13
1991	12
1992	13
1993	15
1994	17
1995	20

SOURCES: United Nations, *Industrial Commodity Statistics Yearbook* (New York: various years); IMMA, *Statistics Production, Sales, PARC, 1997* (Geneva: 1998); IRF, *World Road Statistics 1991–1995* (Geneva: 1996).

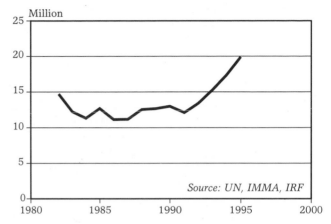

Figure 1: World Motorbike Production, 1982–95

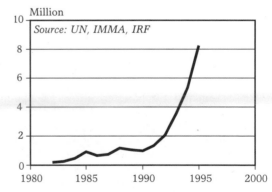

Figure 2: Motorbike Production in China, 1982–95

Global bicycle production decreased to 101 million units in 1996, the last year for which global data are available.[1] (See Figure 1.) The global slump, a 7-percent decline from 1995 levels and the first drop since 1990, is attributed to sluggish sales and excess inventories worldwide.[2]

Virtually all the major producing countries saw production declines. In China, the world's leading manufacturer, output fell some 7 percent from 1995.[3] The next four producers—India, the European Union, the United States, and Taiwan—saw production declines of 2, 11, 13, and 27 percent, respectively.[4] Southeast Asian producers were doubly crippled: tariffs in the European Union kept them out of that market, and rising prosperity in domestic Asian markets turned consumer attention to motorcycles and cars.[5] Asian countries are still the major producers and consumers of bicycles, however; China and India alone accounted for nearly half of global production.[6]

Often overlooked in transportation planning, bicycles are well suited for urban use. Bikes use only 2 percent as much energy as cars per passenger-kilometer, cost 2–3 percent as much to purchase, are entirely nonpolluting, are better for the health of the users, and are often the fastest way to get around urban centers.[7] They are also easy on transportation budgets: research in the Netherlands showed that providing for bicycle traffic cost 5 percent as much per kilometer traveled as providing for municipal public transport.[8]

One bright spot in the global bicycle picture is electric bicycles, which continued the explosive growth that began with their market debut in 1993. Production increased by 78 percent in 1997, to 338,000 bicycles.[9] (See Figure 2.) Japan is the leading producer, accounting for 75 percent of 1997 production.[10] A series of joint manufacturing and marketing agreements between companies in Asia, Europe, and the United States in 1997 could expand the market still further.[11] Indeed, market watchers expect the double-digit growth to continue, leading to more than 2 million electric bikes on streets worldwide by the year 2000.[12]

The success of this new technology could be a boon for cycling. Battery-powered electric bikes allow cyclists to achieve speeds of up to 15 miles per hour without pedaling, and much faster if pedaling and battery power are used together.[13] This could extend a bike's range or allow it to tackle hilly terrain, thereby increasing its attractiveness for commuting. Electric bikes might also become a viable replacement for mopeds and scooters, which are typically noisy and highly polluting. Indeed, electric bikes are expected to proliferate in Shanghai now that authorities have stopped issuing permits for mopeds, whose numbers they seek to curb by 80 percent over three years.[14]

Many factors affect levels of bicycle use, but perhaps the most important is public policy.[15] In the United States and Canada, where cycling is rarely promoted, only 1 percent of all trips are made by bicycle.[16] By contrast, systematic pro-biking policies have pushed cycling rates to 20 percent of all trips in Danish cities and 30 percent in Dutch ones.[17] In western Germany, aggressive policies increased bicycle use by 50 percent in the last 20 years, in spite of unfavorable weather and high incomes, which typically dampen enthusiasm for cycling.[18] These policies often combine measures to facilitate cycling, such as special pathways or traffic signals that favor cyclists, with those that discourage car use, such as limiting parking space or banning auto use in certain urban zones. Largely because of such policies, five pro-biking European countries now boast cycling rates of 10 percent or more of urban trips.[19]

Outside of Europe, trends in biking policies are mixed. The province of Quebec is constructing a huge network of bikeways—more than 3,000 kilometers' worth—within and between cities, some of which will connect with cycling routes in the United States.[20] But governments in many Asian nations continue to be hostile to bicycles and bicycle rickshaws, especially in Hanoi, Dhaka, Manila, and Jakarta.[21]

WORLD BICYCLE PRODUCTION, 1950–96

YEAR	PRODUCTION (million)
1950	11
1955	15
1960	20
1965	21
1966	22
1967	23
1968	24
1969	25
1970	36
1971	39
1972	46
1973	52
1974	52
1975	43
1976	47
1977	49
1978	51
1979	54
1980	62
1981	65
1982	69
1983	74
1984	76
1985	79
1986	84
1987	98
1988	105
1989	95
1990	92
1991	99
1992	102
1993	106
1994	108
1995	109
1996 (prel)	101

SOURCES: United Nations, *The Growth of World Industry 1969 Edition*, Vol. I, *Yearbooks of Industrial Statistics 1979 and 1989 Editions*, Vol. II, and *Industrial Commodity Statistics Yearbook 1994*; *Interbike Directory*, various years.

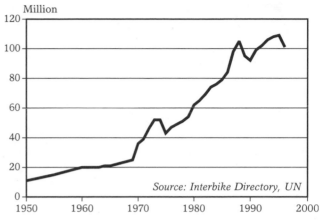

Figure 1: World Bicycle Production, 1950–96

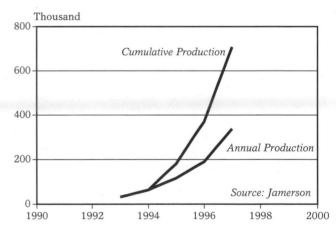

Figure 2: World Electric Bicycle Production, 1993–97

Communications
Trends

Satellite Launches Rebound   Molly O'Meara

In 1997, a total of 133 satellites were launched, up from 82 in 1996.[1] (See Figure 1.) This figure includes satellites for science research, earth observation, communications, navigation, and surveillance.[2]

Satellites got their first boost from the cold war. When scientist and science-fiction author Arthur Clarke wrote in 1945 about the possibility of satellites for communications, World War II was waning and he believed the first satellite launch was still "a half century ahead."[3] But just 12 years later the Soviet Union successfully put up Sputnik, sparking a space race with the United States.[4] (See Figure 2.) From 1965 to 1990, the total number of satellites launched each year remained relatively steady.[5]

With the end of the cold war, the number of launches has declined, but there are more countries involved—18 industrial and 13 developing nations.[6] In 1997, for instance, Argentina, China, France, Germany, Hong Kong, India, Indonesia, Japan, Luxembourg, the Netherlands, Norway, the Philippines, Spain, and Thailand all saw satellites launched.[7]

The nature of satellites has changed over time. As the number launched for defense purposes has decreased, the number of communications satellites has risen. Reconnaissance, surveillance, and other military uses accounted for 52 percent of launches in 1967, while communications satellites constituted just 14 percent.[8] Thirty years later, the share of military satellites had dropped to 8 percent, while communications satellites had rocketed to 69 percent.[9]

Communications satellites themselves are rapidly evolving. Since 1965, Intelsat, a treaty-based cooperative that now has 140 member nations, has dominated commercial satellite communications with a fleet of satellites that are "geostationary," orbiting the equator high enough to remain over the same point on Earth.[10] The first satellite provided 240 telephone circuits (or one television channel) between Europe and the United States; within two decades, Intelsat satellites were providing the bulk of the world's interconti-

nental telephone and television links.[11]

A new generation of privately owned satellites designed for low orbit (700–1,400 kilometers from the surface) has the potential to further revolutionize communications.[12] Low-orbiting satellites are cheaper to launch, can reach the most remote parts of the world, and are better suited than geostationary satellites for interactive voice and video connections because they are close enough to the Earth's surface to eliminate the time lag in transmission.[13] A new space race will be fueled by the 1,700 communications satellites—10 times the number now in orbit—scheduled for launch in the next decade.[14] Teledesic, which is to be the largest constellation of low-orbiting satellites, plans to reserve some of its capacity to extend communications links to rural parts of the developing world.[15]

Satellite-assisted navigation is also moving into a new era, with a growing number of nonmilitary uses. The Global Positioning System, a network of 24 satellites operated by the U.S. Department of Defense, now aids commercial pilots, automobile drivers, boaters, and even backpackers.[16]

Satellite remote sensing technology, too, has advanced into new uses.[17] Vegetation types, land use patterns, surface water, soil quality, roads, and urban sprawl can all be monitored by satellite.[18] In 1998, the United States will launch a new series of earth observation satellites that will aid scientists studying climatic change.[19]

Advances in computer software now allow satellite imagery to be combined with other data in geographic information system computer programs that create maps for a variety of planning purposes.[20] For instance, the technology can be used to show water and fertilizer needs for specific areas on a given field, to identify changes in environmental conditions that determine vector-borne disease transmission, or to map the ocean floor.[21]

As demand for satellite applications grows, launch costs are expected to drop. Future concerns may include the equitable distribution of radio spectrum and the accumulation of satellite-related debris in space.[22]

SATELLITE LAUNCHES WORLDWIDE, 1957–97

YEAR	TOTAL (number)
1957	2
1958	6
1959	10
1960	16
1961	29
1962	63
1963	68
1964	95
1965	143
1966	121
1967	140
1968	123
1969	109
1970	121
1971	136
1972	120
1973	116
1974	113
1975	141
1976	149
1977	129
1978	146
1979	113
1980	119
1981	148
1982	131
1983	147
1984	150
1985	151
1986	129
1987	126
1988	128
1989	123
1990	150
1991	128
1992	114
1993	95
1994	107
1995	92
1996	82
1997 (prel)	133

SOURCES: Jos Heyman, *Spacecraft Tables 1957–1990* (San Diego, CA: Univelt, 1991) and *Spacecraft Tables 1957–1995*, computer diskette, 1996; Jos Heyman, Astronautical Society of Western Australia, letters to author.

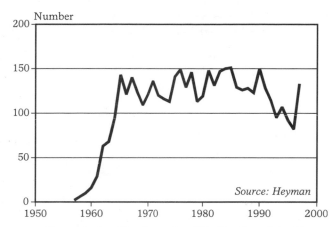

Figure 1: Satellite Launches Worldwide, 1957–97

Figure 2: Satellite Launches in the United States, Russia, and Rest of World, 1957–97

The number of lines that link telephones directly to the global phone network increased 7 percent to more than 740 million in 1996, the latest year for which data are available.[1] (This figure does not include cellular telephones.) (See Figure 1.) The fixed-line network has been growing at this rate throughout the 1990s.[2] Steady expansion has occurred over the last several decades: as world population has doubled since 1960, the telephone network has increased eightfold.[3]

Beginning with the first public telephone exchange in New Haven, Connecticut, in 1878, the telephone network transformed societies as it spread throughout the United States and Europe in the late nineteenth and early twentieth centuries.[4] It built on the progress of telegraphs and railways to overcome the barrier of distance in communications.[5] The network links widely scattered communities, provides a way to get help in emergencies, permits rural farmers and businesses to reach urban markets, and generally allows one-to-one information exchange that promotes social, cultural, and economic development.[6]

Although undersea cables and satellite systems now connect every continent in the world, the vital communications web is far from evenly distributed.[7] Nearly 70 percent of all phone lines are in industrial nations.[8] While the United States has more than 60 lines per 100 people, the "teledensity" of China is just 4.5 lines per 100 people.[9] Today, growth in the network has shifted to the underserved developing world: in 1996, the number of installed lines increased 4 percent in industrial countries and 18.7 percent in developing ones.[10]

Tumultuous changes in today's communications industry, reminiscent of the telephone explosion of a century ago, may have particular benefit for developing nations. When Alexander Graham Bell's patent on the telephone expired in the 1890s, competition in the United States surged for a short period, resulting in lowered costs that made the telephone affordable to more people.[11] Although state-controlled monopolies have dominated the phone business for most of its history, the World Trade Organization ushered in a new era in February 1997 when 69 nations, accounting for more than 90 percent of world telecommunication revenues, agreed to open their long-distance markets to foreign competitors.[12]

Competition is arising not only from phone companies entering new markets but also from new technologies converging with traditional, fixed-line service.[13] For instance, cellular mobile subscribers, who use radio waves rather than an installed line to use the network, have increased by an average 52 percent a year since 1991; by 1996, there were 135 million cell phone subscribers worldwide.[14] (See Figure 2.)

The cellular boom was initially fueled by urban professionals in industrial countries, who still account for more than 80 percent of subscribers. But the technology is quickly catching on in developing countries, where people sometimes must wait decades for a traditional phone line.[15] A number of countries are poised to leapfrog directly into the wireless era.[16] Cambodia, where 60 percent of telephone subscribers now use mobile cellular phones, is the most extreme example.[17]

Expansion of the fixed-line network in industrial countries is increasingly driven by Internet demand. Companies' use of the Internet to compete with traditional fax and telephone services will be another factor helping to lower long-distance rates.[18]

The expanding telephone and related communications network contributes to social change, often in contradictory ways.[19] The telephone, by obviating the need to move goods and people, averts resource use and transportation-related pollution.[20] Together with the automobile, however, the telephone allows migration to the suburbs and necessitates more transportation.[21] One of the challenges of the next century will be using communications technologies to increase the efficiency with which scarce resources are used.[22]

TELEPHONE LINES WORLDWIDE, 1960–96

YEAR	TELEPHONE LINES (million)
1960	89
1965	115
1970	156
1975	229
1976	244
1977	259
1978	276
1979	294
1980	311
1981	339
1982	354
1983	370
1984	388
1985	407
1986	426
1987	446
1988	469
1989	493
1990	519
1991	545
1992	573
1993	606
1994	646
1995	692
1996 (prel)	741

SOURCES: International Telecommunication Union, *World Telecommunication Indicators on Diskette*, (Geneva: 1996); ITU, *Challenges to the Network* (Geneva: September 1997).

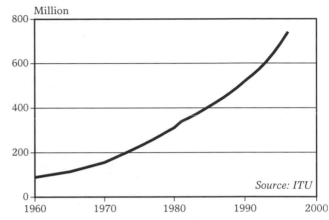

Figure 1: Telephone Lines Worldwide, 1960–96

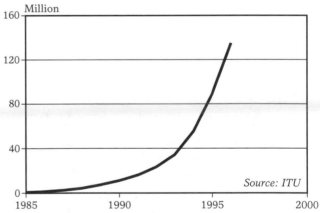

Figure 2: Cellular Mobile Telephone Subscribers Worldwide, 1985–96

Internet Use Grows Exponentially   Payal Sampat

The Internet, a global network of electronically linked computers, has more than doubled in size each year in the last decade.[1] In 1997, nearly 30 million host computers—and more than 100 million people—were connected to the Internet.[2] (See Figure 1.) A host computer can represent one or more Internet user, just as office telephone connections can serve multiple phone extensions.[3]

Conceived in 1969 to link U.S. military and, later, university computers, the Internet took root as an integral part of communications less than five years ago, when it became available commercially.[4] Still in its infancy, the Net today serves as a marketplace, library, post office, telephone, and source of entertainment and information for millions.

But with more than 90 percent of Internet users in industrial countries, these benefits have thus far been unevenly available.[5] (See Figures 2 and 3.) Of the estimated 107 million people online, more than half—62 million—are in the United States; 20 million live in Europe, and 8 million each are in Canada and Japan.[6] By contrast, developing countries—home to 80 percent of humanity—have only 8 percent of Internet users.[7] Africa has fewer than 2 host computers for every 10,000 people; Finland, on the other hand, has 877 per 10,000 people—making it the "most wired" nation per person.[8] Poor telecommunications infrastructure, lack of computers, and high Internet access fees pose obstacles. And the language of the Internet is predominantly English, spoken by less than 15 percent of the world's population.[9]

Despite these hurdles, the developing world is rapidly catching up.[10] Internet access in Russia and Brazil has grown fivefold in the last two years, each now with 7 host computers per 10,000 people.[11] Among the fastest-growing Internet markets are China and India, where the number of people online is projected to multiply 15-fold, to 4 million and 1.5 million respectively by 2000.[12] Thanks to cornerstore telecommunications centers, which offer access to the Internet, telephone, and fax for a fee, soon every African may have Internet access less than 10 kilometers from home.[13]

What does the Internet mean for developing countries? For some, it has been an economy booster. Software programmers in Bangalore, India, telecommute daily to Silicon Valley via the Internet, and will generate an estimated $4 billion a year in software exports for India by 2000.[14] For the millions of developing-world inhabitants who lack access to more essential services such as health care and education, Internet access may seem a remote priority. Ironically, these are the lives it is changing most profoundly.

Indigenous groups like the Kuna nation of Panama, the Assyrians of the Middle East, and the Sami of northern Scandinavia have used the Internet to protest human rights and environmental violations, communicate with scattered members of their tribes across the world, and uphold their languages and traditions.[15] Telemedicine projects now provide low-cost online medical assistance and health education to doctors in Uganda, Mexico, and Bhutan.[16]

A rural Internet project helped a Peruvian agricultural cooperative sell organically grown potatoes to clients in New York, bringing in 10 times the usual profits.[17] Dominican farmers now help their Guatemalan counterparts with irrigation questions posted on the Internet.[18] And the Internet empowers local activists by linking them with supporters across the globe, which is why authoritarian governments fear it. The government of Myanmar (formerly Burma), for instance, threatens unauthorized owners of networked computers with 15 years in jail.[19]

British scientist Arthur C. Clarke observes that people usually exaggerate the short-term impacts and underestimate the long-term effects of technological change.[20] The automobile transformed the twentieth century in complex and momentous ways, changing our habitats, bridging distances, and unleashing environmental hazards.[21] With 500 million people—8 percent of humanity—projected to be online by 2001, we can barely guess how the Internet phenomenon will shape the twenty-first century.[22]

INTERNET HOST COMPUTERS, 1981–97

YEAR	HOST COMPUTERS (number)
1981	213
1982	235
1983	562
1984	1,024
1985	2,308
1986	5,089
1987	28,174
1988	80,000
1989	159,000
1990	376,000
1991	727,000
1992	1,313,000
1993	2,217,000
1994	5,846,000
1995	14,352,000
1996	21,819,000
1997	29,670,000

SOURCE: Network Wizards, "Internet Domain Surveys, 1981–1998," < http://www.nw.com >, viewed 6 February 1998

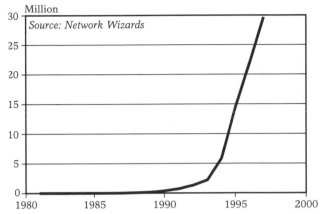

Figure 1: Internet Host Computers, 1981–97

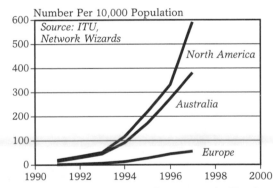

Figure 2: Internet Host Computers in North America, Australia, and Europe, 1991–97

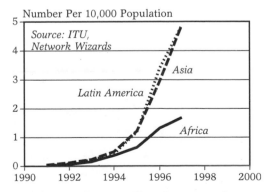

Figure 3: Internet Host Computers in Asia, Latin America, and Africa, 1991–97

Social
Trends

Population Growth Continues
Jennifer D. Mitchell

In 1997, 80 million people were added to the world's population—slightly more than in the previous year—bringing the total to 5.85 billion.[1] (See Figures 1 and 2.) Virtually all the added people live in the developing world, already home to some 4.7 billion people.[2] Approximately 60 percent—roughly 50 million people—were added in Asia alone.[3]

While the total number of people continues to increase, the annual rate of growth has slowly dropped from its historical high of 2.2 percent in 1963 to 1.4 percent in 1997.[4] (See Figure 3.) This global average, however, masks regional variations. Developing countries are growing much faster than industrial ones: 1.7 percent versus 0.3 percent.[5] In sub-Saharan Africa the rate of growth is even higher: 2.7 percent.[6]

The decline in the number of people added to the world in the 1990s is partly the result of falling fertility rates in several developing countries. A 1997 Demographic and Health Survey in Bangladesh, for example, showed that the average number of children per woman there has dropped from 4.8 in 1987 to 3.3 today.[7]

In other countries, however, new data indicate that fertility rates are higher than earlier estimates. The Indian government, for instance, announced that India's total fertility rate for 1995 was approximately 3.4 children per woman, not roughly 3.2, as previously projected.[8] Although the difference may seem small, in a country of more than 950 million the effect could be substantial.[9] (These new data have not yet been integrated into U.N. or U.S. Census Bureau estimates.)

The United Nations projects that over the next 50 years world population will reach 9.4 billion—some 3.55 billion more people than today.[10] Nearly 60 percent of the projected population growth is expected to occur in Asia, which could grow from 3.4 billion people in 1995 to more than 5.4 billion in 2050.[11] By then, China's population of 1.2 billion is expected to exceed 1.5 billion, while India's is projected to soar from 930 million to 1.53 billion.[12] And the population of the Middle East and North Africa is likely to more than double, while that of sub-Saharan Africa will triple.[13] By 2050, Nigeria alone is expected to have 339 million people—more than all of Africa had 35 years ago.[14]

Controlling population growth depends on the international community's willingness to make population issues a priority. At the 1994 International Conference on Population and Development (ICPD) in Cairo, the governments of the world agreed to a 20-year population and reproductive health program.[15] Some have made some progress toward the agreements made at the ICPD. Women in Zambia are now able to receive family planning services without their husband's consent.[16] Nevertheless, more than 120 million married women in the developing world, and many more unmarried sexually active adults and teens, still do not have access to the family planning services that they desire.[17]

Funding for the ICPD program is also lagging. The United Nations estimates that $17 billion a year will be needed for population programs by 2000 and $21.7 billion by 2015.[18] (In both cases, this is less than the world spends every two weeks on military expenditures.)[19] Developing countries and countries in transition have agreed to cover two thirds of the price tag, while donor countries have promised to pay $5.7 billion a year by 2000 and $7.2 billion by 2015.[20]

Unfortunately, while developing countries are on track with their part of the expenditures, donor countries are not. A recent U.N. Population Fund study reports that the assistance of bilateral donors, multilateral agencies and banks, and charitable foundations amounted to only $2 billion in 1995.[21] Although donors' contributions in 1995 were 24 percent more than in 1994, preliminary estimates indicate that contributions declined some 18 percent in 1996.[22] And it is likely that funding levels in 1997 fell even further.[23] International population assistance by the United States, the largest donor, dropped from $547 million in 1995 to $385 million in 1998.[24]

WORLD POPULATION, 1950–97

YEAR	TOTAL (billion)	ANNUAL ADDITION (million)
1950	2.556	37
1955	2.780	51
1960	3.039	42
1965	3.345	69
1966	3.416	70
1967	3.485	70
1968	3.557	72
1969	3.631	75
1970	3.707	75
1971	3.784	77
1972	3.861	77
1973	3.937	76
1974	4.013	76
1975	4.086	73
1976	4.158	72
1977	4.231	72
1978	4.303	72
1979	4.378	75
1980	4.454	76
1981	4.530	76
1982	4.610	80
1983	4.690	80
1984	4.770	79
1985	4.850	81
1986	4.933	82
1987	5.018	86
1988	5.105	86
1989	5.191	86
1990	5.278	87
1991	5.361	83
1992	5.444	83
1993	5.526	82
1994	5.606	81
1995	5.687	81
1996	5.766	79
1997 (prel)	5.847	80

SOURCE: U.S. Bureau of the Census, *International Data Base*, electronic database, Suitland, MD, updated 10 October 1997.

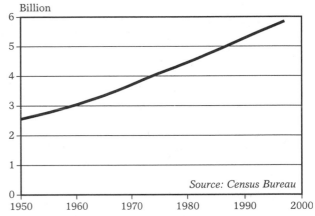

Figure 1: World Population, 1950–97

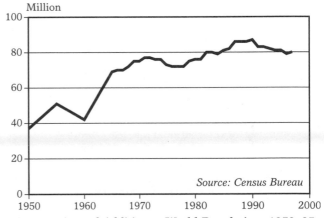

Figure 2: Annual Addition to World Population, 1950–97

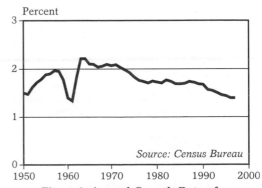

Figure 3: Annual Growth Rate of
World Population, 1950–97

Refugee Flows Drop Steeply

Jennifer D. Mitchell

Between January 1996 and January 1997, 22.7 million people qualified for and were given refugee assistance, according to the U.N. High Commissioner for Refugees (UNHCR).[1] (See Figure 1.) Of this total, some 13.2 million people had been forced to flee their countries, 4.9 million were internally displaced, and 3.3 million had recently returned to their home countries.[2] The remaining 1.3 million were considered "others of concern."[3]

The number of people receiving refugee assistance worldwide reached an all-time high of 27.4 million in 1995, but then declined two years in a row.[4] The drop of 3.4 million between 1996 and 1997 was the largest decline on record.[5]

Africa provided asylum to the largest number of refugees receiving U.N. assistance—more than 8 million last year.[6] But Asia is not far behind.[7] While the number of refugees in Asia rose, the number in Africa and Europe dropped by 1 and 2 million, respectively.[8] (See Figure 2.) The three countries that hosted the largest number of refugees are Iran (2 million), Germany (1.3 million), and Pakistan (1.2 million).[9]

Afghanistan was the source of the largest number of international refugees—some 2.7 million people.[10] Liberia, with 778,000 in exile, and Bosnia and Herzegovina, with 673,000, followed Afghanistan.[11] In 17 other countries, more than 100,000 people were forced to flee their homelands.[12] Overall, however, the number of people who fled their countries declined in 1997, and 10 million have returned home since 1990.[13]

Official statistics do not include everyone forced to flee from their homes or in need of shelter and assistance, however. While the number of international refugees has been shrinking, the number of people living in refugee-like situations within their own countries continues to rise. UNHCR estimates that roughly 30 million people may be internally displaced.[14] Of these, approximately 16 million are in Africa, 7 million in Asia, 5 million in Europe, and 3 million in the Americas.[15] These people, however, are not protected under international refugee law and therefore can only receive assistance if their governments allow them to receive it. Consequently, most internally displaced people did not receive such help.

Civil wars and unrest, economic turmoil, and environmental pressures are some of the factors responsible for the large numbers of displaced people.[16] But recently, many displaced people have been forced to remain in their own countries even when victimized because they could not find a safe asylum.[17] Despite the official statistics indicating that the number of refugees has declined, UNHCR reports that "the number of people forced to flee their homes because of fear and hardship is rising, but refugees are increasingly being shut out of safe havens—especially in Europe."[18]

Fear of a massive movement of people from poor to richer nations has prompted several industrial countries to tighten their borders.[19] Since the mid-1980s, more than 5 million people have applied for asylum in industrial countries, but many were turned down.[20] For example, several European countries have denied asylum to Algerians, even though 65,000 people have died in the last six years as a result of the political violence in Algeria.[21] Moreover, many countries are forcibly returning refugees, as has happened to nearly 300 Bosnians in Germany.[22]

With industrial countries closing their doors, refugees attempt to flee to poorer countries. But many of these nations are also tightening their borders.[23] And even when refugees are given asylum, they are often treated so badly that they return home, even though conditions have not improved.[24] In September 1996, for example, when Iraq launched an offensive against the Kurdish population, tens of thousands of Iraqi Kurds fled into Iran. Although they were given asylum, evidence suggests that officials withheld food and heating oil in order to force them out.[25] The closing of borders along with this new battery of techniques forces many refugees to remain in dangerous situations and to forgo much needed assistance.

REFUGEES RECEIVING U.N. ASSISTANCE, 1961–97[1]

YEAR	TOTAL (million)
1961	1.4
1962	1.3
1963	1.3
1964	1.3
1965	1.5
1966	1.6
1967	1.8
1968	2.0
1969	2.2
1970	2.3
1971	2.5
1972	2.5
1973	2.4
1974	2.4
1975	2.4
1976	2.6
1977	2.8
1978	3.3
1979	4.6
1980	5.7
1981	8.2
1982	9.8
1983	10.4
1984	10.9
1985	10.5
1986	11.6
1987	12.4
1988	13.3
1989	14.8
1990	14.9
1991	17.2
1992	17.0
1993	19.0
1994	23.0
1995	27.4
1996	26.1
1997 (prel)	22.7

[1]All data are as of January 1 of the year indicated.
SOURCE: United Nations High Commissioner for Refugees, various data series.

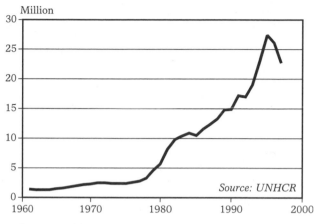

Figure 1: Refugees Receiving U.N. Assistance, 1961–97

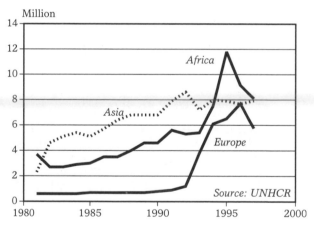

Figure 2: Refugees Receiving U.N. Assistance in Asia, Africa, and Europe, 1981–97

HIV/AIDS Pandemic Far From Over Brian Halweil

Nearly 6 million people contracted HIV—the virus that causes AIDS—in 1997, eclipsing the previous year's record of 5.6 million.[1] (See Figure 1.) More than 30 million people are now living with HIV/AIDS, and the number infected since the beginning of the epidemic in the late 1970s has topped 40 million.[2] Approximately 15 million of these people have developed full-blown AIDS, and 11.7 million have died.[3] (See Figure 2.) Even these figures may be dwarfed in the near future, however, for one fifth of those living with HIV/AIDS contracted the virus in the past year.[4]

While HIV infection rates and AIDS deaths have declined or stabilized recently in industrial nations, the epidemic grows unabated in the rest of the world.[5] In many ways, HIV/AIDS has become two epidemics. In industrial nations, it is treated with expensive drug regimens as a "manageable" chronic condition. In poorer nations—where more than 90 percent of all cases occur—infection still means gradual wasting and death.[6]

Sub-Saharan Africa—home to two of every three people living with HIV/AIDS—continues to be the region most ravaged by the virus.[7] HIV infection among adults in this region stands at an unprecedented 7.4 percent.[8] Yet much higher infection rates are found in areas such as Nairobi, Kenya, and Harare, Zimbabwe, where adult prevalence tops 25 and 30 percent, respectively.[9] Moreover, 8 of every 10 women with HIV/AIDS live in sub-Saharan Africa, as do 9 of every 10 children born with HIV infection.[10]

In India and China, high HIV prevalence is still limited to high-risk populations, such as prostitutes and intravenous drug users.[11] HIV prevalence among sex workers in Bombay, India, has been estimated at over 50 percent, while intravenous drug users in parts of China have similar infection rates.[12] However, since these groups can form centers for wider diffusion of HIV, enormous epidemics are poised to develop in these highly populated regions.[13]

Typically, second-class citizens—marginalized by society and lacking equal access to health care, education, and other human ser-vices—are most susceptible to the disease.[14] Even in the United States, AIDS prevalence is six times greater among blacks and three times greater among Hispanics than among whites.[15]

More than 40 percent of new infections in 1997 occurred in women, who now account for at least 40 percent of those living with HIV worldwide.[16] Young women seem to be most at risk.[17] Up to 60 percent of HIV-infected women worldwide are under the age of 20.[18] Holding lower social, economic, and legal positions in many nations, women often lack the means to refuse risky sexual encounters and protect themselves from infection.

People under 25 years of age account for three out of five new infections worldwide and constitute the fastest-growing segment of the epidemic.[19] In Latin America and the Caribbean, AIDS is on target to become the leading cause of death among youths.[20] Throughout the world, cultural taboos and lack of resources deny young people access to HIV/AIDS education and condoms—the primary means of prevention.[21]

Both Uganda and Thailand have seen HIV prevalence drop significantly in recent years as a result of aggressive government campaigns to increase public HIV/AIDS awareness.[22] Measures by these nations to reduce new infections have ranged from promotion of safe sex practices to treatment of sexually transmitted diseases, which facilitate the spread of HIV.[23]

Prevention remains a top priority for the more than 3 billion people living in parts of the world where HIV is still relatively uncommon.[24] Dr. Richard Feachem of the World Bank notes that "the best time to spend a dollar on HIV control is when you've got no HIV in your country."[25] At these early stages, low-cost, low-tech steps, such as condom distribution and needle exchange programs, can prevent a national epidemic from escalating.[26] Yet less than 5 percent of global HIV/AIDS funding currently goes for prevention and education.[27] The lion's share goes to pharmaceutical research and costly drug treatments, which are inaccessible to most of those living with HIV.

ESTIMATES OF CUMULATIVE HIV/AIDS CASES WORLDWIDE, 1980–97

YEAR	HIV INFECTIONS (million)
1980	0.2
1981	0.6
1982	1.2
1983	1.9
1984	2.8
1985	3.9
1986	5.4
1987	7.1
1988	8.9
1989	10.9
1990	13.3
1991	15.8
1992	18.8
1993	22.2
1994	26.2
1995	30.9
1996	36.5
1997 (prel)	42.3

YEAR	AIDS CASES (million)
1980	0.0
1981	0.1
1982	0.1
1983	0.1
1984	0.2
1985	0.4
1986	0.7
1987	1.1
1988	1.6
1989	2.3
1990	3.2
1991	4.2
1992	5.5
1993	6.9
1994	8.5
1995	10.4
1996	12.5
1997 (prel)	15.1

SOURCE: UNAIDS, *Report on the Global HIV/AIDS Epidemic* (Geneva: December 1997).

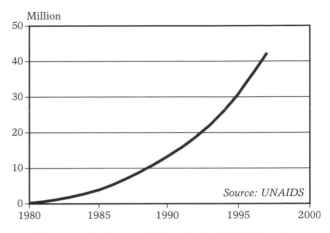

Figure 1: Estimates of Cumulative HIV Infections Worldwide, 1980–97

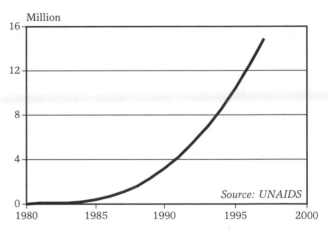

Figure 2: Estimates of Cumulative AIDS Cases Worldwide, 1980–97

Urban Areas Swell

Jennifer D. Mitchell

Since 1950, the number of people living in urban areas has jumped from 750 million to 2.64 billion people.[1] (See Figure 1.) Currently, some 61 million people are added to cities each year through rural-to-urban migration, natural increase within cities, and the transformation of villages into new urban areas.[2]

In most countries, the number of city dwellers is growing faster than the national population.[3] As a result, people living in urban areas account for a steadily growing share of world population. Today's city dwellers represent 46 percent of the global total, up from less than 30 percent in 1950.[4] (See Figure 2.) And according to U.N. estimates, more than half the world will live in urban areas within the next decade.[5]

One third of all city dwellers live in industrial countries while the rest live in the developing world—mostly in poor countries that do not have the resources to support large populations.[6] (See Figure 3.)

Like the number of city dwellers, the number of urban areas is also increasing rapidly. In 1800, London was the only city with more than 1 million people.[7] Today, 326 cities have passed this milestone.[8] Some 14 of these are "megacities": urban areas with populations in excess of 10 million.[9] By 2000—just two years from now—there will be 20 megacities, 17 of which will be in the developing world.[10]

Tokyo holds the title as the world's most populous city: with more than 27 million inhabitants, it is home to nearly one fourth of Japan's total population.[11] Mexico City, São Paulo, and New York trail Tokyo, with some 16 million people each.[12]

While the megacities in the industrial world grew slowly, the newly emerging megacities are exploding. It took London 130 years to grow from 1 million to 8 million, while Mexico City gained this many people in just 30 years, from 1940 to 1970, and then grew by another 7 million over the next 16 years.[13] Two of the fastest growing cities are Bombay and Lagos. Bombay, with a 3.5-percent annual growth rate, is projected to grow from 15 million to 18 million between 1995 and 2000, while Lagos, with a growth rate of 5.4 percent a year, will probably grow from 10.3 million to 13.5 million in this same period.[14] By 2015, Lagos may be home to nearly 25 million people, rising in rank from the world's thirteenth largest city to the third largest.[15]

Still, less than 10 percent of urban dwellers live in megacities.[16] Instead, 64 percent of city dwellers live in areas with populations under 1 million.[17] The challenges they face are similar, however. While urban areas usually have better access to health care and sanitation, increasingly these comparative advantages are being overwhelmed by sheer numbers.[18] According to a recent study by the Population Council, the quality of life in many urban centers of the developing world is poorer today than in rural areas.[19]

Every week, more than 1 million people are added to urban centers.[20] Many are poor people lured by the prospects of jobs, better education, or improved services. The United Nations estimates that nearly half of the world's poorest people, some 420 million, will live in urban settlements by the year 2000.[21] Unfortunately, these large influxes of people often lead to high levels of homelessness and unemployment, pollution and congestion, the loss of agricultural land, and the accumulation of nutrients and waste. A study of Bombay, for example, estimates that the city needs 500,000 public toilets, yet as of the beginning of 1995 only about 200 were in operation.[22] And due to the more than 10 million commuters using the city's bus and train system daily, people in Bombay spend on average two hours a day commuting.[23]

Massive infrastructure investments will be needed if the comparative advantages of cities are to be preserved. In the megacities of Asia alone, the Asian Development Bank estimates that $20–40 billion will be needed annually over the next decade to sustain productivity and improve the quality of life moderately.[24]

WORLD URBAN POPULATION, 1950–96

YEAR	POPULATION (billion)
1950	0.750
1955	0.872
1960	1.017
1965	1.185
1970	1.357
1975	1.543
1980	1.754
1985	1.997
1990	2.280
1996 (prel)	2.636

SHARE OF WORLD POPULATION THAT IS URBAN, 1950–96

YEAR	SHARE (percent)
1950	29.7
1955	31.6
1960	33.6
1965	35.5
1970	36.7
1975	37.8
1980	39.4
1985	41.2
1990	43.2
1996 (prel)	46.0

SOURCE: United Nations, *World Population Prospects: The 1996 Revision* (New York: draft, 1 May 1997).

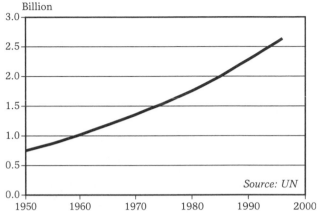

Figure 1: World Urban Population, 1950–96

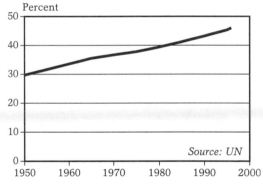

Figure 2: Share of World Population That Is Urban, 1950–96

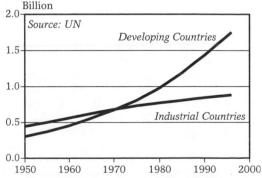

Figure 3: Urban Population in Industrial and Developing Countries, 1950–96

Cigarette Production Hits All-Time High   Brian Halweil

World cigarette production climbed to 5.8 trillion pieces in 1997—setting a record for the fourth consecutive year.[1] (See Figure 1.) Production lagged behind population growth, however, as the number of cigarettes manufactured per person fell to 982, a 4-percent drop from the all-time high in 1990.[2] (See Figure 2.)

China is the world's largest producer, responsible for 1.7 trillion pieces a year—30 percent of global production.[3] The United States follows, with 760 billion cigarettes, and Japan produces 266 billion cigarettes annually.[4] In 1997, production remained stable in China and the United States, while in Japan— the nation that smokes the most cigarettes per person—it dipped by 5 billion pieces due to a cigarette tax increase and growing health consciousness.[5]

In Asian nations, cigarette production has increased strongly over the last few years, fueled by unprecedented economic growth and demand for this luxury good. Indonesia— where production increased on average 6 percent over the past five years—boosted output by 10 billion pieces to a total of 208 billion in 1997.[6] India, Malaysia, and South Korea also raised production in 1997.[7] In contrast, an aggressive government drive against smoking and a new tax reduced output in the Philippines by 11 billion pieces—a drop of 16 percent.[8]

Production in the ex-Soviet nations and Eastern Europe continues to rebound from the dramatic drop in output following the breakup of the Soviet Union. In Bulgaria it jumped by 22 percent, to 70 billion pieces, in 1997.[9] In Croatia, the Czech Republic, and Slovakia, production rose by 5 percent; smaller increases were seen in Armenia, Romania, Russia, Ukraine, and Georgia.[10] In recent years, U.S.-based tobacco firms have entered this market—where about half of all men and women smoke—to make sure that the fierce appetite for cigarettes is not constrained by supply.[11]

Despite strong anti-tobacco policies and declining numbers of smokers in Europe and the United States, cigarette production in these areas continues to rise.[12] Increased exports fill the growing gap between production and consumption, as American and European tobacco firms look to overseas markets that are underregulated, underinformed, and underaged. Exports as a share of production have doubled in the last decade to 60 percent in the United Kingdom and 30 percent in the United States—the two largest exporters.[13] Since 1992, the percentage of tobacco revenue derived from international sales has climbed from 43 to 57 percent for Philip Morris and from 32 to 44 percent for R.J. Reynolds—the multinational tobacco companies with the first and third largest market shares, respectively.[14]

It is increasingly clear that smoking is hazardous not only to smokers—approximately half of whom are eventually killed by the habit—but also to nonsmokers.[15] Secondhand smoke increases the risk for virtually every life-threatening disease caused by smoking, including various cancers, heart disease, and respiratory conditions.[16] Passive smokers increase their risk of lung cancer by 30 percent and their risk of heart disease by 34 percent.[17]

Of the 3 million tobacco-related deaths each year, nearly 70 percent occur in the industrial world.[18] But as tobacco firms shift to Third World markets and as smoking rates increase in developing nations (see Figure 3), an epidemic of tobacco-related deaths will follow.[19] If current smoking trends persist, by 2020 the annual tobacco-related death toll will soar to 10 million, with 70 percent of deaths occurring in the developing world.[20] The enormous future medical costs of smoking will cripple the health care systems of these poorer nations.

More women and young people in developing nations are taking up smoking, in large part because tobacco firms increasingly target these groups with promotional giveaways and seductive advertising.[21] This trend threatens to erode years of health improvements and efforts to save impoverished children from diseases that are largely preventable. As Carol Bellamy, director of UNICEF, notes, "there is no cause of death more preventable than smoking."[22]

WORLD CIGARETTE PRODUCTION, 1950–97

YEAR	TOTAL (billion)	PER PERSON (number)
1950	1,686	660
1955	1,921	691
1960	2,150	707
1965	2,564	766
1966	2,678	784
1967	2,689	772
1968	2,790	785
1969	2,924	805
1970	3,112	840
1971	3,165	836
1972	3,295	853
1973	3,481	884
1974	3,590	895
1975	3,742	916
1976	3,852	926
1977	4,019	950
1978	4,072	946
1979	4,214	962
1980	4,388	985
1981	4,541	1,002
1982	4,550	987
1983	4,547	969
1984	4,689	983
1985	4,855	1,001
1986	4,987	1,011
1987	5,128	1,022
1988	5,240	1,026
1989	5,258	1,013
1990	5,419	1,027
1991	5,351	998
1992	5,363	985
1993	5,300	959
1994	5,478	977
1995	5,605	986
1996	5,713	991
1997	5,743	982

SOURCES: USDA, FAS, *World Cigarette Database,* electronic database, December 1997; data for 1950–58 estimates based on U.S. data.

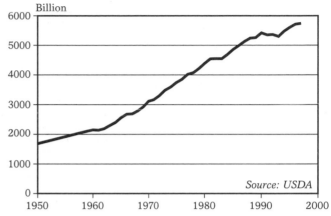

Figure 1: World Cigarette Production, 1950–97

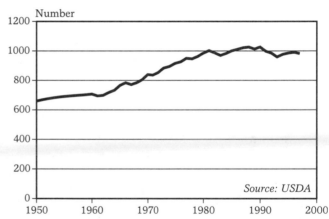

Figure 2: World Cigarette Production Per Person, 1950–97

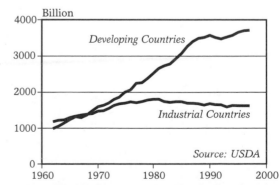

Figure 3: Cigarette Consumption in Developing and Industrial Countries, 1962–97

Military

Trends

Military Expenditures Continue to Decline   Michael Renner

By a preliminary estimate, world military expenditures fell by 4 percent in 1996, to $701 billion.[1] (See Figure 1.) They are now 39 percent below the peak level of $1,144 billion that they reached in 1984. (All data are expressed in 1995 dollars unless otherwise noted.) Relative to global economic output, military spending now stands at 2.6 percent, down from 5.7 percent in the mid-1980s.[2]

The end of the cold war and of several regional and local hot wars in recent years has brought military expenditures down in many countries, although the quality and reliability of information made available by national governments are still poor. Many governments—China prominent among them—reveal only a portion of their full expenditures, hiding other relevant items in the budgets of civilian agencies.[3]

As a consequence, military budget watchers report widely different figures. For 1995, the U.S. Arms Control and Disarmament Agency (ACDA) puts global spending at $865 billion, the International Institute for Strategic Studies (IISS) says the figure is $828 billion, but the Bonn International Conversion Center (BICC) pegs it at $728 billion.[4]

The biggest uncertainties are Russian and Chinese expenditures. Given its methodology, ACDA tends to inflate these outlays; for Russia, it relies on estimates of what it would cost in the United States, in dollars, to outfit and maintain Russia's military. For China, it uses purchasing power estimates of the Chinese yuan. Even if reliable local currency expenditure estimates were available, converting these into dollars—applying proper exchange rates—creates still more problems.[5]

For 1995, ACDA pegs Russian spending at $76 billion, and Chinese expenditures at $63.5 billion.[6] IISS believes the figures are $82 billion and $33 billion, respectively.[7] Trying to correct for the problems just mentioned, BICC puts Russia's budget at a mere $13 billion—perhaps too low—and China's at $34 billion.[8]

But there is no disputing that the single largest spender by far is the United States. According to the Pentagon's National Defense Budget Estimates, which provides more recent data than in other countries, U.S. outlays came to $243 billion, or 35 percent of global military expenditures, in 1997.[9] (See Figure 2.) Almost a full decade after the end of the cold war, the decline in U.S. military spending is just beginning to bring outlays back to the levels prevalent before the Reagan buildup.

Besides the United States, Russia, and China, other big spenders (in 1995) include Japan ($43.9 billion), France ($43.1 billion), Germany ($37.8 billion), and the United Kingdom ($33.9 billion)—all close allies of the United States.[10]

A third tier of large military spenders includes Italy ($19.8 billion), Saudi Arabia ($16.8 billion), South Korea ($13.6 billion), Taiwan ($12.6 billion), and Canada ($10.7 billion).[11] They are followed by India ($9.8 billion), Switzerland ($8.2 billion), Australia ($8.1 billion), Spain ($7.7 billion), Israel ($7.5 billion), Netherlands ($7.1 billion), Turkey ($6.1 billion), and North Korea ($5.6 billion).[12] All other countries spend less than $5 billion per year on their militaries.[13] Among the top 20 military spenders, only North Korea is hostile toward western countries.

On a regional level, East Asia is the only area that has witnessed a growth in military expenditures from 1985 to 1995, from about $100 billion to $129 billion.[14] (See Figure 3.) Yet the region's economic crisis has now forced several governments to cut their military budgets.[15] In the Middle East and North Africa, except for a brief spending bulge related to the 1991 Gulf War, countries have seen their outlays decline, from $93 billion to $52 billion.[16]

Western Europe's military budgets have declined gradually, from $232 billion in 1987 to $193 billion in 1995, yet they are still the largest of any region outside North America.[17] But the most dramatic decline has occurred in Eastern Europe and the successor states to the Soviet Union: expenditures plummeted from $247 billion in 1985 to just $21 billion in 1995.[18]

WORLD MILITARY EXPENDITURES, 1950–96

YEAR	EXPENDITURE (bill. dollars)
1950	267
1955	462
1960	475
1965	598
1966	653
1967	720
1968	765
1969	779
1970	765
1971	763
1972	771
1973	865
1974	891
1975	918
1976	931
1977	945
1978	974
1979	1,001
1980	1,008
1981	1,032
1982	1,093
1983	1,123
1984	1,144
1985	1,078
1986	1,071
1987	1,064
1988	1,056
1989	1,034
1990	1,012
1991	955
1992	837
1993	787
1994	750
1995	728
1996 (prel)	701

SOURCES: Worldwatch, based on Rita Tullberg, "World Military Expenditure," *Bulletin of Peace Proposals*, no. 3–4, 1986; ACDA, *World Military Expenditures and Arms Transfers 1996* (GPO, July 1997); BICC, *Conversion Survey 1997* (Oxford, 1997); IISS, *The Military Balance 1997/98* (Oxford: October 1997).

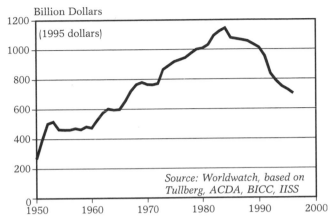

Figure 1: World Military Expenditures, 1950–96

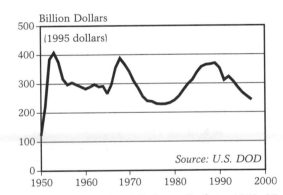

Figure 2: U.S. National Defense Outlays, 1950–97

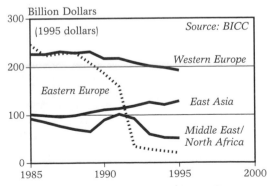

Figure 3: Regional Military Expenditures, 1985–95

The number of armed conflicts declined from 28 to 25 in 1997—half the peak number of 51 recorded during 1992.[1] (See Figure 1.) These data are being collected by the Unit for the Study of Wars, Armaments, and Development at the University of Hamburg in Germany.

Other analysts report slightly different numbers, due to definitional and methodological questions, along with the frequent lack of reliable information. The Conflict Data Project at the University of Uppsala, Sweden, puts the peak in 1992 at 55 and pegs the number of conflicts in 1997 at 24.[2] The regional figures here and those on size of conflict are based on the Uppsala project findings.

During 1989–96, there were a total of 101 separate armed conflicts.[3] Almost all of them—95—took place among combatants within countries rather than between different states.[4] This is reflected in the large number of conflict parties—254 in all, including government armies, paramilitary forces, guerrilla bands, drug warlords, and others.[5]

An estimated 250,000 children are serving as soldiers, often against their own will.[6] Children under 18 years of age were among the combatants in 33 current or recent conflicts, while 26 of these involved children younger than 15.[7] Taking a snapshot of 1995, Project Ploughshares in Canada found that children participated in fighting in more than 80 percent of the countries that were at war during that year.[8]

Although the number of conflicts is still high, few of them are full-fledged wars, killing more than 1,000 persons per year. Rather, most are "intermediate" armed conflicts (fewer than 1,000 deaths in any one year) or "minor" ones (fewer than 1,000 deaths during the conflict).[9] During 1996, there were 17 minor conflicts, 13 intermediate ones, and 6 wars.[10] By contrast, as recently as 1989, the respective numbers were 15, 14, and 18.[11]

Of the 101 conflicts during 1989–96, two thirds had ended by the close of 1996.[12] Conflict termination was due to one party's victory in 23 cases, the result of a peace

agreement in 19, and halted by a cease fire in another 7.[13] But in the remaining 17 cases, fighting simply ebbed away—and it is unclear whether the violence is gone for good or whether hostilities might resume at a later point.[14] (For definitional purposes, a conflict is considered "terminated" if there is no fighting for at least one year.)

Many of the still-active conflicts have lasted many years, although in some cases the fighting is sporadic. Most were initiated during the 1970s and 1980s, but some—like the violence in Myanmar (formerly Burma)—originated in the 1940s.[15]

More than half of the 19 peace agreements during 1989–96 were achieved in Africa.[16] Four agreements were concluded in the Americas, 3 in Europe, but only 1 each in the Middle East and Asia.[17] Most of the conflicts active since 1989 in the latter two regions remain unresolved.

Yet every region has seen a reduction in warfare since 1992. Of the 34 conflicts active in 1996, 14 were in Asia, 14 in Africa, 5 in the Middle East, 2 in the Americas, and 1 in Europe.[18] In 1996, the heaviest fighting took place in Afghanistan, Algeria, Sri Lanka, Sudan, and Turkey.[19]

Of course, the number of armed conflicts alone is not a sufficient indicator of the loss of human life or the disruption of societies. A single major conflict may cause far greater suffering than a large number of small ones.

During the first half of the 1990s, at least 3.2 million people died of war-related causes (either due to fighting or to hunger and disease caused by the fighting).[20] This is one of the highest death tolls of any five-year period since the end of World War II.[21] (See Figure 2.) Since 1946, at least 25 million people have been killed.[22] Some analysts contend that the number is far higher: according to Milton Leitenberg of the University of Maryland, it may be as high as 44 million.[23] Civilians account for a growing share of the victims, rising from 14 percent in World War I to 67 percent in World War II, 75 percent in the 1980s, and 90 percent in the 1990s.[24]

ARMED CONFLICTS, 1950–97

YEAR	ARMED CONFLICTS (number)
1950	12
1955	14
1960	10
1965	27
1966	28
1967	26
1968	26
1969	30
1970	30
1971	30
1972	29
1973	29
1974	29
1975	34
1976	33
1977	35
1978	36
1979	37
1980	36
1981	37
1982	39
1983	39
1984	40
1985	40
1986	42
1987	43
1988	44
1989	42
1990	48
1991	50
1992	51
1993	45
1994	41
1995	37
1996	28
1997	25

SOURCE: Arbeitsgemeinschaft Kriegsurachenforschung, Institute for Political Science, University of Hamburg.

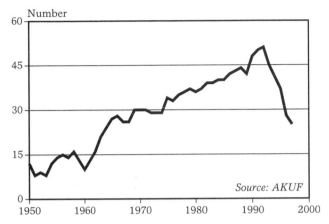

Figure 1: Armed Conflicts, 1950–97

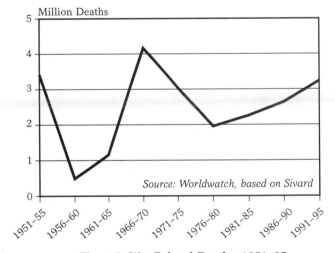

Figure 2: War-Related Deaths, 1951–95

U.N. Peacekeeping Contracts Further
Michael Renner

Continuing their rapid decline, expenditures for United Nations peacekeeping fell to an estimated $1.3 billion in 1997, down 29 percent from 1996.[1] (See Figure 1.) The number of soldiers, military observers, and civilian police involved in U.N. peacekeeping also declined, from 24,919 in December 1996 to 18,798 in September 1997.[2] (See Figure 2.)

This latest reduction is primarily due to the scaling back of operations in Angola, where a smaller observer mission replaced a peacekeeping operation that had been the largest mission in 1996. Although the prospects for lasting peace in Angola are still uncertain, the Security Council expects activities to be wrapped up by the end of April 1998.[3]

Other significant reductions in expenditures and personnel took place in Croatia and Haiti. In its latest incarnation, the mission in Haiti—which runs to the end of 1998—now consists of a police force rather than military troops.[4] And smaller missions to Liberia and Guatemala were completed during 1997.[5]

A significant portion of the peacekeeping boom was due to the conflict in the former Yugoslavia. Though scaled back substantially, the United Nations still had four ongoing missions there in 1997—two in Croatia, one in Bosnia, and one in Macedonia—involving almost 6,000 peacekeepers.[6] Half of them were part of a mission in eastern Croatia that in January 1998 was replaced with a small group of 180 civilian police monitors.[7]

The dramatic expansion of peacekeeping in the early 1990s now appears to have been a short-lived bubble. Indeed, it is telling that the largest single remaining mission at the end of 1997 was the UNIFIL deployment in Lebanon that was set up in 1978.[8]

Since the inception of peacekeeping a half-century ago, a total of 45 U.N. peacekeeping and observer missions have been initiated to help contain or settle 33 distinct conflicts.[9] Some 15 operations were still active at the end of 1997, of which 5 were initiated prior to the 1990s.[10]

Activity in the U.N. Security Council has mirrored the trends in peacekeeping. The total number of resolutions brought before the council rose dramatically—from 29 in 1988 to 93 in 1993—before dropping to 54 in 1997.[11] Even as the number of introduced resolutions skyrocketed, far fewer were blocked by the veto of a permanent member. With the end of the cold war, the United States and the former Soviet Union have adopted a more cooperative stance, allowing the Security Council to take a more active role in questions of international peace and security. Back in 1954, vetoes were cast against a record 90 percent of all resolutions; from the late 1960s to the late 1980s, an average of 26 percent were vetoed, but in 1997, fewer than 6 percent of resolutions met that fate.[12] (See Figure 3.) All in all, 256 vetoes were cast in 1946–97, while 1,134 resolutions were passed.[13]

Curiously, what did not decrease along with expenditures, troops, and council actions is the amount of money owed by member states for peacekeeping operations. Arrears rose from about $350 million in 1991 to a peak of $1.72 billion in 1995, declining just slightly to $1.57 billion in 1997, when members paid only two thirds of their dues.[14]

By far the biggest debtor is the United States. Congressional opposition has kept U.S. arrears at record levels.[15] The U.S. debt to U.N. peacekeeping hovered between $900 million and $1.1 billion during 1996–97—more than half of the arrears in this category owed by all members.[16]

As in 1996, a single non-U.N. operation was larger in 1997 than all U.N. peacekeeping missions combined. The NATO-led force implementing the Dayton Peace Agreement for Bosnia involved some 34,000 troops.[17] This is symptomatic of the current situation: the major powers on the Security Council have repeatedly declined to launch new U.N. missions, preferring either to act through ad hoc coalitions of states or not act at all. This attitude will limit U.N. peacekeeping for the foreseeable future.

U.N. PEACEKEEPING OPERATION EXPENDITURES, 1986–97

YEAR	EXPENDITURE (mill. dollars)
1986	242
1987	240
1988	266
1989	635
1990	464
1991	490
1992	1,767
1993	3,059
1994	3,342
1995	3,364
1996	1,840
1997 (prel)	1,300

SOURCES: U.N. Department of Peacekeeping Operations; Office of the Spokesman for the U.N. Secretary-General.

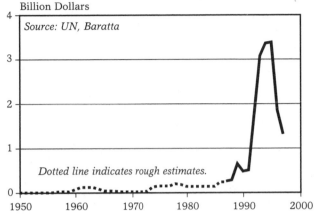

Billion Dollars

Source: UN, Baratta

Dotted line indicates rough estimates.

Figure 1: U.N. Peacekeeping Expenditures 1950–97

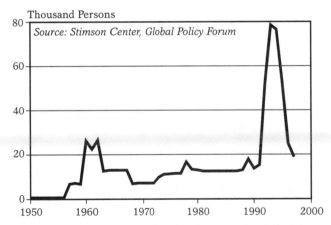

Thousand Persons

Source: Stimson Center, Global Policy Forum

Figure 2: U.N. Peacekeeping Personnel, 1950–97

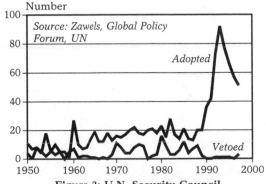

Number

Source: Zawels, Global Policy Forum, UN

Adopted

Vetoed

Figure 3: U.N. Security Council Resolutions, 1950–97

Part **TWO**

Special Features

Environmental Features

Forest Decline Continues

Janet N. Abramovitz

The world's forests have declined significantly in both area and quality in recent decades. Almost half of the forests that once blanketed Earth—3 billion hectares—are gone.[1] At least 200 million hectares of forest were lost between 1980 and 1995 alone—an area larger than Mexico or Indonesia, or three times the state of Texas.[2] Each year there is a net loss of another 16 million hectares as forests are converted to other uses.[3] Between 1990 and 1995, at least 107 countries had a net loss of forest cover.[4]

Today, forests cover more than one quarter of the world's total land area, excluding Antarctica and Greenland.[5] Slightly more than half of the world's forests are in the tropics; the rest are in temperate and boreal (coniferous northern forest) zones.[6] Seven countries hold more than 60 percent of the world's remaining forests: in order of forest area, they are Russia, Brazil, Canada, the United States, China, Indonesia, and Congo (formerly Zaire).[7]

Until recent decades, most forest loss occurred in Europe, North Africa, the Middle East, and temperate North America. By the early part of the twentieth century, these regions had been largely stripped of their original cover. Now forest cover in Europe and the United States is stabilizing, as secondary forests and plantation forests fill in.[8] In the last 30–40 years, in contrast, the vast majority of deforestation has occurred in the tropics, where the pace has been accelerating. Indeed, between 1960 and 1990, one fifth of all tropical forest cover was lost.[9] Asia lost one third of its cover, and Africa and Latin America lost about 18 percent each.[10] During the first half of the 1990s, these regions continued to lose significant portions of forest cover.[11] (See Table 1.)

Broad regional overviews such as these can mask even more severe forest loss that is taking place in some countries and forest types. Well over half (57 percent) of the net forest loss from 1980 to 1995 took place in just seven countries: Brazil, Indonesia, Zaire, Bolivia, Mexico, Venezuela, and Malaysia.[12]

Tropical dry forest types, mangrove forests, and the temperate rainforests of the Americas have experienced very high losses.[13]

Deforestation is not the only threat. Serious declines in forest quality are affecting much of the world's forests. The temperate forests are the most fragmented and disturbed of all forest types. For example, 95–98 percent of forests in the continental United States have been logged at least once since settlement by Europeans.[14] And in Europe, two thirds of the original forest cover is gone, while less than 1 percent of old growth remains.[15]

The secondary forest and plantations that are filling in are a very different type than the original. The forests are highly manipulated and highly fragmented. Plantations and even-aged stands occupy substantial areas of forestland. Worldwide, at least 180 million hectares of forest have been converted to tree plantations.[16] In the last 15 years, the area of tree plantation doubled and is expected to double again in the next 15 years.[17]

Atmospheric pollution is also taking a toll on the world's forests. This is particularly evident in Europe, North America, and Asia, as well as near cities throughout the world. More than one quarter of European trees show moderate to severe defoliation from exposure to pollution and its related stresses, according to regular surveys conducted by the U.N. Economic Commission for Europe.[18]

The extent of forest loss and fragmentation was made clear in a recent study by the World Resources Institute that identified what it calls "frontier forests"—areas of "large, ecologically intact, and relatively undisturbed natural forests."[19] The study found that while 40 percent of the world's forests are frontier, only 22 percent of the world's original forest cover remains in these large expanses, about evenly divided between boreal and tropical forest.[20] Only 3 percent of the frontier forests are entirely within temperate zones, much of which is in Chile and Argentina.[21]

More than 75 percent of the world's frontier forest is in three large areas: the boreal forests of Canada and Alaska, the boreal forests of Russia, and the tropical forests of the northwestern Amazon Basin and the Guyana shield (Guyana, Suriname, French Guiana, northeastern Brazil, Venezuela, and Colombia).[22]

Just eight countries—Brazil, Suriname, Guyana, Canada, Colombia, Venezuela, Russia, and French Guiana—have large portions of their original forests in vast undisturbed blocks.[23] Other countries that have lost much of their original forests—Indonesia, the United States, and Congo—still hold frontier forest by virtue of their size.[24] Seventy-six countries have no frontier forest remaining; 11 others are about to lose theirs.[25] In Europe, only 1 percent of the original forest cover is in large patches, in Sweden and Finland.[26]

The size and remoteness of most frontier forests does not isolate them from threats. Logging has been identified as the major danger in most forests, including the frontier ones. Mining and energy and infrastructure developments are also threats. Logging and these other developments play an important role in opening up frontiers to other activities, such as large-scale clearing for agriculture and ranching. The record-setting fires in Indonesia and Brazil in 1997 to clear forest for large plantations and ranches, the roads under construction through the remote forests of South America, and the logging that is occurring in every region—tropical, temperate, and boreal—make it clear that even remote forests are under threat.[27]

A major opportunity for international cooperation lies in improving monitoring of global forest conditions and threats. In order to assess the state of the world's forests accurately, data collection procedures and classifications need to be improved, satellite monitoring used, in-country capacity strengthened, and an independent monitoring mechanism put in place.

TABLE 1: FOREST COVER AND FRONTIERS BY REGION, MID-1990S

REGION	ORIGINAL FOREST	TOTAL REMAINING	NET ANNUAL CHANGE 1991–95	TOTAL REMAINING AS SHARE OF ORIGINAL FOREST	FRONTIER FOREST AS SHARE OF TOTAL REMAINING FOREST
	(thousand square kilometers)		(percent)	(percent)	(percent)
Africa	6,799	2,302	−0.7	34	23
Asia	15,132	4,275	−0.7	28	20
North and Central America	12,656	9,453	−0.1	75	41
Central America	1,779	970	−1.2	55	18
North America	10,877	8,483	0.2	78	44
South America	9,736	6,800	−0.5	70	65
Russia and Europe	16,449	9,604	—	58	36
Europe	4,690	1,521	0.3	32	1
Russia	11,759	8,083	0.1	69	43
Oceania[1]	1,431	929	−0.1	65	34
World	62,203	33,363	−0.3	54	40

[1] Papua New Guinea, Australia, and New Zealand.
SOURCES: Dirk Bryant, Daniel Nielsen, and Laura Tangley, *The Last of Frontier Forests: Ecosystems and Economies on the Edge* (Washington, DC: World Resources Institute, 1997); net annual change from U.N. Food and Agriculture Organization, *State of the World's Forests 1997* (Oxford, U.K.: 1997).

Tree Plantations Taking Root Ashley T. Mattoon

In 1997, the U.N. Food and Agriculture Organization (FAO) reported that between 1980 and 1995 the global extent of tree plantations roughly doubled—from approximately 90 million hectares to 180 million hectares, which is just slightly smaller than the land area of Mexico.[1] (See Table 1.) In addition, most developing countries with large plantation estates reported plans to double their plantation area by 2010.[2]

Tree plantations, as defined by FAO, are analogous to agricultural crops. They are artificially created and usually consist of one or a few species that are chosen for fast growth and high yields of wood fiber.[3] Often the species is not indigenous to the area in which it is planted. One 1990 assessment by FAO concluded that tree plantations in tropical countries primarily consisted of eucalyptus (23 percent of cover), pines (10.5 percent), acacias (7.7 percent), and teak (5.0 percent).[4]

Records of plantation cover do not account for tree plantations that provide what have been traditionally thought of as agricultural commodities—products such as palm oil, coconuts, and rubber. These plantations cover close to 14 million hectares in tropical Asia and another 2 million hectares in Africa and Latin America.[5]

FAO estimates do not distinguish between plantations established for industrial and non-industrial use. For example, a plantation could be a 10,000-hectare pulpwood production farm or a small-scale agroforestry plot designed for agricultural enhancement.[6] In addition, some plantations may be established for environmental purposes, such as carbon sequestration or watershed protection.[7]

Quantifying the extent of the many different types of plantations subsumed by FAO's assessment is not an easy task—the term "plantation" itself has no universally accepted definition. Nevertheless, the recent proliferation of large-scale industrial tree plantations has led forestry consultants and environmental groups to try to put a more precise number to this type of land use.[8]

One study, done for a joint project between Shell Petroleum and the World Wide Fund for Nature, concluded that close to 100 million hectares of the global plantation estate is for industrial use.[9] Approximately three quarters of this is planted in relatively slow-growing species—everything from slower-growing pines to teak.[10] These stands are used primarily for producing sawnwood and panels used in building construction and furniture making. The remaining 25 percent of the industrial plantation area has fast-growing species characterized by yields of more than 12 cubic meters per hectare a year (mostly eucalyptus and faster-growing pines).[11] These plantations are largely aimed at supplying pulpwood to the paper industry.[12]

Over the last three decades, the growing role of industrial plantations in providing a source of raw material for industry has been widely recognized and encouraged. Forest products industries are looking less to natural forests as sources of wood fiber, and more toward tree farms—

TABLE 1: WORLD TREE PLANTATION COVER, 1980 AND 1995

REGION	1980	1995
	(million hectares)	
Developing countries		
Africa	3.1	5.2
Latin America and the Caribbean	4.5	9.1
Asia/Oceania	32.6	66.9
Industrial countries (estimated range)[1]	45–60	80–100
Total	85–100	161–181

[1]FAO does not distinguish between natural forest and plantation forest in industrial countries. However, it does provide "rough estimates" of plantation cover in these regions.
SOURCE: FAO, *State of the World's Forests 1997* (Oxford, U.K.: 1997).

especially in southern regions where growth rates are faster, land and labor are cheaper, and environmental regulations are sometimes weaker.[13]

Annual growth rates of 3–5 cubic meters per hectare in eastern Canada and 10 cubic meters per hectare in the southeastern United States pale in comparison to rates as high as 25 cubic meters in Indonesia and 30–40 in Brazil.[14] And while it takes at least 15 years in Alabama to grow pine large enough to cut, rotations of eucalyptus in Brazil can be as short as 4–6 years.[15] It can take up to 16 times as much area to feed a 500,000-ton-per-year pulp mill in a Nordic country as it does in Brazil.[16]

As fast-growing plantations have spread in countries such as Brazil, Chile, Indonesia, and New Zealand, the role of the traditional major suppliers of pulpwood for the paper industry, such as Canada, the United States, and Scandinavia, has been gradually eroded.[17] In the 1960s and 1970s, these northern producers supplied more than 80 percent of the world's market pulp.[18] Today, this share has decreased to roughly 65 percent.[19]

In many countries, the prospect of garnering a larger share of the wood products market has led to heavily subsidized plantation programs and a rush of foreign investment.[20] Plantation cover in Latin America has increased by 50 percent in just the last 12 years, and is now found on 7.5 million hectares in Argentina, Brazil, Chile, and Venezuela.[21] Argentina, with approximately 800,000 hectares of plantation today, is expected to expand this cover by 50,000 hectares a year in order to increase its export market share.[22] Brazil has roughly 3 million hectares of eucalyptus plantations, a genus native to Australia.[23] Chile has close to 1.4 million hectares of radiata pine plantations and 250,000 hectares of eucalyptus.[24]

Indonesia, with nearly 1.5 million hectares of plantation today, plans to establish another 4.5 million hectares.[25] In September 1997, Australia launched a major national initiative to triple plantation area by 2020, requiring a plantation establishment rate of about 80,000 hectares a year.[26] And in New Zealand, plan-

tations currently cover close to 1.6 million hectares and are expanding by about 70,000 hectares annually.[27]

Given the high growth rates and yields of industrial plantations, it is widely believed that they have the potential to "protect" the world's remaining natural forests by concentrating the production of wood fiber for industry on a much smaller amount of land than would otherwise be needed. In some developing countries with large plantation estates, plantations produce 50–95 percent of the industrial wood harvest.[28] Some argue that the global shift to tree farming is the forester's equivalent of the Green Revolution, which favored high-yield crop varieties and large, mechanized farms instead of smaller, more diverse operations.[29]

Plantations established on lands that have been degraded by agricultural use or logging have potential to provide services such as erosion control and carbon sequestration while also supplying a source of wood fiber and other forest products. However, there are many cases in which plantation development has come at the cost of natural forest or has displaced rural communities.[30] Many of the fires that burned close to 2 million hectares of Indonesian forests and scrubland in 1997 (up to 100,000 hectares of which was primary forest) were set to clear land for industrial plantations (in this case, including plantations for products such as palm oil).[31] In Chile, 132,000 hectares of native forests have been replaced by pine plantations in the last 30 years.[32] In the southeastern United States, experts predict that 70 percent of the native pine forests will be converted to plantations by 2020—a doubling of the region's current plantation area.[33]

Although the potential for plantations to relieve the pressures on the world's remaining forest frontiers is promising, past and current practices—combined with the rate and scale at which plantations are being established—give cause for concern. In addition, the potential benefits of plantations may not come to fruition if the demands humans make of them do not decrease.

Vertebrates Signal Biodiversity Losses   John Tuxill

How much biological diversity is the world in danger of losing? Even for scientists, this question is difficult to answer. Most of the estimated 4–40 million species of life on Earth are unknown and unmonitored, and other elements of biodiversity—genes, populations, communities, and habitats—are equally hard to assess.[1] In this murky situation, one of the clearest windows on the status of biodiversity is offered by the organisms we already know the most about—birds, mammals, reptiles, amphibians, and fish, collectively known as vertebrate animals. Vertebrates total about 50,000 species and inhabit nearly all environments on Earth.[2] Since they tend to have large habitat requirements and occupy the top rungs of food chains, vertebrates provide a good indication of the general health of natural communities.

The conservation status of birds (nearly 10,000 species) and mammals (about 4,400 species) has been comprehensively assessed by the World Conservation Union.[3] The status of reptiles (6,300 species), amphibians (4,000 species), and fish (nearly 24,000 species, the most diverse vertebrate group) is relatively well known in North America, Australia, and Europe, but still largely obscure in many species-rich habitats in the tropics and—for fish—in marine habitats.[4] As a result, the proportion of species assessed for conservation status in these three groups ranges from 20 percent (reptiles) to less than 10 percent (fish).[5]

Together, these surveys yield some alarming numbers. The proportion of species judged threatened with extinction ranges from 11 percent for birds to 34 percent for fish.[6] (See Table 1.) In addition, another 5–14 percent of species in these groups are near-threatened—these are species clearly declining in numbers and range and likely to soon qualify for threatened status without a change in their current condition.[7] These numbers suggest that about one in every four vertebrate species is currently on a road to extinction unless we work to change their circumstances.[8]

Declines in all vertebrate groups are due to similar causes. The single largest problem is habitat loss—humankind's conversion and fragmentation of forests, thornscrub, coral reefs, rivers, and many other habitats that species call home. At least 70 percent of threatened vertebrate species are declining because they can no longer find suitable habitat.[9]

Although habitat loss receives the most attention on land—an old-growth forest is

Table 1: Conservation Status of Vertebrates, 1996

STATUS	BIRDS	MAMMALS	REPTILES	AMPHIBIANS	FISH	ALL VERTEBRATES
			(number)			
Species Assessed	9,615	4,355	1,277[1]	497[1]	2,158[1]	17,902[1]
			(percent)			
Not currently threatened	80	61	74	70	61	72
Nearing threatened status	9	14	6	5	5	9
Threatened (vulnerable to or in immediate danger of extinction)	11	25	20	25	34	19

[1]Numbers reflect only the species surveyed for conservation status, not the total number of species known in each group.
SOURCE: Jonathan Baillie and Brian Groombridge, eds., *1996 IUCN Red List of Threatened Animals* (Gland, Switzerland: World Conservation Union, 1996).

converted to a uniform timber plantation, for instance, or a farm hedgerow is leveled to make room for more crops—it is an equally severe problem underwater. Freshwater systems worldwide have been heavily altered by drainage and channelization projects, tens of thousands of dams, and widespread agricultural and industrial pollution. The highest price for such disruption of natural hydrological patterns has been paid by freshwater species in semiarid regions such as North America's Colorado River basin, where 29 of 50 native fish species are either endangered or already extinct.[10] Throughout Mexico, 68 percent of the fish native to arid-region river systems are threatened with extinction.[11]

A second major problem for about one fifth of all declining species is overexploitation.[12] Ocean fish are particularly hard hit, with some 39 percent of threatened species overharvested.[13] Large reptiles and large mammals also face particularly heavy hunting pressure. The most serious instances of overexploitation arise where unregulated commercial markets exist for wildlife meat, hides, ivory, musk, and other products.

Of particular concern are the "bushmeat" trade now flourishing in Central and West Africa and the booming demand in East Asia for traditional medicinal products derived from animals.[14] For instance, the demand for tiger body parts in traditional Asian medicine is such that an individual tiger can be worth more than $5 million—dead, not alive.[15] The result has been an upsurge in poaching in recent years, and wild tiger numbers have dwindled to as few as 3,000 individuals.[16]

The decline of vertebrates like tigers, whales, and elephants is particularly worrisome because such large creatures also have outsized ecological roles—their disappearance is likely to have serious ecological side effects. Research in Panama and Peru suggests that jaguars, the top rainforest predators, help control populations of smaller forest mammals, many of which feed on fruits of forest trees.[17] In the absence of jaguars, smaller mammals may increase in numbers and in essence overharvest the forest fruits, stifling the regenera-

tion of certain tree species and, over time, changing the forest's composition. Eliminate the large vertebrates from a forest or marine food web, and the end result could be a less diverse, less productive community.

The third major problem facing threatened species is competition and predation from invasives—highly adaptable animals and plants that spread outside their native ranges, usually with human help, and do well in disturbed habitats. As many as 10 percent of threatened vertebrates may face pressure from invasives, which cause the most problems on islands and in freshwater systems, where endemic, long-isolated species are often unprepared to face competitors.[18]

If the trends evident in vertebrates also hold for other organisms, then extinction could be an unnaturally close possibility for about one quarter of the world's entire complement of species. This number could well rise further, for it does not consider global changes in climate that most scientists suspect are in store for our planet. A major climate shift, such as a global warming trend, will probably mean changes in seasonal timing, rainfall patterns, ocean currents, and other parts of Earth's life-support systems. Although species have responded to climate changes in the past by migrating or shifting their ranges, such adaptive responses will be more difficult in today's degraded habitats, where many species are already hard-pressed to maintain their numbers.[19]

In the end, the struggle to reverse vertebrate declines is but part of a larger struggle to protect all elements of biodiversity, from individual populations to entire native landscapes. Conserving species is as much a cultural as a biological endeavor, and action can be taken on all levels, from improving the management of forest reserves and national parks to reducing our imprint on the planet by creating a more energy and resource-efficient society where we live and work.[20] Scientists may keep track of the numbers, but safeguarding biodiversity is a task for all of us.

Organic Waste Reuse Surging Gary Gardner

Communities are returning organic material to soils at a growing rate in the 1990s, especially in industrial countries.[1] Although global data are not available, the United States and Europe have seen a sharp increase in composting of municipal organic waste and the reuse of human waste.[2] (See Table 1.) U.S. composting facilities grew more than fourfold between 1989 and 1996.[3] And in both regions, roughly one third of the sewage sludge is land-applied.[4] Despite the rapid growth in recycling, however, organic waste remains largely untapped. Composting rates for this waste in major industrializing nations averaged only about 11 percent in the early 1990s.[5]

Once commonly practiced, organic recycling was increasingly abandoned this century as urbanizing societies turned to chemical fertilizer to enrich soils, and to dumping areas to eliminate organic wastes.[6] But fertilizer is now a major source of water pollution in industrial countries, and disposal areas in some countries have become scarce or are so badly polluted that dumping is increasingly discouraged.[7] In the United States, for example, 23 states have prohibited or restricted the flow of organic material to landfills since 1990.[8] Ocean dumping of sewage became illegal throughout the country in 1992, and is banned in Europe as of 1998.[9]

Compost provides multiple benefits to soils. It shelters nutrients that would otherwise be leached or eroded away.[10] It helps soils retain water, which can see crops through periods of low rainfall. And it suppresses plant diseases: compost has been shown to limit the spread of root rot, for example, as effectively as many fungicides.[11] But compost is a challenge to manage. Composts vary from place to place and by season, as the composition of waste flows changes. This complexity allows compost makers to tailor their products to diverse customer needs, but it also means users must understand how particular composts will work in particular soils and with given crops.[12]

Human waste is also increasingly recycled, especially in industrial countries. Europe as a whole applied roughly one third of its sewage sludge—the muck from a treatment plant that is processed to reduce the level of pathogens—to agricultural land in the early 1990s, while the United States applied 28 percent.[13] In developing countries, sewer coverage is much less extensive, and only 10 percent of wastes from sewers receive treatment.[14] These nations often recycle by diverting sewage, in raw form, directly into irrigation canals.[15] In many developing-country cities, however, human waste is not recycled, but is simply dumped into rivers or bays.

Reuse of human waste on crops carries risks. Human waste is teeming with pathogens, and using it without treatment or composting can lead to widespread sickness.[16] Even so, irrigation with untreated wastewater continues in many developing countries.

In industrial countries, the risk from pathogens is greatly reduced due to sewage treatment. But health risks still exist from the toxic chemicals and heavy metals that leave homes and industry and then mix with human waste in modern sewer systems. Standards are set for some of these contaminants in Europe and the United States, but the rules are criticized for insufficient coverage and lax enforcement. Safe recycling may require that human waste be separated from industrial flows.

Because recycled municipal and human waste supply soils with nutrients and organic matter, recycling can reduce applications of manufactured fertilizer. In the major industrial countries, unrecycled municipal organic waste and human waste could have provided some 15 percent of the nutrients applied with commercial fertilizer in the early 1990s.[17] Because fertilizer is commonly overapplied, however, the potential contribution of urban nutrients is likely greater than the 15-percent figure indicates.[18] And unlike fertilizer, organic wastes enrich soils with organic matter, which is essential for soil health.

Organic recycling has proven economic benefits as well. Middlebury College in

TABLE 1: INCREASE IN COMPOSTING ACTIVITIES IN THE 1990S

ACTIVITY	LOCATION	DESCRIPTION
Construction of composting facilities	United States	Facilities increased more than fourfold between 1989 and 1996, from some 700 to more than 3,200.
	Germany	More than 500 composting facilities have been built since 1985.
Regulations issued	South Korea	National goal set to increase food scrap recycling rate from 2 percent in 1995 to 21 percent by 2001.
	Germany	Landfilled material cannot contain more than 5 percent organic material. This is only one quarter to one fifth as much organic matter as found in most industrial-country landfills.
	United States	23 states have laws to reduce waste inflows to landfills by up to 50 percent; goal pursued in large part by composting, rather than disposing of, organic wastes.
	Canada	Organic material to be banned from all landfills in Nova Scotia starting in 1999.
Composting of municipal solid waste	Belgium	Flanders region saw a doubling of organic waste composting between 1995 and 1996. Goal for 2001 of 23-percent participation in home composting programs.
Composting of food scraps	United States	1997 survey of food residuals composting by institutions found 48 percent more projects than in 1996. Of projects that listed start dates, 91 percent had begun since 1990.
Information and research	International	Trade publication *Biocycle* set to launch an international edition in 1998 to cover rapid growth in composting worldwide. *Compost Science and Utilization*, a peer-reviewed journal on composting, began publication in 1993.

SOURCE: See endnote 2.

Vermont reports annual savings of some $25,000 through composting food scraps, while the New York State Department of Corrections has saved more than $1 million at 31 sites around the state.[19] A backyard composting program in Sonoma County in California has cut participants' landfilled wastes by 18 percent and cost the county 60 percent less than landfilling would have.[20]

Composters do well, too: a southern California recycling company has prospered by composting spoiled fruits and vegetables from supermarkets with yard wastes, and selling the finished product to farmers in the region.[21] The program grew from 28 pilot supermarkets in 1994 to more than 750 in 1997—and has cut disposal costs for participating grocers by more than 85 percent.[22]

Further growth in organic recycling will depend in part on increasing user confidence in recycled organics. Compost of consistent quality, and farmers trained in its use, are the keys to successful recycling. And if human waste is isolated from other sewage flows, confidence in reuse of this nutrient-rich resource will also increase.

Nitrogen Fixation Continues to Rise
Gary Gardner

Human activities continue to increase the supply of nitrogen that can be used by plants around the world, a trend that effectively raises the fertility of Earth.[1] As humans cultivate more leguminous crops, burn more fossil fuels, and manufacture more chemical fertilizer, the rate of nitrogen fixation—the conversion of atmospheric nitrogen to a form plants can use—has more than doubled over its natural, preindustrial level.[2] This increased fertility is necessary for high-yield agriculture, but it also pollutes land and water, and disrupts the natural cycling of nitrogen.[3]

Nitrogen availability is a key factor for plant growth. Although nitrogen accounts for 78 percent of the atmosphere, only fixed nitrogen is useful to plants.[4] Nitrogen is fixed naturally by lightning and by specialized bacteria and algae; before the industrial era, production of crops (and all other biomass) was largely limited by the nitrogen made available through these sources.[5] But as human activities have increased the supply of fixed nitrogen over the past two centuries, the nitrogen limit to plant growth has been relaxed.

Burning fossil fuels fixes a small amount of nitrogen, but it also releases large quantities of fixed nitrogen that have been locked in geological deposits for eons. Today, fossil fuel consumption accounts for some 6 percent of human and natural sources of nitrogen fixation.[6] (See Table 1.) Other nitrogen-releasing human activities include burning wood fuel, forests, and grasslands; draining wetlands; and clearing land for agriculture.[7] These various activities account for roughly 21 percent of natural and human sources of nitrogen availability.

Most of the human-origin increase in nitrogen comes from activities related to agriculture. The oldest of these is the use of leguminous crops. Clover, alfalfa, peas, beans, and other legumes have roots that support nitrogen-fixing bacteria.[8] Cultivation of these crops increases soil fertility, which is why farmers often rotate legumes such as soybeans with nonlegumes such as corn. As demand for livestock feed and cooking oil—both of which are derivatives of soybeans—has surged since 1970, world soybean production has more than tripled, adding substantially to the global supply of fixed nitrogen.[9]

The greatest human impact on nitrogen fixation, however, comes from production of synthetic nitrogen fertilizer, which has increased ninefold since mid-century.[10] The growth is driven in part by the use of high-yielding grain varieties, which need extra nutrients for optimal growth. As these varieties were adopted widely in the past 15 years, fertilizer use surged as well: half of the manufactured fertilizer ever used has been applied since 1982.[11] Although saturation in some industrial countries and depression in the former Soviet Union and Eastern Europe caused global fertilizer use to drop in recent years, consumption has picked up again on strong demand in developing countries.[12]

Overfertilization of the planet is more damaging than might be expected. The Organisation for Economic Co-operation and Development lists nitrate pollution as one of the most serious water quality problems in Europe and North America.[13] Indeed, every country in the European Union has areas that regularly exceed maximum allowable levels of nitrates in drinking water.[14] These pollutants can be converted to potential carcinogens when digested by humans, and can cause brain damage or even death in infants by affecting the oxygen-carrying capacity of the blood.[15]

Excess nitrogen also poses a threat to ecosystem health. Along with phosphorus (another key fertilizer ingredient), nitrogen can promote overgrowth of algae in rivers, lakes, and bays.[16] As the algae die and decay, they use up large amounts of the water's oxygen, depriving other species of the oxygen they need to survive.[17] The incidence of this "hypoxia" in coastal regions now appears to be on the increase globally.[18] The coastal areas of Denmark, Sweden, Germany, and the states of Louisiana and Texas, along with areas of the Black and Baltic Seas, have had to deal with hypoxia for at least a decade.[19] In the case of the U.S. Gulf Coast, the hypoxic

TABLE 1: SOURCES OF FIXED NITROGEN

SOURCE	QUANTITY (teragrams per year)	AS SHARE OF TOTAL NITROGEN FIXED[1] (percent)
Natural Sources of Nitrogen Fixation		
Lightning	< 10	3
Microbes	90–140	34
Human Sources of Nitrogen Fixation		
Nitrogen Fertilizer	80	24
Leguminous Crops	32–53	13
Release of Previously Fixed Nitrogen		
Burning fossil fuels	20	6
Clearing land, draining wetlands	70	21
Total Human Fixation and Release	213	63

[1]Share calculation uses midpoint values for range data in quantity column.
SOURCE: Based on Peter Vitousek et al., *Human Alteration of the Global Nitrogen Cycle: Causes and Consequences* (Washington, DC: Ecological Society of America, 1997).

"dead zone" that now appears each summer—at the peak of fertilizer runoff from the Corn Belt—is the size of New Jersey.[20]

Plant diversity is also reduced by excess levels of nitrogen. A 12-year study completed in 1996 documented declines in species diversity of more than 50 percent after nitrogen fertilizer was applied to test plots of Minnesota grasslands.[21] The fertilizer spurred the growth of plants that were best able to take it up—but at the expense of plants that were less well adapted.[22] This loss of diversity is consistent with the experience of areas of northern Europe, where high levels of nitrogen deposition have converted heathlands rich in diversity to grasslands with relatively few species.[23]

Nitrogen is also implicated in the production of acid rain. Nitric oxide, which is released when fossil fuels are burned, can be transformed in the atmosphere to nitric acid, a key component (along with sulfuric acid) of acid rain.[24] As this fallout raises the acidity of water and soils, organisms from bacteria to frogs are increasingly threatened.[25] The increased acidity also consumes the finite supply of a soil or lake's alkaline material—the buffer that protects fauna from excessive acidity.[26]

Excessive levels of fixed nitrogen may also affect the global cycling of carbon. Because plants store carbon, the increase in plant growth spurred by excess nitrogen may be capturing substantial amounts of carbon that would otherwise escape to the atmosphere and likely influence climate.[27] If true, this surplus nitrogen could account for the planet's "missing carbon": the imbalance between the amount of carbon emitted during the burning of fossil fuels and the clearing of land, and the lesser amount that accumulates in the atmosphere.[28] Thus the increase in nitrogen availability may have had a dampening effect on the rise in global temperatures seen over the past century.

Acid Rain Threats Vary

Molly O'Meara

etween 1980 and 1995, emissions of sulfur dioxide (SO_2) from fossil fuel burning fell by 47 percent in Europe and 31 percent in the United States; at the same time, they more than doubled in Asia, despite reductions in Japan.[1] (See Table 1.) Along with nitrogen oxides, sulfur dioxide forms acids in the atmosphere that fall back to Earth as dry particles or precipitation—a phenomenon known as acid rain. These acids corrode the metal and stone of buildings and monuments, impair human health, and damage forests, lakes, and crops.[2]

Industrial countries began to recognize the acid rain threat in the 1960s and 1970s, as scientists showed that tall smokestacks, while reducing local smog, allowed pollutants to be carried longer distances.[3] Fish declines in acidified lakes and streams in Scandinavia, northeastern United States, and Canada, along with forest die-offs in Germany's Black Forest and the Appalachians, were among the events that heightened public concern.[4]

In 1979, the United States, Canada, and Western Europe produced a model treaty on acid rain: the Convention on Long Range Transboundary Air Pollution.[5] Parties to the treaty have taken their own routes to achieve emissions reductions. In the United States, for example, a tradable sulfur permit system for utilities led to a 13-percent decrease in sulfur emissions nationwide between 1994 and 1995, while in Sweden a tax resulted in a 30-percent decrease in total emissions between 1990 and 1995.[6]

Today, falling SO_2 emissions in industrial nations stem from gains in energy efficiency, cleaner technologies, and cleaner fuels.[7] (Nitrogen pollution has proved more difficult to prevent, because much of it comes from gasoline burned by vehicles.) As a result, acid rain attracts less attention in North America and Western Europe now.

In contrast, the countries of Central and Eastern Europe, plagued by pollution during the Soviet era, are at an earlier stage in addressing acid rain. However, analysts at the Austria-based International Institute for Applied Systems Analysis (IIASA) project that as the region emerges from economic crisis, efficiency measures and the adoption of European Union standards will result in declines in sulfur emissions and more modest declines in nitrogen emissions from 1990 levels by 2010.[8]

Acid rain is now a growing problem in Asia.[9] China's coastal areas in 1990 were blanketed in 830–1,480 tons of SO_2 per square kilometer, as much as 40–45 times greater than the levels in Japan in 1975—that nation's worst air pollution year.[10] According to IIASA's Regional Air Pollution and Information Simulation model, SO_2 emissions in Asia will surpass those of Europe and North America combined by 2000.[11]

Variations in vegetation, soil, topography, and climate make some areas more vulnerable to acid rain than others.[12] For instance, southwestern China is more acidified than the northeast not only because of the region's high-sulfur coal consumption, but also because the winds in the northeast tend to disperse the pollution and the alkaline soils there neutralize the acids.[13] Although soils and water

TABLE 1: SULFUR DIOXIDE EMISSIONS FROM FOSSIL FUEL BURNING IN ASIA, EUROPE, AND THE UNITED STATES, 1980–2010

	1980	1990	1995	2000	2010
	(million tons of sulfur dioxide)				
Europe	59	42	31	26	18
United States	24	20	16	15	14
Asia	15	34	40	53	79

SOURCE: See endnote 1.

can buffer acids, continued acid assault can wear down the buffering capacity of natural systems.[14]

Acid rain can hasten forest decline by corroding leaves, acidifying soils, and promoting the uptake of heavy metals by tree roots.[15] Forests weakened in this way may be more vulnerable to ground-level ozone (formed by nitric oxides and hydrocarbons) and to climatic stresses.[16] Early reports in North America emphasized that acid rain was one of several contributors to forest damage, although European studies found a more direct link.[17]

In China, acid rain is implicated in large-scale die-offs in southwestern forests.[18] And in an interim report in April 1997, a Japanese government study group announced that unprecedented levels of acid deposition were damaging trees and plants.[19]

Crops are also at risk. A survey by China's National Environment Protection Agency found that about 40 percent of China's agricultural land is affected by acid rain.[20] According to the World Bank, annual forest and crop losses there are estimated at $5 billion.[21]

Acidified lakes suffer decreased productivity. As lakes acidify, the concentration of trace toxic metals increases, some fish populations die out, and the composition of the plankton and microbial populations shifts to those that can tolerate high acidity.[22] According to the Japanese government, that nation's lakes and ponds could become too acidic for freshwater life in the next 30 years.[23]

The problem of acid rain demands a regional solution. For instance, Japan has reduced sulfur emissions through gains in efficiency, heavier reliance on oil and nuclear power, and stringent pollution control laws, but it cannot stop China's emissions from drifting across the Sea of Japan.[24] In 1990, at least 37 percent of Japan's sulfur deposition came from China.[25]

Although Asia lacks a formal treaty to combat transboundary air pollution, Japan has taken the lead in forming a region-wide network to collect and exchange data on acid deposition.[26] Since the mid-1990s, Japan has offered low-interest loans to China for pur-

chasing desulfurization equipment for power stations and instituting other environmental reforms.[27] In 1997, for the first time, China was willing to accept a loan from Japan of $1.7 billion for energy conservation technology and equipment, reforestation, prevention of air pollution, and the building of environmental model cities.[28] And in 1998, China announced new plans to fine polluters and restrict the burning of high-sulfur coal (the nation has a great deal of low-sulfur coal).[29]

One lesson learned in Western Europe and North America is that acid rain is linked with other environmental problems that stem from fossil fuel burning, such as local air pollution, global climate change, and stratospheric ozone layer depletion. An isolated response to one threat might actually worsen another. For instance, the catalytic converters on cars that decrease nitric oxide emissions help to reduce acid rain and urban smog, but they also release higher levels of nitrous oxide—a potent greenhouse gas and contributor to depletion of stratospheric ozone.[30]

Another example of the interactions between air pollution problems is that sulfate aerosols in the upper atmosphere contribute to acid rain but mask greenhouse warming. To reduce sulfur emissions, power plant owners have switched to low-sulfur coal or attached "scrubbers" to their smokestacks. But a decline in sulfur emissions without a corresponding decrease in carbon dioxide concentrations has exacerbated the problem of climate change.[31] The ultimate solution to these related atmospheric problems lies in reforming the world's pollution-generating energy, transportation, and industrial systems.

Economic Features

Private Capital Flows to Third World Slow   Hilary F. French

The amount of private capital flowing into the "emerging markets" of the developing world exploded in the early 1990s, rising from $44 billion at the beginning of the decade to an all-time high of $244 billion in 1996 (in current dollars), according to the World Bank.[1] Meanwhile, during the first half of the 1990s, spending on official development assistance fell by more than a quarter in the face of large government budget deficits in donor countries and declining political support for aid.[2] The shrinking public presence and expanding private flows dramatically changed the complexion of North-South development finance. Whereas in 1990 less than half the international capital moving into the developing world came from private sources, by 1996 this share had risen to 86 percent.[3]

But in the wake of the Asian economic crisis of 1997, the international capital that had been pouring into that region suddenly reversed course as investors raced for the exit. This turnaround brought total private capital flows to emerging markets down to $175 billion in 1997, according to preliminary estimates by the International Monetary Fund (IMF).[4] (See Figure 1.) The IMF expects the slowdown to continue into 1998.[5]

Most of the private funds have so far gone to a relatively small group of countries, mainly in Asia and Latin America: in the first half of the 1990s, just 12 nations received some three quarters of all private inflows—led by China, Mexico, and Brazil.[6] These dozen countries have an enormous impact on the health of the planet by virtue of their relatively large populations, economies, and land masses.

But when foreign capital inflows are measured as a percentage of gross domestic product rather than in absolute terms, it becomes clear that foreign capital is also shaping the environmental futures of many smaller countries. For example, Angola, Ghana, and Papua New Guinea receive higher inflows relative to their size than do Brazil, China, and Mexico—the three largest recipients in absolute terms.[7]

Private capital flows take three principal forms: foreign direct investment (FDI) by companies, often through joint ventures with local firms; "portfolio investment," in which stocks and bonds are purchased on local capital markets by individuals and large institutional investors such as insurance companies, mutual funds, and pension plans; and commercial bank loans.[8]

Foreign direct investment in developing countries is the largest category, as well as the best documented. It added up to $110 billion in 1996—45 percent of total private flows—and has been growing fast, having more than quadrupled since 1990.[9] Although investment from domestic sources is still 10 times as large—$1.2 trillion in 1995—the foreign share has climbed steadily.[10]

After FDI, the next largest category is portfolio investment—accounting for just under 40 percent of the total.[11] This includes stocks, in which investors own shares in companies,

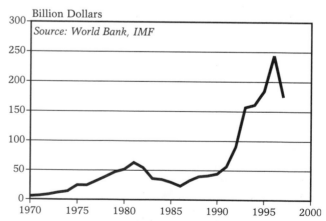

Figure 1. International Private Capital Flows to Developing Countries, 1970–97*

*Numbers for 1996 and 1997 are preliminary

as well as bonds, in which private investors make long-term loans to governments or businesses at fixed interest rates. In 1996, each of these two categories amounted to $46 billion.[12]

Commercial bank lending is the third major category of private capital flowing into the developing world—it accounted for 14 percent of total private flows in 1996, or $34 billion.[13] Commercial loans climbed to this level from just $3 billion at the beginning of the decade.[14] But the increase may have been short-lived: early estimates indicate that commercial loans declined substantially in volume in 1997 as a result of Asia's troubles.[15]

The quest for natural resources historically has drawn international investors into distant ventures in the developing world.[16] Over the last several decades, however, manufacturing has gradually risen in importance as has, more recently, the services sector, including construction, electricity distribution, finance, retailing, and telecommunications. The World Bank estimates that the "primary" sector, which includes agriculture, forestry, and mining, now accounts for some 20 percent of all FDI flows to developing countries, while manufacturing makes up less than half of the total, and services more than a third.[17]

In the wake of Asia's crisis, economic experts who just months earlier were extolling the virtues of global economic integration are urgently warning that international financial flows have outgrown existing financial regulatory structures.[18] But few people are paying attention to another critical issue: the extent to which the decade's massive international financial flows to the developing world have undermined the economy's ecological foundations.

The inflows of foreign capital fueled a record-breaking economic takeoff in the countries receiving them. China, for instance, which has attracted the greatest volume of funds, expanded its economy at double-digit annual rates in the first half of the 1990s. Several other countries were not far behind.[19] Though the booming economies of the developing world raised national incomes, they left ecological devastation in their wake. Urban air pollution levels in many Asian and Latin American cities are among the worst in the world, and natural resources such as forests and fisheries are badly depleted on both continents.[20]

Understanding the role of private capital flows in all of this is no simple matter, for the environmental implications of this decade's massive movements of money into the developing world, while enormous, are also complex and somewhat contradictory. As investors search the globe for the highest return, they are often drawn to places endowed with bountiful natural resources but handicapped by weak or ineffective environmental laws.[21] Many people and communities are harmed as the environment that sustains them is damaged or destroyed—villagers are displaced by large construction projects, for example, and indigenous peoples watch their homelands disappear as timber companies level old-growth forests.

Foreign-investment-fed growth also promotes western-style consumerism, pushing car ownership, paper use, and Big Mac consumption rates toward the untenable levels found in the United States—with grave potential consequences for the health of the natural world, the stability of Earth's climate, and the security of food supplies.[22]

Yet international capital brings environmental benefits as well, such as access to cutting-edge technologies that minimize waste generation and energy use. These new processes can help developing countries leapfrog over the most damaging phases of industrialization, and avoid the kind of costly cleanup bills that many industrial countries are now saddled with.[23]

Several "green" international investment strategies taking shape today aim to shift private capital out of environmentally damaging activities and into the cleaner technologies and enterprises of tomorrow.[24]

Taxation Shifting in Europe

David Malin Roodman

Since 1991, six national governments in Western Europe have made small cuts in conventional taxes on income and raised taxes that discourage environmental harm.[1] (See Table 1.) As would be expected of policies that raise some taxes and cut others, several concerns have motivated European legislators to make environmental tax shifts. To date, the uppermost concern has been to remedy problems with conventional taxes, such as complexity, high rates, and the way payroll taxes destroy jobs by raising the cost of workers. To pay for cuts in these taxes, governments have sought new revenue sources—and have discovered that taxes on polluters have become, if not popular, one of the least unpopular ways to raise revenue.

Sweden implemented the world's first environmental tax shift, in 1991.[2] In the postwar era, Sweden charted a middle course between capitalism and communism, building a market-based economy but with a large government role in everything from child care to housing. But by the early 1990s, structural flaws had appeared in the "Swedish Model." Economic growth stopped. Unemployment rose.[3] Taxes captured 55 percent of economic output but were full of exemptions.[4] That forced tax rates on nonexempt income as high as 85 percent, and deterred work.[5]

By 1990, Swedish politicians had decided to simplify the tax code in order to eliminate exemptions and lower overall tax rates—a task made politically easier if it resulted in a net income tax cut. One appealing option for replacing the lost revenue was to use environmental taxes more. In the previous decade, signs of global warming, the discovery of the ozone hole, and televised images of mass seal deaths due in part to pollution in waters along the Swedish coast had raised environmental concern to unprecedented levels among the Swedish public.[6] As a result, the electorate became more open to environmental taxation.

The tax reform package that became law

TABLE 1: TAX SHIFTS FROM WORK AND INVESTMENT TO ENVIRONMENTAL DAMAGE

COUNTRY, YEAR INITIATED	TAXES CUT ON	TAXES RAISED ON	REVENUE SHIFTED[1]
			(percent)
Sweden, 1991	Personal income	Carbon and sulfur emissions	1.9
Denmark,1994	Personal income	Motor fuel, coal, electricity and water sales; waste incineration and landfilling; motor vehicle ownership	2.5
Spain, 1995	Wages	Motor fuel sales	0.2
Denmark, 1996	Wages, agricultural property	Carbon emissions; pesticide, chlorinated solvent, and battery sales	0.5
Netherlands, 1996	Personal income and wages	Natural gas and electricity sales	0.8
United Kingdom, 1996–97	Wages	Landfilling	0.2
Finland, 1996–97	Personal income and wages	Energy sales, landfilling	0.5

[1]Expressed relative to tax revenue raised by all levels of government.
SOURCE: See endnote 1.

included two major environmental revenue raisers, which together allowed a 1.9-percent shift in total taxation from income to environmental damage. One was a tax on emissions of carbon from fossil fuel burning. By 1994, the Swedish government estimates, this tax had cut the country's carbon emissions 2–3 percent below what they would have been without the tax.[7] The other measure was a tax on sulfur dioxide emissions, which contribute to the country's severe acid rain problem. The government attributes 12 points of the 40-percent sulfur emissions decline between 1989 and 1995 to the levy.[8]

As Western Europe's unemployment crisis deepened during the 1990s, jobs became the driving concern behind tax shifts in other countries. In the European Union, unemployment reached 10.6 percent in 1997, representing 18 million people, up from a mere 2.6 percent in 1973.[9] This trend has been tied to international capital mobility, trade-induced competition, immigrants willing to accept low wages, and the rise of information technologies—each perhaps with some cause.[10]

But taxes appear to contribute too. Wage taxation has been rising in almost all western industrial countries in recent decades. Between 1970 and 1995, taxes' share of labor costs climbed from 30 to 43 percent in Germany, from 18 to 26 percent in Japan, and from 20 to 26 percent in the United States.[11] Economic studies have been reasonably consistent in concluding that this added to joblessness. One found that wage tax increases explained 0.5 percentage points of the unemployment rise in France between 1956–66 and 1980–83 and 2.0 points in the United Kingdom.[12]

In response to studies like these, tax shifts in the mid-1990s have focused more exclusively on cutting payroll taxes. Denmark, Finland, the Netherlands, Spain, and the United Kingdom have all made modest cuts in wage taxes and paid for them with new taxes or tax increases on sales of energy, water, pesticides, or batteries; on incineration or landfilling; or on car ownership.[13] Denmark executed two tax shifts totaling 3 percent of revenues in the mid-1990s, making it

the largest tax shifter to date.[14] After a solid waste charge went into effect, the share of the country's demolition refuse that was not recycled crumpled from 88 to 18 percent.[15]

Many countries outside of Western Europe have also raised environmental taxes. Australia and the United States, for example, have combined taxes and regulations to phase out ozone-depleting chemicals.[16] China is developing a tax system to control sulfur emissions, and the Philippines is beginning to tax water pollution.[17] And although none of these tax increases is explicitly linked to across-the-board cuts in conventional taxes, all indirectly reduce the need for other taxes to fund government programs. Some have paid for water treatment plants, some for subsidies to private businesses to reduce pollution, and some for tax breaks to other industries.[18]

In the long run, the largest potential environmental revenue source would be taxes on carbon emissions. Various studies have suggested that shifting toward carbon taxation could eventually allow cuts in conventional taxes of 10–20 percent.[19]

Unlike most regulations, which set minimum standards, environmental taxes create an ongoing prod for conservation and pollution reduction without restricting people's flexibility in responding. They allow governments to push an economy toward environmental soundness without taking on the impossible task of planning all the major changes that will be needed in how people use resources—thus where they live, how they move about, and how they make everything from bottles to buildings.[20]

Moreover, since environmental tax shifts do not increase the overall tax burden, they allow policymakers to protect the environment essentially without hurting the economy overall—and when the tax cuts are properly targeted, they can address problems such as unemployment.[21] Environmental taxes thus seem so essential to the creation of an environmentally sound society that Europe's tax shifts likely represent the beginning of a major historical trend.

Fossil Fuel Subsidies Falling

David Malin Roodman

Government subsidies for fossil fuels—coal, oil, and natural gas—fell dramatically during the first half of the 1990s. Since fossil fuel use is by far the largest source of greenhouse gas emissions from human activities, and since it also causes other problems from acid rain to water pollution, this is a welcome development for the global environment.

Fossil fuel subsidies are aimed at two main groups: users and producers. Those for users, which work by keeping prices artificially low, are found mainly in developing and former Eastern bloc nations, even though western industrial countries account for most fossil fuel use. In total, they slowed from roughly $200 billion per year in the 1990–91 period to $84 billion five years later.[1] (See Table 1.) (All figures in 1997 dollars.)

Subsidies for consumers are often defended as reducing the cost of living. They can do some good by saving money for low-income families, but most of the benefits go to better-off people, who spend more on fuel.[2] This makes them inefficient and costly, which is one reason they are increasingly seen as unaffordable.

In 1990–91, governments in the former Eastern bloc spent an elephantine $130 billion a year, roughly 10 percent of their gross domestic product, to hold fuel prices to small fractions of what they were in the West.[3] (This figure has to be interpreted cautiously, however, since hyperinflation made estimating fuel prices—and hence subsidies—extremely difficult.) Although prices governed buying decisions much less than in more capitalist countries, cheap energy nevertheless induced waste—from grossly inefficient factories to overheated apartment buildings that could only be cooled by opening windows.[4]

Since 1991, however, market reforms and budget squeezes have redrawn the region's subsidy map. For industry, energy subsidies have mostly ended, which is partly why energy use and air pollution have dropped sharply.[5] In contrast, subsidies for household energy buyers have generally failed to fall.[6] In 1990–91, Russian families paid only 10 percent of the world price for natural gas. By 1995–96, that figure had barely budged: they paid 9 percent.[7]

Subsidies for energy use are high in developing countries too. Popular objects of subsidy include kerosene, a heat and lighting source for many people, and diesel fuel, which is used in public buses. Here too, subsidies have fallen in the 1990s, reflecting the worldwide trend toward a smaller government role in many industries.[8] In 1996, for example, Venezuela slashed the $500 million a year it once pumped into its popular gasoline subsidies, subsidies that made gas so cheap (3.4¢ a liter or 13¢ a gallon) that buyers used it to clean floors.[9]

China implemented especially dramatic subsidy cuts between 1990–91 and 1995–96, from $24 billion a year to $10 billion.[10] Higher coal prices in particular have led to more-efficient energy use, one reason Chinese economic output has grown 30 percent faster than energy use since 1985, reversing the typical pattern for newly industrializing countries.[11] India, another coal giant, also cut subsidies, from $3.3 billion to $1.9 billion, as part of a larger move to make its economy more market-driven.[12]

The other family of fossil fuel subsidies, for producers, has not been so comprehensively surveyed, but it appears relatively more common in western industrial countries. Spending to protect uncompetitive coal mines, for example, amounted to $13.2 billion a year in 1990–91 in Germany, Japan, Spain, and the United Kingdom.[13] The overall trend for these subsidies is also downward: coal aid in these countries fell to $9.5 billion in 1995–96.[14] Nevertheless, many western nations offer additional support for fossil fuel producers, from tax breaks to military spending in the Middle East—and this may not be declining.[15]

Historically, subsidies like these have been defended on several grounds. Some, particularly those for oil drilling, have been offered in the name of national security, since they can reduce a country's dependence on imported supplies. Most others are granted in the name of protecting the jobs of coal, oil, and natural gas workers.[16]

Yet the very forces that necessitate the subsidies—dwindling oil reserves, job-destroying automation—undermine them as time passes. In the United States, for example, a clutch of tax breaks worth $5 billion a year to domestic oil producers has not kept the companies' reserves from dwindling.[17] As a result, output has dropped by a quarter since 1970 and producers' domestic market share has fallen below 50 percent.[18] All that such incentives do is shift production from the future, when oil will be scarcer.

In Germany, resource depletion and automation are combining to make coal subsidies increasingly costly and untenable. As miners have delved deeper into the country's sole hard coal deposit, the time and equipment needed to raise a ton of coal have climbed. In 1982, the government granted the industry $42 in subsidies for each ton of coal it sold; by 1996, the price of protection had nearly quadrupled, to $153.[19] Since total subsidies climbed about half as fast—from $4.1 billion to $7.3 billion—production had to fall 50 percent, and employment 54 percent.[20] Overall, the cost of "protecting" a mining job rose from $21,700 to $85,800 a year.[21] It would be cheaper now to shut down the mines and pay miners not to mine.

Sooner or later, Germany will have to cut back support, as many coal subsidizers have already done. In addition to Japan and the United Kingdom, East European nations such as Poland, Hungary, and the Czech Republic have all begun reforming their coal sectors, a painful job since it entails eliminating jobs in societies still picking up the pieces of the old communist system.[22] And China cut aid to state-owned mines from $750 million in 1993 to $240 million just two years later.[23]

Overall, poorer nations have seized the lead in ending subsidies for the largest source of greenhouse gases. If the global community is ever to cooperate effectively to slow climate change, western industrial nations will need to make at least as much progress in cutting their own subsidies.

TABLE 1: SUBSIDIES FOR FOSSIL FUEL CONSUMPTION, DEVELOPING AND FORMER EASTERN BLOC COUNTRIES, 1990–91 AND 1995–96

REGION/ COUNTRY	SUBSIDIES		CHANGE (percent)
	1990–91	1995–96	
	(billion 1997 dollars per year)		
Former Soviet Union[1]	115.3	32.8	−72
Russia	62.5	14.8	−76
Eastern Europe[1]	15.1	7.2	−52
Developing Asia	36.7	19.6	−46
China	25.7	10.8	−58
India	4.5	2.8	−37
Indonesia	1.9	1.4	−28
Middle East	17.2	13.9	−19
Iran	12.2	10.1	−17
Saudi Arabia	3.6	1.8	−50
Africa	5.4	3.9	−28
Egypt	1.9	1.4	−28
Nigeria	0.9	0.6	−28
South Africa	0.9	0.4	−58
Latin America	12.8	6.8	−47
Mexico	5.0	2.4	−53
Venezuela	3.2	2.5	−22
Total	202.5	84.2	−58

[1]Estimates for Eastern bloc nations are particularly rough because of hyperinflation in the early 1990s and because, in some of them, widespread nonpayment of energy bills creates hard-to-measure de facto subsidies.
SOURCE: Worldwatch Institute, based on World Bank sources. See endnote 1.

Paper Recycling Climbs Higher Ashley T. Mattoon

Between 1975 and 1995, world recovered-paper volume more than doubled, from 49 million to 114 million tons.[1] During that time, the wastepaper recovery rate—the share of paper used that is recovered—increased from approximately 38 percent to 41 percent.[2] The U.N. Food and Agriculture Organization predicts that by 2010, global use of recovered paper will reach 181 million tons, with a projected recovery rate of 46 percent.[3]

These data do not differentiate between pre- and post-consumer waste. Pre-consumer waste includes scraps generated during the production of products such as envelopes and books as well as publications that are returned unsold. Post-consumer waste is material such as cardboard, newspapers, printing and writing papers, and so on that is collected from homes and offices.[4] While it is significant that the industry reroutes pre-consumer waste back into paper production rather than discarding it, many argue that this has been routine practice for the industry and that pre-consumer material does not represent a legitimate source of solid waste. This has led to increased demand for products containing post-consumer fiber.[5]

Wastepaper recovery rates vary dramatically among countries due to differences in environmental regulations, pulpwood supply, cost effectiveness, access to local markets, and existing infrastructure. (See Table 1.) For example, aggressive legislation to reduce solid waste in Germany has resulted in recovery rates above 65 percent.[6] And in Japan and the United Kingdom—two major paper producers—limited pulpwood resources have encouraged a heavy dependence on recovered paper.[7]

In many countries, a primary motivation for increasing recovery rates has been the need to reduce the flow of waste to landfills and incinerators. Paper accounts for a significant proportion of municipal solid waste (MSW) in industrial countries. In the United States, it makes up 39 percent (by weight) of MSW generated, and in Europe, it is 30–40 percent.[8]

In the 1970s and early 1980s, wastepaper recovery rates in the United States were fairly stagnant, ranging between 22 and 27 percent.[9] But the mid-1980s surge in recycling brought recovery rates close to 34 percent in 1990, and to 45 percent by 1995.[10] The American Forest and Paper Association has set a goal of a 50-percent recovery rate by 2000.[11] And a 1994 European Union Directive targeted a recovery rate of 50–65 percent for packaging waste by 2001.[12]

Due to the large amount of trade in recovered paper, recovery rates do not necessarily indicate the amount of recovered paper a particular country actually uses to produce more paper. The "wastepaper utilization rate" is the ratio of recovered paper used in a given year to the total volume of paper produced. Although Sweden recovers well over half of what it consumes, for instance, the country is such a large producer and exporter that the relative contribution of recovered paper to overall paper production is less than 16 percent.[13] In the United States, the wastepaper utilization rate remained close to 23 percent between 1965 and 1985 (down from nearly 40 percent in the 1940s).[14] By 1990, it passed 27 percent, and in 1995, the rate neared 38 percent.[15] In Japan, efforts to make up for limited pulpwood supplies and to reduce dependence on imports have encouraged the industry to set a goal of a 56-percent utilization rate by 2000, up from 53 percent in 1995.[16]

International trade in recovered paper has more than tripled in volume since 1975.[17] In 1995, about 16 percent of all recovered paper entered world trade.[18] The United States, by far the largest exporter, accounted for 53 percent of total trade in 1995.[19] In 1996, recovered paper represented close to 6 percent of U.S. paper industry exports and was worth $804 million.[20] Recovered paper from the United States is sent to more than 75 markets around the world.[21] Major export destinations include, in order of importance, Canada, Mexico, South Korea, Taiwan, Japan, China, Indonesia, Venezuela, Thailand, and the Philippines.[22]

TABLE 1: PAPER RECOVERY, TOTAL AND TOP 10 PAPER PRODUCERS, 1995

COUNTRY	TOTAL RECOVERED	EXPORTS	IMPORTS	RECOVERY RATE[1]	UTILIZATION RATE[2]
		(thousand tons)		(percent)	
United States	39,305	9,430	464	45	37
Japan	15,473	42	479	52	53
Germany	10,531	2,986	1,054	67	58
China	8,246	16	906	31	38
France	3,702	787	1,245	38	48
South Korea	3,662	0	1,317	56	72
Canada	2,694	465	1,923	40	22
Italy	2,351	57	1,083	29	50
Sweden	1,079	182	614	58	16
Finland	492	35	66	32	5
World	114,283	17,784	19,207	41	41

[1] Total recovered paper volume divided by paper and paperboard consumption. [2] Recovered paper consumption divided by paper and paperboard production.
SOURCE: PPI, *International Fact and Price Book 1997* (San Francisco, CA: Miller Freeman, Inc., 1996).

In recent years, Asia has been home to the world's fastest-growing paper producers. In many countries, such as Indonesia, the Philippines, South Korea, and Taiwan, the domestic paper industry has developed on the basis of recovered-paper imports.[23] In 1995, Asian countries accounted for nearly 40 percent of all such imports.[24] According to one industry analyst, Asia's recovered-paper imports will rise from the current 7 million tons a year to about 20 million tons by 2005.[25] (In early 1998, however, analysts were speculating that at least for the first half of the year there would be a substantial drop in Asian imports due to the recent currency crises there.)[26] Another growing market for recovered-paper imports is Eastern Europe, where increasing demand for paper combined with dwindling timber reserves and the higher cost of processing virgin pulp have led to a recent focus on recovered paper.[27]

Global consumption of recovered paper is now increasing at a faster rate than consumption of wood pulp. Although use of recovered paper more than doubled since 1975, that of wood pulp increased by less than two thirds.[28] Greater recycling has slowed growth in the demand for wood pulp, but it has served more as a supplement than a substitute for total fiber supply to industry. This is largely because global paper and paperboard consumption is increasing so rapidly that it has overwhelmed gains made by recycling. In addition, paper fibers can only be recycled four to six times before they become too weak for use in paper production.[29]

The long-term potential for increased recycling to relieve pressures on the world's forest resources is not well understood and is the subject of debate.[30] Yet as waste disposal problems grow, as paper consumption rises, and as pulpwood supply declines in various regions of the world, reusing and recycling paper and paperboard products will become increasingly important.

Cigarette Taxes on the Rise   Anne Platt McGinn

Currently, some 90 countries regulate tobacco in various fashions, but only about a third of these use direct fiscal policy to reduce smoking.[1] Tobacco taxes help reduce smoking and thus lower smoking's costs to society.[2] They also reinforce nonfiscal policies that are beginning to take hold worldwide.[3]

Cigarette taxes are highest in Europe.[4] (See Table 1.) Smokers in Norway pay the most in the world—$5.23 in taxes per pack, which is 74 percent of the total price.[5] Danish smokers, however, pay a higher portion of taxes: 85 percent of the price is tax.[6]

In 1997, U.S. smokers paid an average of $1.90 per pack of cigarettes, less than half as much as many Europeans; of that total, 35 percent of the price was taxes.[7] The rate of federal excise taxes on cigarettes has dropped from 35 percent in 1955 to 12 percent in 1997.[8] Although the absolute amount of tax tripled during this time (from 8¢ to 24¢ a pack) as cigarette prices steadily increased, cigarettes in the United States are taxed at the lowest rate of any industrial country, and lower than in several developing countries.[9]

Experience in many countries has shown that each 10-percent increase in cigarette prices leads to a 5-percent decrease in smoking among adults.[10] And teenagers, with less disposable income, demonstrate an even stronger connection—a 10-percent price hike reduces smoking by 6–8 percent among young adults.[11]

Evidence that taxes discourage smoking is overwhelming. In Belgium, for example, a 46-percent increase in cigarette prices between 1985 and 1995 was linked to a 25-percent decline in per capita cigarette consumption.[12] Between 1973 and 1986, Papua New Guinea increased tobacco excise taxes by 10 percent, which resulted in a 7-percent decline in cigarette consumption.[13]

Similarly, between 1980 and 1991 New Zealand increased cigarette taxes by almost $2, nearly doubling the overall price.[14] During this time, the number of cigarettes purchased per person dropped from 4,100 annually to just over 1,500.[15] Currently, smokers in New Zealand pay nearly $3 per pack in taxes, with revenue from additional tax increases channeled into a three-year campaign against teen smoking.[16]

Between 1979 and 1991, real cigarette prices in Canada increased by 159 percent while the prevalence of teen smoking dropped from 42 percent to 16 percent.[17] But after more than 12 years of rising prices and falling rates of consumption, Canada did an about-face. In 1994, Canadian lawmakers—concerned about cigarette smuggling from the United States— slashed prices by one third.[18] Within a year, teenage smoking rates increased from 16 to 20 percent.[19] Lower prices have since encouraged higher rates of smoking among adults as well.[20] In late 1996, the Canadian Parliament voted for a modest tax increase and four provinces followed suit with slightly higher increases, but the resulting prices are much lower than

TABLE 1: CIGARETTE TAXES AND PRICES PER PACK, SELECTED COUNTRIES, 31 DECEMBER 1996			
COUNTRY	TAX[1]	PRICE	TAX SHARE OF PRICE
	(dollars)		(percent)
Norway	5.23	7.05	74
United Kingdom	4.30	5.27	82
Denmark	4.02	4.75	85
Finland	3.48	4.54	77
New Zealand	2.76	4.17	66
France	2.61	3.47	75
Canada	1.97	3.00	66
Netherlands	1.94	2.66	73
Singapore	1.87	3.72	50
Italy	1.59	2.17	73
Brazil	1.06	1.43	74
Thailand	0.89	1.58	56
United States	0.66	1.90	35
Taiwan	0.62	1.45	43
South Africa	0.47	1.04	45

[1]All applicable taxes and other fees on the product.
SOURCE: David Sweanor, Smoking and Health Action Foundation, Ottawa, ON, Canada, letter to author, 5 December 1997.

those in the early 1990s.[21]

Increasing cigarette taxes can also help fund public health efforts and raise revenue for government coffers. Tobacco taxes constitute at least 5 percent of government revenues in Bangladesh, Côte d'Ivoire, and Indonesia, and nearly 20 percent in Singapore.[22]

As many communities are learning, pairing tobacco taxes with other control efforts strengthens the positive effects on health. In 1993, cigarette excise taxes in South Africa had dropped to an all-time low of 20 percent of price, and per capita consumption was up.[23] With the passage of the Tobacco Products Control Act of 1993, which instituted health warnings and advertising restrictions and increased excise taxes, the situation was reversed.[24] In 1997, cigarette taxes accounted for more than half of the price of a pack, while annual per capita consumption dropped by 20 percent.[25]

Voters in Massachusetts in the United States approved a ballot measure to double cigarette taxes (from 26¢ to 51¢) beginning in January 1993.[26] Data collected between 1990 and 1996 demonstrate that shortly after the new tax was implemented, prices increased by 25 percent.[27] Mass media campaigns and local health education programs combined with the tax increase to reduce consumption among adults by 20 percent.[28]

Many countries now allocate a share of taxes specifically to anti-smoking activities. Since 1985, Iceland has put 0.2 percent of revenue from cigarettes sales into such programs.[29] In 1987, the Australian state of Victoria established a health foundation paid for by a 5-percent levy on all cigarette sales.[30] VicHealth, as the program is known, involves representatives from government agencies, community development groups, schools, sports teams, and the arts, housing, and transport sectors who coordinate anti-smoking efforts in their respective fields. Currently, VicHealth sponsors more than 1,000 arts and sporting events that have traditionally been paid for by tobacco companies.[31]

Tax revenue is also used to support broader public health goals. After spending nearly $1 billion on tobacco-related health care in 1995, U.S. taxpayers in Oregon approved an initiative to increase the tax on each pack of cigarettes from 38¢ to 68¢ beginning in February 1997.[32] According to voter surveys, the measures passed in large part because a portion of the revenue is earmarked for smoking prevention, health education, and expanded medical coverage for people without insurance.[33]

Nearly a dozen developing countries spend a portion of tobacco taxes on health care, research, and education.[34] In recent years, the Iranian government increased tobacco excise taxes and earmarked a portion of tax revenue for health education and primary health care.[35] Latvia dedicates 30 percent of tobacco tax revenue to health care programs, and in Nepal and Peru a share of cigarette tax revenue supports cancer research and treatment.[36] Nearly one fourth of tobacco taxes in Ecuador support the National Program for Free Children's Medicine.[37]

While notable, these efforts are not enough to counter subsidies in favor of tobacco production and use. Despite some of the highest prices in the world, the European Union currently spends 115 times as much subsidizing tobacco growing ($1.5 billion) as it does fighting the results of tobacco use through the Europe Against Cancer program ($13 million).[38]

The governments of China, Poland, Russia, and Ukraine, among others, support national tobacco companies. By no coincidence, people living there are among the heaviest smokers in the world. To keep their national companies afloat, these governments tax foreign cigarettes at a higher rate than national brands, so the domestic products remain cheaper.[39] If policymakers are serious about reducing smoking, they need to raise taxes for all brands and to dismantle government support for domestic tobacco production.

As Finnish researchers pointed out more than a decade ago, "Every tobacco price decision is also a health policy decision."[40] By following the lead of countries that tax tobacco use heavily, policymakers can take advantage of an important tool to reduce smoking and improve public health.

Metals Exploration Explodes in the South　　Payal Sampat

Spending on nonferrous metals exploration has more than doubled worldwide in the last five years, exceeding $5 billion in 1997.[1] Most of this growth has been in developing regions. (See Figure 1.) Between 1991 and 1997, exploration investment expanded six times in Latin America, almost quadrupled in the Pacific region, and doubled in Africa.[2] (See Figure 2.)

Gold has long dominated exploration budgets, and in 1997 accounted for two thirds of all exploration. Copper claimed an additional 17 percent.[3] Prices for both metals plummeted last year, leaving analysts guessing about trends in 1998.[4] If prices stay low, mines that are expensive to operate may be forced to close.[5] This may spur exploration, as companies seek out new, low-cost deposits.[6]

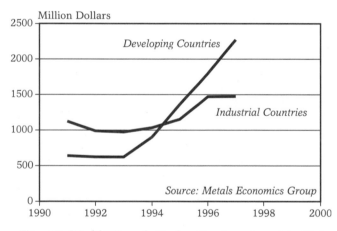

Figure 1: World Minerals Exploration Investment by Major Mining Companies, 1991–97

The southern investment boom has been spurred by new mining laws and rapid privatization in several developing countries.[7] Since the beginning of this decade, 70 nations in Latin America, Africa, Asia, Eastern Europe, and the Pacific region have modified their mining codes in order to attract investors.[8] Others have abolished mining taxes and introduced generous economic incentives.[9] Where the minerals sector was once a state monopoly, several countries have thrown open their doors to private mining companies in recent years.[10]

Latin America has been at the forefront of this new exploration activity. In 1997 the region received a staggering 29 percent of world exploration budgets, swelling from an 11 percent share in 1991.[11] Mining giants have flocked to mineral-rich Andean nations such as Chile and Peru, which allow private ownership of mines and the option to repatriate all profits.[12] Although mining has long dominated their economies—nearly half of their total export earnings come from this sector—their neighbor Argentina jumpstarted its mining sector this decade, with a series of inviting reforms.[13] In 1997 it was rated the most attractive developing country for mining investors.[14]

Exploration spending in Africa soared in 1997, growing at 54 percent over 1996.[15] Gold has been the major draw in West Africa, notably in Ghana.[16] In the Asia and Pacific region, Indonesia is the largest recipient of foreign exploration dollars and has increased gold production 10-fold in the last decade.[17] As large consumers of metals, several industrializing Asian countries, including China and India, are developing their mining sectors to reduce growing minerals imports.[18]

With the opening up of unexplored mining grounds in the developing world, investment in the four major mining nations has not been as buoyant. Australia, where exploration spending doubled in the last five years, is the exception.[19] But with declining gold prices and ore-grades in South Africa, companies there have downscaled production locally, investing instead in other African nations.[20] And spending in Canada and the United States—both heavily mined—has leveled off; companies now concentrate on expanding existing mines.[21] Also, it can take up to five years to get an exploration license in the United States; in some parts of Latin America, this process takes just one month.[22]

Almost all 279 major mining companies come from these four mining nations.[23] With their large capital base, these have been the primary beneficiaries of the incentives offered by southern nations. A growing band of junior companies has also entered the fray, and in 1997 accounted for 21 percent of global exploration.[24] Collapsing metals prices may make it uneconomical for them to remain in this capital-intensive industry.[25] Of late, a handful of southern firms have emerged, including the Malaysian firm Delcom Services Sdn Bhd, now prospecting for gold in northeast Cambodia.[26]

Although sometimes advocated as a means of spearheading economic growth, studies show slower growth rates in economies dependent on mining and extractive industries.[27] Often heavily subsidized, the mining sector employs few people and has high environmental and social costs.[28] The extraction and processing of minerals require vast quantities of energy and water resources.[29] The 2,402 tons of gold produced in 1997, for instance, generated 725 million tons of waste, which could fill enough 218-ton dump trucks to circle the globe.[30] This waste is contaminated with an assortment of other metals, acids, and solvents, including cyanide-solution and mercury that are used to extract gold from ore.[31]

Most new mining development is taking place in some of the world's most ecologically fragile regions, leaving behind clogged rivers, decapitated mountains, and contaminated soils and groundwater. The International Labour Organization calls mining one of the most hazardous occupations. For each ton of gold mined in South Africa, one person is killed and 12 are injured.[32] Furthermore, an estimated 50 percent of gold produced in the next 20 years will come from indigenous peoples' lands.[33]

Governments and international organizations have gradually responded to these warning signs. In 1997, the Costa Rican government ordered Canadian giant Placer Dome to suspend part of its environmentally damaging gold exploration activities in the northern part of the country.[34] In 1995, the U.S. Overseas Private Investment Corporation (OPIC) can-

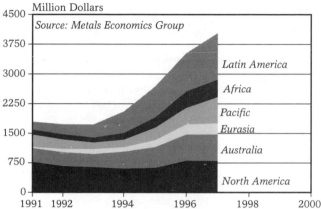

Figure 2: **World Minerals Exploration Investment by Major Mining Companies, by Region, 1991–97**

celed its political risk insurance to Freeport McMoran's Grasberg mine in Indonesia because of environmental and human rights concerns.[35] South America's largest gold deposit—estimated to be worth $4 billion—lies beneath the Sierra Imataca Reserve in Venezuela, home to indigenous communities and rare plants and fauna.[36] The Venezuelan Supreme Court has temporarily banned new concessions in this rainforest following protests by indigenous peoples and local environmentalists.[37]

But these victories are still tentative: In 1996, for instance, OPIC offered to reinstate Freeport's insurance policy.[38] A more enduring strategy is for nations to strengthen environmental regulations and reform wasteful mining subsidies, for project financiers to insist on stringent environmental risk assessments, and for industry to realize the economic potential of recycling and increased materials efficiency. For example, the 3.3 million tons of aluminum recovered from scrap in the United States in 1996 was worth $5 billion, and saved enough energy to meet the annual electricity needs of a city about the size of Philadelphia.[39]

Pollution Control Markets Expand   Michael Renner

The world market for pollution control technologies and other environmental goods and services grew from $295 billion in 1992 to $408 billion in 1994 and then to a projected $426 billion in 1997, or 2 percent of global gross domestic product, according to Environmental Business International (EBI).[1] Spending may reach $572 billion by 2001.[2] This group of companies thus easily outclasses the global aerospace products and arms industries (each with annual revenues of about $200 billion), and is drawing close to the chemical industry ($500 billion in revenues).[3]

The bulk of the operations captured in these figures concern pollution control, waste management, and remediation (cleaning up waste sites, for example). Pollution prevention, recycling, and alternative energy sources account for no more than about 10 percent of the global total, and about 12 percent of the U.S. market.[4] (See Table 1, which provides data for the last year for which a breakdown of this sector is available.)

EBI projects that revenues from process and prevention technologies in the United States will rise by 88 percent in 1994–99—the steepest increase of any environmental market segment; energy efficiency and renewable energy are expected to grow by 46 percent.[5] But there is strong reason to believe that

spending in the latter areas is being undercounted in existing studies. One study estimated global export markets alone for energy efficiency products and technologies at $8.4 billion annually in the 1990s and double that in the decade ahead.[6]

The EBI figures represent the most comprehensive survey available. Yet they do not capture many activities critical to preserving the environment—partly because they are hard to document, and partly because many companies make internal changes in their operations that never register as a "market." For instance, at least 42 percent of global steel production is derived from recycling scrap metal.[7] Achieving this rate required investments in new furnaces—a change unlikely to be fully reflected in the EBI data.

So far, the global pollution control industry is overwhelmingly centered in western industrial countries; they represent more than 90 percent of the current global market.[8] The United States alone accounts for 40 percent.[9] EBI reports that the U.S. market grew from $126 billion in 1990 to $171.7 billion in 1995.[10] And Management Information Services, Inc., projects it will reach $258 billion by 2010.[11]

Facing a mix of environmental challenges arising from persistent poverty, unplanned urbanization, careless industrialization, and

TABLE 1: POLLUTION CONTROL MARKET COMPONENTS, 1994

COMPONENT	SPENDING (billion dollars)	SHARE[1] (percent)
Water equipment	161.1	39
Solid waste management	132.0	32
Resource recovery (including recycling)	34.5	8
Analytical services, instruments, and consulting	34.4	8
Air pollution control equipment	25.4	6
Remediation services	14.6	4
Environmental energy[2]	4.4	1
Process and prevention technology	2.0	0.5

[1]Column does not add up to 100 due to rounding. [2]Includes renewable energy and cogeneration.
SOURCE: Compiled from Environmental Business International, *The Global Environmental Market and United States Environmental Industry Competitiveness* (San Diego, CA: undated).

overburdened soils and water resources, pollution control markets are now growing rapidly in many developing countries as well. By 2001, EBI expects these nations to increase their share of the global market from the current 8 percent ($32.8 billion) to 13 percent ($68.2 billion).[12]

In 1994, Asian countries (excluding Japan) accounted for just 3.5 percent of the global market.[13] But this is the fastest-growing market in the world, projected to triple to $43 billion by 2001, when it might account for more than 7 percent of the world total.[14] Taiwan, South Korea, Hong Kong, and Singapore have been the leaders in environment-related spending in Asia. Burdened by heavy pollution, China is now rapidly increasing its investments, planning to spend between $26.5 billion and $38.5 billion on equipment over the five years to 2000.[15] Whether the strong growth of Asian markets will in fact continue is open to some question, however, as the region's economic crisis may lead governments to give the environment less priority. Even in September 1997, a report by the Association of South-east Asian Nations, found that "the use of less-polluting processing technologies has been limited by the lack of capital."[16]

Latin America now accounts for only 1.6 percent of world environmental spending.[17] But the region's markets are growing at about 12 percent annually, a rate second only to Asian countries, and are projected to more than double to $14.6 billion by 2001.[18] Brazil and Mexico are by far the leading countries in the region, accounting for two thirds of the total.[19] The Mexican government projects spending to rise to at least $7.3 billion by 2010, up from just $2 billion in 1994.[20]

In Eastern Europe and Russia, environmental needs are enormous—a legacy of decades of abusive industrial practices. Unfortunately, the lack of financing limits what would otherwise be a huge market for both cleanup and the introduction of the latest technologies. Poland's environment-related investments, for example, have risen to about $1.5 billion annually.[21] But a 1997 World Bank assessment concluded that in order to catch up with environmental standards in the European Union (which Poland is eager to join), the country will need to triple its current spending.[22] And the U.S. Office of Technology Assessment reported in 1994 that environmental cleanup in Poland might require a total of $260 billion over the next 25–30 years.[23]

International trade in pollution control and other environmental goods and services is rising as well, though there are few reliable figures. Based on EBI data, the global environmental export market might be on the order of $40–45 billion a year, or about 10 percent of total industry revenue.[24]

The environment industry is generating substantial numbers of jobs, both in traditional industries such as iron and steel and in emerging ones such as wind power and energy efficiency technologies. U.S. environment-related spending has created a rapidly growing number of jobs—rising from 700,000 in 1970 to 4.3 million in 1995, and growing to a projected 5.3 million by 2010.[25] In Germany, a recent study found that close to 1 million jobs are supported by environmental spending.[26]

Developing countries in particular have a unique opportunity to "leapfrog" by taking advantage of emerging technologies instead of following the old route of "pollute first, then clean up." In doing so, they could limit the extent to which they would have to introduce costly pollution abatement measures.

Fully addressing environmental challenges—averting climate change, reducing materials use, and boosting water efficiency and soil conservation, to name but a few—provides investment opportunities that are likely to be several orders of magnitude larger than the current pollution control market.

Social
Features

Female Education Gaining Ground   Jennifer D. Mitchell

Worldwide, female education is increasing. Female enrollment in primary school jumped from 226 million to 254 million between 1990 and 1995.[1] As a result of this increase, nearly 70 percent of girls worldwide were enrolled in primary school in 1995.[2]

The U.S. Agency for International Development found a growing share of educated women in the 47 developing countries they surveyed.[3] In 30 of these countries, the percentage of women with no formal education was more than halved in a single generation.[4] The greatest improvements have been seen in Tanzania, Jordan, and Kenya, where more than four out of five women aged 20–24 have at least a primary school education.[5] (See Table 1.)

But in many countries, little progress has been made. In Burkina Faso, Burundi, Mali, Nepal, Niger, Pakistan, and Yemen, more than three quarters of women aged 20–24 have no education at all.[6] And in Bangladesh, Guinea, Morocco, and Senegal, more than half of the younger women still have no education.[7] Despite worldwide increases in female education, it is estimated that some 90 million girls—approximately 25 percent—are still not enrolled in primary school.[8]

Female education is associated with increased economic productivity, better family health and nutrition, lower maternal and child death rates, and lower birth rates.[9] Studies in several developing countries show that an extra year of schooling reduces fertility rates by 5–10 percent.[10] And in India, infants of mothers who have received primary education are half as likely to die in their first year as children whose mothers are illiterate.[11]

For many girls, however, access to schooling is difficult. Often the nearest school is not within safe walking distance.[12] Lack of sanitary facilities for girls and the scarcity of female teachers also discourages female attendance.[13] And unfortunately, even when females attend school, the quality of the education is frequently poor. This often does a disservice to the female student by limiting access to information that is important to her well-being and her future.[14] Additionally, females do not always stay in school very long. African women, for example, have an average of less than one year of formal education.[15]

Obstacles like these have led to significant gender disparities in many developing countries.[16] In Yemen, for example, 39 percent of girls are enrolled in primary school, compared with 73 percent of boys.[17] In industrial nations, however, there is little gender disparity at the primary and secondary school levels.[18] In fact, in many wealthy nations, such as the United States, more females than males complete secondary school.[19] Moreover, female enrollment in colleges and universities is greater than male enrollment in many industrial nations, including Iceland, Portugal, France, New Zealand, Norway, Sweden, and the United States.[20]

At the graduate school level in industrial nations, females outnumber males in several programs, such as in veterinary schools.[21] Overall, however, women still lag behind men in most professional schools, including law and business, though they are approaching gender parity.[22] In the fields of math, computer science, engineering, and architecture, men still dominate in all industrial nations.[23]

Worldwide, however, among children not attending school, there are twice as many girls as boys, and among illiterate adults, there are twice as many women as men.[24] A 1993 study by Population Action International estimated that that it would cost more than $18 billion a year (in 1990 dollars) to close the gender gap in primary education by 2005.[25] Yet in many countries, closing the gender gap would still leave female enrollment at very low levels. In sub-Saharan Africa, for example, nearly half of the young boys are not enrolled in primary school either.[26]

Although the number of children enrolled in primary school is rising, about a third of the children in the developing world fail to complete even four years of education, either because they never enroll or because they drop out of school early.[27] And despite an increase in education for both boys and girls, the current advances will not meet the goal of the 1990 World Summit for Children: universal access to basic education by the year 2000 and completion of primary school by at least 80 percent of primary-school-aged children.[28]

Most countries could achieve basic education for all if they stepped up funding. Even though many countries are increasing the amount spent on education, their budgets are not keeping pace with rapid population growth. Consequently, the amount spent per capita on education is falling. In Africa, for instance, it dropped from $41 per person in 1985 to $28 in 1995.[29]

In many countries, therefore, international aid is desperately needed. Unfortunately, however, the proportion of international aid dedicated to education has declined from 17 percent in 1975 to 11 percent in 1994.[30] Yet some significant investments have been made. The World Bank's lending for basic education has more than tripled since 1990.[31] And in 1996, the Asian Development Bank approved a $45-million loan to Pakistan specifically for primary education for girls.[32] As a result of this loan, approximately 7,500 more girls will enroll in grades 1 and 2 each year.[33] Individual countries are also providing aid for female education. In 1996, Norway gave $24 million to increase female education in Africa, and Canada has pledged $75 million over five years for the same goal.[34]

TABLE 1: SHARE OF WOMEN EDUCATED IN DIFFERENT GENERATIONS, SELECTED COUNTRIES, EARLY 1990s

COUNTRY	EDUCATED WOMEN AGED 45–49[1] (percent)	EDUCATED WOMEN AGED 20–24[1] (percent)	DIFFERENCE (percentage points)
Tanzania	26	84	58
Jordan	37	94	57
Kenya	43	94	51
Viet Nam	40	86	46
Nigeria	15	58	43
Morocco	11	45	34
Indonesia	59	92	33
Senegal	6	33	27
Guinea	5	30	25
Mexico	70	94	24
Bangladesh	25	47	22
Yemen	1	23	22
Nepal	3	22	19
Burkina Faso	5	22	17
Mali	2	18	16
Pakistan	11	25	14
Niger	1	15	14
Brazil	84	96	12
Egypt	40	52	12
Burundi	13	21	8

[1]Having at least a primary school education.
SOURCE: UNICEF, The Progress of Nations 1995 (New York: 1995).

Sanitation Access Lagging

Gary Gardner

The share of developing-country populations with access to adequate sanitation fell from 36 to 34 percent between 1990 and 1994, the last year for which comprehensive data are available.[1] (See Table 1.) Global data are less precise, but the World Health Organization (WHO) estimates that half the people in the world do not have access to a decent toilet.[2] Such poor sanitation coverage, especially in cities, increases the risk of illness; in some countries, the sanitation gap is the greatest threat to public health.

The unserved population in developing countries grew by 274 million people between 1990 and 1994.[3] This is a rapid acceleration of the trend in the 1980s, when the number inadequately covered increased by 50 million.[4] The backsliding runs counter to the goal of the U.N.-declared International Drinking Water Supply and Sanitation Decade (1981–90), which sought to broaden access to safe water and adequate sanitation.[5] While the decade was successful in increasing access to safe water, and while availability of sanitation grew absolutely, access to sanitation fell in percentage terms as population growth outstripped the decade's gains.[6]

In some countries, less than half the population is adequately covered: Afghanistan, Brazil, Cambodia, China, Congo, Egypt, Haiti, India, and Senegal are all examples of this.[7] This dismal picture is partly a question of definition, however. Brazil, for instance, defines adequate sanitation as flush toilets that connect to sewers or septic tanks.[8] Yet simpler technologies such as latrines and composting toilets would meet the WHO definition of adequate sanitation, which is any excreta disposal facility that interrupts the transmission of fecal contaminants to humans.[9]

Preventing such transmission is the chief health benefit of adequate sanitation. Human waste is full of bacteria, viruses, and parasites that can cause widespread sickness if they contaminate drinking water.[10] Indeed, WHO reports that half the people in developing countries suffer from one of the six diseases associated with poor water supply and sanitation.[11] One of these diseases, diarrhea, is the biggest killer of children today—taking an estimated 2.2 million young lives each year.[12]

The greatest shortage of sanitation is found in rural areas, where some 2.3 billion people did not have adequate access in 1994.[13] In rural India, for example—home to more than 70 percent of the country's population—fewer than 10 percent of houses have toilets.[14] Yet the need for sanitation is most urgent in cities, because of the greater potential there for mass infections from pathogen-tainted water.[15] Rapid urban expansion in the nineteenth century, in combination with inadequate sanitation, spawned the world's first pandemics of cholera. In each of the world's seven cholera pandemics—including the current one, which began in 1961 and spread to Latin America in the early 1990s—waterborne fecal material has played a key role.[16] Despite the clear health risks of inadequate urban coverage, some 589 million city dwellers were estimated to be without adequate sanitation in 1994.[17] The situation was especially worrisome in urban Africa, where coverage plummeted from 65 to 55 percent between 1990 and 1994.[18]

One reason for the lag in sanitation coverage is its expense. WHO estimates that adequate sanitation in urban areas of developing countries costs $145 per person—which represents at least 10 percent, and sometimes much more, of the real gross domestic product per capita in 24 of the world's poorest countries.[19] The high costs leave developing countries spending less than a third of what they should in order to provide adequate sanitation, according to WHO.[20] Another drag on sanitation investment is burdensome debt, which restricts investment options, especially in Africa.[21]

Despite these barriers, many developing countries boast high levels of sanitation access. Among those with sanitation coverage at industrial-country rates are Iran, Jamaica, Jordan, Malaysia, the Philippines, Saudi Arabia, Thailand, Trinidad and Tobago, and

TABLE 1: ACCESS TO ADEQUATE SANITATION, 1990 AND 1994

REGION	SHARE OF POPULATION WITH ACCESS TO ADEQUATE SANITATION	
	1990 (percent)	1994
Rural Areas		
Africa	23	24
Latin America	33	34
Asia and the Pacific	18	15
Western Asia	60	66
Urban Areas		
Africa	65	55
Latin America	83	73
Asia and the Pacific	62	61
Western Asia	68	69
All Areas		
Africa	36	34
Latin America	69	63
Asia and the Pacific	30	29
Western Asia	65	68
All Developing Countries	36	34

SOURCE: World Health Organization (WHO), Water Supply and Sanitation Collaborative Council; and UNICEF, *Water Supply and Sanitation Sector Monitoring Report, 1996* (New York: WHO, 1996).

all of Central America except Nicaragua.[22]

Adequate sanitation, however, does not always require flush toilets and underground sewers—the most expensive way to manage human waste, especially when combined with a treatment plant.[23] Even in some countries in Europe, where access to adequate sanitation is widespread, a high proportion of the population is not served by sewers: in Belgium it is 42 percent; in France, 35 percent; in Ireland, 34 percent; and in Spain, 20 percent.[24]

In cash-strapped developing countries, forms of sanitation that do not involve sewers offer a relatively cheap but effective means of processing human waste. On-site systems such as composting toilets cost a fraction as much as flush toilets, sewers, and treatment plants, and they produce a nutrient-rich composted fertilizer that can be safely recycled to farms.[25] One system of household- and neigh-borhood-level sanitation in Mexico has proved to be not only inexpensive and workable, but also a money-maker for families who sell their composted waste to nearby farmers.[26]

Prospects for providing universal access to sanitation are dismal in the near to medium term. Just to keep from losing ground, the rate of provision of service to urban dwellers needs to more than double in Asia.[27] In Africa, it would have to increase by 33 times.[28] And to achieve full coverage by 2020, service provision would have to triple in Asia and increase by 46 times in Africa.[29] Despite the attention focused on sanitation, governments have not demonstrated the will to meet this growing challenge.

Military
Features

Small Arms Proliferate

Michael Renner

Assault rifles and other so-called small arms and light weapons—principally defined by their small size and weight, which allows them to be carried by an individual—are now easily available in such abundance that they seem like casual accessories. The spread of these arms has encouraged a habitual recourse to violence that threatens the cohesion and well-being of many societies.

Small arms are the weapons of choice in today's typical armed conflict—fighting that rages within, rather than between, countries. But the proliferation of small arms also fuels criminal violence. It threatens the consolidation of still-weak democracies, compromises the reconstruction of war-torn societies, and obstructs social and economic development.

The same characteristics that have long led policymakers to underestimate the importance of small arms make these weapons easy to acquire and handle—and hard to track and control.

Low cost means that small arms do not figure prominently in arms-trade statistics but are affordable to many armies, guerilla forces, organized crime groups, or individuals. For just $50 million—roughly the cost of a single modern jet fighter—an army the size of the United Kingdom's military can be equipped with some 200,000 assault rifles at prevalent black market prices.[1]

Easy to handle, small arms do not require any complex organizational, logistical, or training capacities. Their easy use has boosted the ability of children to participate in armed conflicts.[2] Their light weight and small size make them easy to conceal and smuggle, and therefore easy to obtain on black markets.[3]

Small weapons are sturdy enough to have a long life, making it possible for them to be circulated from one conflict to another. Weapons of World War II or earlier vintage are still in use today.[4]

No one really knows how many small arms may be in circulation worldwide, but one estimate says the number may be some 500 million.[5] Of these, more than 100 million are assault rifles.[6] (See Table 1.) The most notorious and numerous is the AK-47, also known by its inventor's name, Kalashnikov. Manufactured in the former Soviet Union and in nine other countries, more than 70 million Kalashnikovs have been produced in some 100 different versions since 1947; this assault rifle is in service in the armies of 78 countries and in countless guerrilla groups the world over.[7]

Other assault rifles include the U.S. M-16, of which 8 million copies have been made, the German G-3 (7 million), the Belgian-designed FN-FAL (5–7 million), and the Israeli Uzi machine pistol (10 million).[8] In addition to licensed production of these and other small

TABLE 1: PRODUCTION OF SELECTED ASSAULT RIFLES

WEAPON NAME	ORIGIN[1]	NUMBER PRODUCED (million)
Kalashnikov AK-47/-74	Soviet Union/Russia	70+
Uzi machine pistol	Israel	10
M-16	United States	8
G-3	Germany	7
FN-FAL	Belgium	5–7

[1]Country that first developed and produced the weapon. A large number of additional countries are producing these weapons under license or are making illicit copies.
SOURCE: U.N. General Assembly, "Report of the Panel of Governmental Experts on Small Arms," A/52/298 (New York: 27 August 1997).

weapons, manufacturers from several coun-·
tries are apparently flooding the world market
with counterfeit (unauthorized) versions.[9]

The United States and the former Soviet
Union have been the leading proliferators.
But China, Belgium, Switzerland, Germany,
and Israel are also important suppliers.[10]

Given a multitude of legal and illegal trading networks, there is no telling in whose
hands the weapons will end up. Not only are
embargoes difficult to enforce, but the original suppliers have come to be haunted by a
boomerang effect, with weapons intended for
friendly recipients ending up in the hands of
adversaries.

Trade in secondhand arms flourishes. Now
that the cold war is over, armies in North
America, Europe, and the former Soviet
Union are shrinking; much of their excess
equipment is given away or sold cheaply to
other countries.[11] Since the 1950s the U.S.
government, for instance, has transferred
some 3 million military-style firearms to foreign governments.[12] In the 1990s, Turkey
received 304,000 formerly East German
Kalashnikovs from Germany.[13]

And weapons left over at the end of civil
wars often enter the black market and frequently resurface in new hotspots when big
parts of government armies and insurgent
forces are demobilized. Arms originally supplied to combatants in Nicaragua and El
Salvador, for example, have found their way
into Colombia and other parts of Latin
America.[14]

The dispersal of arms to private armies
and militias, insurgent groups, criminal organizations, and other nonstate actors feeds
political, communal, criminal, and personal
violence in many societies. And it poses a
particular challenge for countries struggling to
emerge from long years of debilitating warfare, including several in Central America and
southern Africa. Contending with limited economic opportunities, these countries find that
discontent is strong and crime is rising.
Demobilized ex-combatants, with few civilian
skills, may be tempted to turn to banditry.
And ordinary citizens use leftover weapons of
war to carry out crimes or settle personal
scores.[15]

In South Africa, criminal violence has
increased even as political violence is on the
decline. Military-style weapons such as the
AK-47 are increasingly used in robberies and
in the "taxi wars"—clashes between competing taxi fleet owners.[16]

El Salvador has been formally at peace
since 1992. Yet the number of violent deaths
since that year—some 20,000—comes close,
on an annual basis, to rivaling the number of
people killed during the war (about 75,000
over 13 years).[17] "Peacetime" has seen sky-
rocketing numbers of murders, kidnappings,
robberies, and other forms of violent crime
throughout the country.[18]

Long ignored, small arms have garnered
growing attention from academic analysts and
nongovernmental organizations (NGOs) in the
last three to four years, and are now beginning to attract policymakers' concern.[19] A
range of NGOs have begun local or national
campaigns against small arms, seeking primarily to curb the unregulated trade in these
weapons. Sympathetic governments, such as
Canada's, are likely to support that effort.[20]

NOTES

GRAIN HARVEST UP SLIGHTLY (pages 28–29)

1. U.S. Department of Agriculture (USDA), Foreign Agricultural Service (FAS), *Grain: World Markets and Trade* (Washington, DC: January 1998).
2. Ibid.; U.S. Bureau of the Census, *International Data Base*, electronic database, Suitland, MD, updated 10 October 1997.
3. USDA, op. cit. note 1; USDA, *Production, Supply, and Distribution (PS&D)*, electronic database, Washington, DC, updated February 1998; USDA, "World Grain Database," unpublished printout, Washington, DC, 1991; Bureau of Census, op. cit. note 2.
4. USDA, op. cit. note 1; USDA, *PS&D*, op. cit. note 3.
5. USDA, op. cit. note 1.
6. Ibid.
7. Ibid.; USDA, *PS&D*, op. cit. note 3.
8. USDA, op. cit. note 1.
9. Ibid.
10. Ibid.
11. Ibid.
12. Ibid.
13. Ibid.
14. Ibid.
15. Ibid.; USDA, *PS&D*, op. cit. note 3; idled land from USDA, Economic Research Service, "AREI Updates: Cropland Use in 1997," No. 5, Washington, DC, 1997.
16. USDA, op. cit. note 1; USDA, *PS&D*, op. cit. note 3.
17. USDA, op. cit. note 1; USDA, *PS&D*, op. cit. note 3.
18. USDA, op. cit. note 1; USDA, *PS&D*, op. cit. note 3; Sandra Postel, *Dividing the Waters: Food Security, Ecosystem Health, and the New Politics of Scarcity*, Worldwatch Paper 132 (Washington, DC: Worldwatch Institute, September 1996).

SOYBEAN PRODUCTION JUMPS (pages 30–31)

1. U.S. Department of Agriculture (USDA), Foreign Agricultural Service (FAS), *Oilseeds: World Markets and Trade* (Washington, DC: December 1997); USDA, *Production, Supply, and Distribution (PS&D)*, electronic database, Washington, DC, updated February 1998.
2. USDA, *Oilseeds*, op. cit. note 1; USDA, *PS&D*, op. cit. note 1; U.S. Bureau of the Census, *International Data Base*, electronic database, Suitland, MD, updated 10 October 1997.
3. USDA, *Oilseeds*, op. cit. note 1; USDA, *PS&D*, op. cit. note 1; Bureau of Census, op. cit. note 2.
4. USDA, *Oilseeds*, op. cit. note 1.
5. Ibid.
6. Ibid.
7. Ibid.
8. Ibid.
9. Ibid.
10. Ibid.
11. Ibid.
12. Ibid.; USDA, *PS&D*, op. cit. note 1.
13. USDA, *Oilseeds*, op. cit. note 1; USDA, *PS&D*, op. cit. note 1.
14. USDA, *Oilseeds*, op. cit. note 1; USDA, *PS&D*, op. cit. note 1.
15. USDA, *Oilseeds*, op. cit. note 1.
16. Ibid.
17. Ibid.
18. Ibid.
19. Ibid.; USDA, *PS&D*, op. cit. note 1.

WORLD MEAT PRODUCTION CLIMBS (pages 32–33)

1. U.S. Department of Agriculture (USDA), Foreign Agricultural Service (FAS), *Livestock*

and Poultry: World Markets and Trade (Washington, DC: October 1997).

2. Ibid.; U.S. Bureau of Census, *International Data Base*, electronic database, Suitland, MD, updated 10 October 1997.

3. USDA, op. cit. note 1.

4. Ibid.

5. Ibid.

6. Ibid.

7. Ibid.

8. Ibid.

9. Ibid.

10. Ibid.

11. Ibid.

12. Ibid.

13. Ibid.

14. Ibid.

15. Ibid.

16. Grain-to-poultry ratio derived from Robert V. Bishop et al., *The World Poultry Market— Government Intervention and Multilateral Policy Reform* (Washington, DC: USDA, 1990); grain-to-pork ratio from Leland Southard, Livestock and Poultry Situation and Outlook Staff, Economic Research Service (ERS), USDA, Washington, DC, discussion with author, 27 April 1992; grain-to-beef ratio based on Allen Baker, Feed Situation and Outlook Staff, ERS, USDA, Washington, DC, discussion with author, 27 April 1992.

17. USDA, op. cit. note 1.

18. Ibid.

19. Ibid.

20. Ibid.

21. Ibid.

22. Ibid.

23. Ibid.

FISH CATCH HITS A NEW HIGH
(pages 34–35)

1. Preliminary estimates for 1996 from Maurizio Perotti, fishery statistician, Fishery Information, Data and Statistics Service, Fisheries Department, U.N. Food and Agriculture Organization (FAO), Rome, letters to Anne Platt McGinn, 5 and 11 November 1997.

2. Ibid; U.S. Bureau of the Census, *International Data Base*, electronic database, Suitland, MD, updated 10 October 1997.

3. Perotti, op. cit. note 1.

4. Worldwatch estimate based on FAO, *Yearbook of*

Fishery Statistics: Catches and Landings (Rome: various years).

5. Worldwatch estimate based on data from Perotti, op. cite note 1.

6. FAO, op. cit. note 4.

7. FAO, *The State of World Fisheries and Aquaculture, 1996* (Rome: 1997).

8. FAO, *Yearbook of Fishery Statistics: Catches and Landings* (Rome: 1994).

9. Ibid.

10. Study by U.S. Agency for International Development cited in Okechukwu C. Iheduru, "The Political Economy of Euro-African Fishing Agreements," *The Journal of Developing Areas,* October 1995.

11. Jonathan Friedland, "Catch of the Day: Fish Stories These Days Are Tales of Depletion and Growing Rivalry," *Wall Street Journal,* 25 November 1997.

12. Ibid.

13. "Fujimori Against El Niño," *The Economist,* 27 September 1997.

14. World Wide Fund for Nature, "Top Fishing Nations Drag Feet on UN Fish Stocks Agreement," press release (Gland, Switzerland: 25 November 1997).

15. Ibid.

16. Ibid.

AQUACULTURE GROWING RAPIDLY (pages 36–37)

1. Meryl Williams, *The Transition in the Contribution of Living Aquatic Resources to Food Security,* Food, Agriculture, and the Environment Discussion Paper 13 (Washington, DC: International Food Policy Research Institute, April 1996). Unless otherwise specified, aquaculture does not include aquatic plant production. It refers to finfish and shellfish farming only.

2. Data for 1984–85 from U.N. Food and Agriculture Organization (FAO), *Aquaculture Production Statistics, 1984–1993,* FAO Fisheries Circular No. 815, Revision 7 (Rome: 1995); data for 1986–95 from FAO, *Aquaculture Production Statistics, 1986–1995,* FAO Fisheries Circular No. 815, Revision 9 (Rome: 1997); data for 1996 from Maurizio Perotti, fishery statistician, Fishery Information, Data and Statistics Unit (FIDI), Fisheries Department, FAO, Rome, letter to author, 11 November 1997.

3. Data for 1995 from FAO, Revision 9, op. cit. note

2; 1984 from FAO, Revision 7, op. cit. note 2.

4. FAO, Revision 9, op. cit. note 2. Note that 1995 data are the most recent available for breakdown of aquaculture production by country, species, and value; 1996 data are available for total aquaculture production only.

5. Williams, op. cit. note 1.

6. Grain conversion data for fish, chicken, pork, and beef from Lester R. Brown and Hal Kane, *Full House* (New York: W.W. Norton & Company, 1994).

7. Bob Holmes, "Blue Revolutionaries," *New Scientist*, 7 December 1996.

8. Manny Ratafia, "Aquaculture Today: A Worldwide Status Report," *World Aquaculture*, June 1995.

9. FAO, *The State of World Fisheries and Aquaculture* (Rome: 1995).

10. FAO, Revision 9, op. cit. note 2.

11. Ibid.

12. Figure of 17 percent is Worldwatch estimate based on data from FAO, Revision 9, op. cit. note 2.

13. Worldwatch Institute estimate based on ibid.

14. Ibid.

15. Holmes, op. cit. note 7.

16. FAO, Revision 9, op. cit. note 2.

17. Biksham Gujja and Andrea Finger-Stich, "What Price Prawn? Shrimp Aquaculture's Impact in Asia," *Environment*, September 1996.

18. Michael L. Weber, "So You Say You Want a Blue Revolution?" *Amicus Journal*, Fall 1996.

19. Holmes, op. cit. note 7.

20. Industrial Shrimp Action Network, "Global Group Formed to Counter Destructive Shrimp Farming," press release (Seattle, WA: Mangrove Action Project, 24 October 1997).

21. N.J. Stephenson and P.R. Burbridge, "Abandoned Shrimp Ponds: Options for Mangrove Management," *Intercoast Network* (Narragansett, RI: Coastal Resources Center), March 1997.

22. Malcolm C.M. Beveridge, Lindsay G. Ross, and Liam A. Kelly, "Aquaculture and Biodiversity," *Ambio*, December 1994.

23. Ibid.

24. Rebecca Goldburg and Tracy Triplett, *Murky Waters: Environmental Effect of Aquaculture in the US* (New York: Environmental Defense Fund, 1997).

25. Mary DeSena, "Integration of Aquaculture and Agriculture Saves Water, Boosts Economy," *U.S. Water News* (Halstead, KS), November 1997.

GRAIN STOCKS REMAIN LOW

(pages 38–39)

1. U.S. Department of Agriculture (USDA), Foreign Agricultural Service (FAS), *Grain: World Markets and Trade* (Washington, DC: January 1998).

2. Idled land from USDA, Economic Research Service, "AREI Updates: Cropland Use in 1997," No. 5, Washington, DC, 1997.

3. Ibid.

4. U.S. Bureau of the Census, *International Data Base*, electronic database, Suitland, MD, updated 10 October 1997.

5. Population Reference Bureau, "1997 World Population Data Sheet," wallchart (Washington, DC: May 1997).

6. USDA, op. cit. note 1; USDA, *Production, Supply, and Distribution (PS&D)*, electronic database, Washington, DC, updated February 1998; USDA, "World Grain Database," unpublished printout, Washington, DC, 1991.

7. USDA, op. cit. note 1; USDA, *PS&D*, op. cit. note 6.

8. USDA, op. cit. note 1; USDA, *PS&D*, op. cit. note 6.

9. Bureau of Census, op. cit. note 4.

10. USDA, op. cit. note 1; USDA, *PS&D*, op. cit. note 6.

GRAIN YIELD RISES (pages 42–43)

1. U.S. Department of Agriculture (USDA), *Production, Supply, and Distribution*, electronic database, Washington, DC, updated February 1998.

2. Ibid.

3. Ibid.

4. Ibid; U.S. Bureau of the Census, *International Data Base*, electronic database, Suitland, MD, updated 10 October 1997.

5. Gary Gardner, *Shrinking Fields: Cropland Loss in a World of Eight Billion*, Worldwatch Paper 131 (Washington, DC: Worldwatch Institute, July 1996).

6. USDA, op. cit. note 1.

7. Ibid.

8. Mark W. Rosegrant et al., "Global Food Markets and US Exports in the Twenty-first Century," revision of paper presented at the World Food and Sustainable Agriculture Program Conference, *Meeting the Demand for Food in the 21st*

Century: Challenges and Opportunities for Illinois Agriculture, Urbana-Champaign, IL, 28 May 1997; Lester Brown, "Higher Crop Yields? Don't Bet the Farm on Them," *World Watch*, July/August 1997.

9. L.T. Evans, *Crop Evolution, Adaptation and Yield* (Cambridge, U.K.: Cambridge University Press, 1993).

10. Ibid.

11. Prabhu Pingali et al., *Asian Rice Bowls: The Returning Crisis?* (New York: CAB International, 1997); P.L. Pingali and P.W. Heisey, "Cereal Crop Productivity in Developing Countries: Past Trends and Future Prospects," Conference proceedings, *Global Agricultural Science Policy for the 21st Century*, 26–28 August 1996, Melbourne, Australia.

12. Pingali et al., op. cit. note 11.

13. Mark W. Rosegrant and Claudia Ringler, "World Food Markets into the 21st Century: Environmental and Resource Constraints and Policies," revision of a paper presented at the RIRDC-sponsored plenary session of the 41st Annual Conference of the Australian Agricultural and Resource Economics Society, Queensland, Australia, 22–25 January 1997.

14. USDA, op. cit. note 1.

15. Rosegrant and Ringler, op. cit. note 13.

16. U.N. Food and Agriculture Organization (FAO), *FAOSTAT Statistics Database*, < http://www.apps.fao.org >.

17. Paul Raskin et al., *Water Futures: Assessment of Long-Range Patterns and Problems*, vol. 3 of *Comprehensive Assessment of the Freshwater Resources of the World* (Stockholm: Stockholm Environment Institute, 1997). The International Food Policy Research Institute projects a slightly higher annual growth rate—0.6 percent—for the period 1995–2020; see Mark W. Rosegrant, Claudi Ringler, and Roberta Gerpacio, "Water and Land Resources and Global Food Supply," paper prepared for the 23rd International Conference of Agricultural Economists on *Food Security, Diversification, and Resource Management: Refocusing the Role of Agriculture*, Sacramento, CA, 10–16 August 1997 (Washington, DC: International Food Policy Research Institute, 1997).

18. FAO, op. cit. note 16.

19. "Winning the Food Race," *Population Reports*, December 1997.

FERTILIZER USE UP (pages 44–45)

1. K.G. Soh and K.F. Isherwood, "Short Term Prospects for World Agriculture and Fertilizer Use," presentation at IFA Enlarged Council Meeting, International Fertilizer Industry Association, Monte Carlo, Monaco, 18-21 November 1997.

2. Ibid.

3. Ibid.; U.S. Bureau of Census, *International Data Base*, electronic database, Suitland, MD, updated 10 October 1997.

4. Soh and Isherwood, op. cit. note 1.

5. Ibid.

6. Ibid.

7. Ibid.; U.N. Food and Agriculture Organization (FAO), *Fertilizer Yearbook* (Rome: various years).

8. Alison Maitland, "Fertilizer Groups See Further Decline," *Financial Times*, 10 September 1997.

9. Ibid.

10. Population Reference Bureau, "1997 World Population Data Sheet," wallchart (Washington, DC: May 1997).

11. Soh and Isherwood, op. cit. note 1; FAO, op. cit. note 7.

12. Soh and Isherwood, op. cit. note 1; FAO, op. cit. note 7.

13. Soh and Isherwood, op. cit. note 1; FAO, op. cit. note 7.

14. FAO, *FAOSTAT Statistics Database*, < http://www.apps.fao.org >, Rome, viewed 26 January 1998, with adjustments to U.S. data from Bill Quinby, Economic Research Service, U.S. Department of Agriculture, Washington, DC, letter to author, 4 December 1997.

15. David Seckler, *The New Era of Water Resources Management: From "Dry" to "Wet" Water Savings* (Washington, DC: Consultative Group on International Agricultural Research, 1996).

16. Soh and Isherwood, op. cit. note 1; FAO, op. cit. note 7.

IRRIGATED AREA UP SLIGHTLY (pages 46–47)

1. U.N. Food and Agriculture Organization (FAO), *FAOSTAT Statistics Database*, < http://www.apps.fao.org >, Rome, viewed 3 December 1997.

2. Worldwatch calculation based on irrigated area from FAO, op. cit. note 1, and on global population from U.S. Bureau of the Census,

International Data Base, Suitland, MD, updated 10 October 1997.

3. FAO, op. cit. note 1.

4. Ibid.

5. Ibid.

6. FAO, "Water and Food Security: Irrigation's Contribution," fact sheet from 1996 World Food Conference, <http://www.fao.org>, Rome, viewed 13 December 1997.

7. Consultative Group on International Agricultural Research (CGIAR), "25 Years of Improvement Part III. The State of Irrigated Agriculture," <http://www.worldbank.org/html/CGIAR/25years/state.html>, Washington, DC, viewed 5 December 1997.

8. Pierre Crosson, "Future Supplies of Land and Water for World Agriculture," revision of a paper presented at a conference of the International Food Policy Research Institute in February 1994 (Washington, DC: Resources For the Future, August 1994).

9. Working Group on Environmental Scientific Research, Technology Development and Training, "The Role of Sustainable Agriculture in China Environmentally Sound Development," Fifth Conference of the China Council for International Cooperation on Environment and Development, Shanghai, China, 23–25 September 1996.

10. Ibid.

11. Tata Energy Research Institute, *Looking Back to Think Ahead: Executive Summary* (New Delhi: 15 August 1997).

12. Ibid.

13. Patralekha Chatterjee, "Water in India: Mismanaging a Vital Resource," *Development + Cooperation*, February 1997.

14. Mark W. Rosegrant, Claudi Ringler, and Roberta Gerpacio, "Water and Land Resources and Global Food Supply," paper prepared for the 23rd International Conference of Agricultural Economists on *Food Security, Diversification, and Resource Management: Refocusing the Role of Agriculture, Sacramento,* CA, 10–16 August 1997 (Washington, DC: International Food Policy Research Institute, 1997).

15. Ibid.

16. India population from Bureau of the Census, op. cit. note 2.

17. Rosegrant, Ringler, and Gerpacio, op. cit. note 14.

18. David Seckler, *The New Era of Water Resources Management: From "Dry" to "Wet" Water Savings* (Washington, DC: CGIAR, 1996).

19. Ibid.

20. Paul Raskin et al., *Water Futures: Assessment of Long-Range Patterns and Problems*, Vol. 3 of *Comprehensive Assessment of the Freshwater Resources of the World* (Stockholm: Stockholm Environment Institute, 1997). The International Food Policy Research Institute projects a slightly higher annual growth rate—0.6 percent—for the period 1995–2020; see Rosegrant, Ringler, and Gerpacio, op. cit. note 14.

OIL AND GAS USE REACH NEW HIGHS (pages 50–51)

1. Data for 1950–96 from United Nations, *World Energy Supplies* (New York: 1976), from United Nations, *Yearbook of World Energy Statistics* (New York: 1983), and from U.S. Department of Energy (DOE), Energy Information Administration (EIA), *International Energy Annual 1996* (Washington, DC: February 1998); 1997 figure is Worldwatch estimate based on ibid., on British Petroleum (BP), *BP Statistical Review of World Energy 1997* (London: Group Media & Publications, 1997), on DOE, EIA, *Monthly Energy Review January 1998* (Washington, DC: 1998), on European Commission, *The Market for Solid Fuels in the Community in 1996 and the Outlook for 1997*, Revision of Commission Report SEC (97) (Brussels: 3 October 1997), on J. Perez Martin, Energy Directorate, European Commission, letter to author, 19 January 1998, on PlanEcon Inc., *PlanEcon Energy Update for 1996–97* (Washington, DC: 1997), and on P.T. Bangsberg, *Journal of Commerce*, letter to author, 26 January 1998.

2. BP, op. cit. note 1.

3. Ibid.

4. Ibid.

5. Ibid.

6. Worldwatch estimate based on American Automobile Manufacturers Association (AAMA), *Motor Vehicle Facts and Figures 1997* (Detroit, MI: 1997), on U.S. Bureau of the Census, *Statistical Abstract of the United States, 1997* (Washington, DC: 1997), and on AAMA, *World Motor Vehicle Data, 1997 ed.* (Detroit, MI: 1997).

7. Keith Bradsher, "Light Trucks Increase Profits But Foul Air More Than Cars," *New York Times*, 30 November 1997.

8. Population Reference Bureau, "1997 World Population Data Sheet," wallchart (Washington,

DC: May 1997); BP, op. cit. note 1.

9. Eurogas, "1997 Natural Gas Consumption in Western Europe 1.5% Below Record Level of 1996," press release (Brussels: February 1998).

10. PlanEcon, op. cit. note 1.

11. "Study: Natural Gas Use Will Double by 2030," *Journal of Commerce*, 11 June 1997.

12. "Toyota's Green Machine," *Business Week*, 15 December 1997; "Detroit's Impossible Dream," *Business Week*, 2 March 1998.

13. DOE, *Monthly Energy Review*, op. cit. note 1.

14. Ibid.

15. Ibid.

16. Ibid.

17. BP, op. cit. note 1.

18. Charles Clover, "Battle for Natural Resources," *Financial Times*, 19 September 1997; Steve LeVine, "Instability by the Barrelful? Central Asia's Coming Oil Bonanza and Its Consequences," *New York Times*, 17 February 1998.

19. Charles Clover, "Superpowers Circle Caspian," *Financial Times*, 18 August 1997.

20. Colin J. Campbell and Jean H. Laherrere, "The End of Cheap Oil," *Scientific American*, March 1998.

COAL USE CONTINUES REBOUND (pages 52–53)

1. Figure for 1997 is Worldwatch estimate based on United Nations, *Energy Statistics Yearbook 1995* (New York: 1997), on British Petroleum (BP), *BP Statistical Review of World Energy* (London: Group Media & Publications, 1997), on U.S. Department of Energy (DOE), Energy Information Administration (EIA), *Monthly Energy Review*, January 1998 (Washington, DC: 1998), on European Commission, *The Market for Solid Fuels in the Community in 1996 and the Outlook for 1997*, Revision of Commission Report SEC (97) (Brussels: 3 October 1997), on PlanEcon Inc., *PlanEcon Energy Outlook, Regional Energy Update for 1996–97* (Washington, DC: 1997), and on P.T. Bangsberg, *Journal of Commerce*, letter to author, 26 January 1998; 1996 number is Worldwatch estimate based on United Nations, op. cit. this note, and BP, op. cit. this note.

2. Worldwatch estimate based on sources cited in note 1; 1950–95 figures from United Nations, *World Energy Supplies 1950-74* (New York: 1976), and from United Nations, *Energy Statistics Yearbook* (New York: various years).

3. Worldwatch estimate based on BP, op. cit. note 1.

4. Bangsberg, op. cit. note 1; BP, op. cit. note 1; Steven Mufson, "Rising Coal Consumption Makes China a World Leader in Pollution," *Washington Post*, 30 November 1997; World Bank, *Clear Water, Blue Skies: China's Environment in the New Century* (Washington, DC: November 1997).

5. Jonathan E. Sinton, ed., *China Energy Databook* (Berkeley, CA: Ernest Orlando Lawrence Berkeley National Laboratory, September 1996); Worldwatch estimate based on BP, op. cit. note 1, and on Bangsberg, op. cit. note 1.

6. Hilary French, "Money and the Future of the Earth," *World Watch*, May/June 1997.

7. Worldwatch estimate based on BP, op. cit. note 1.

8. DOE, op. cit. note 1; Worldwatch estimate based on BP, op. cit. note 1, and on DOE, op. cit. note 1.

9. International Energy Agency, *Asia Electricity Study* (Paris: March 1997).

10. Worldwatch estimate based on BP, op. cit. note 1; Kenneth J. Cooper, "Coal vs. Goals: India's Dilemma," *Washington Post*, 16 October 1997.

11. Anne Counsell, "Rapid Expansion in a Dynamic Decade," *Financial Times*, 24 November 1997.

12. Worldwatch estimate based on BP, op. cit. note 1; European Commission, op. cit. note 1.

13. "Coal in Europe: Yesterday's Fuel," *Economist*, 29 November 1997.

14. "Energy Market Report," *Financial Times Energy Economist*, December 1997; "German Coal Industry Hits the Wall as Bonn Slashes Sales Subsidies," *European Energy Report*, 21 March 1997.

15. PlanEcon Inc., op. cit. note 1.

16. "Ukraine: No Cash to Close Mines," *Journal of Commerce*, 3 July 1997.

17. Jane Perlez, "Poland's Coal Miners, Once Stars, Are Now Surplus," *New York Times*, 2 November 1997.

18. "Energy Market Report," op. cit. note 14.

19. Christopher Flavin, "Banking Against Warming," *World Watch*, November/December 1997.

20. Carol Matlack, "What Happened to the Russian Coal Miners' Dollars?" *Business Week*, 8 September 1997.

21. Institute for Policy Studies, *The World Bank and the G-7: Changing the Earth's Climate for Business* (Washington, DC: June 1997); Daphne Wysham and Jim Vallette, "Changing the Earth's Climate for Business," *Multinational Monitor*, October 1997.

22. Agis Sapulkas, "Energy For a Power Source," *New York Times*, 2 January 1998; Matthew L. Wald, "Coal Nightmares, Electrical Dreams," *New York Times*, 1 December 1997.

23. Matthew L. Wald, "The Keys to Electricity: Cost and Cleanliness," *New York Times*, 2 January 1998.

NUCLEAR POWER STEADY
(pages 54–55)

1. Installed nuclear capacity is defined as reactors connected to the grid as of December 31, 1997, and is based on the Worldwatch Institute database complied from statistics from the International Atomic Energy Agency (IAEA) and press reports, primarily from *European Energy Report, Energy Economist, Nuclear News, New York Times, Financial Times, Reuters*, and Web sites.

2. Worldwatch Institute database, op. cit. note 1.

3. Included in the United States closures is one reactor at Zion that is listed as having closed in 1997. An additional reactor at Zion ceased operating in 1996.

4. Worldwatch Institute database, op. cit. note 1.

5. Ibid.

6. Ibid.

7. "IMF Retrenchment Will Not Affect North Korean Reactors," *Agence France Presse*, 4 December 1997.

8. "Six Nuclear Power Stations to be Operating in China by 2004," *Agence France Presse*, 30 October 1997.

9. Ross Kerber, "Nuclear Plants Face Huge Costs to Fix Problems," *Wall Street Journal*, 18 June 1997.

10. John Earl, Ontario Hydro, Toronto, Canada, discussion with author, 5 January 1998. The Canadian reactors are not considered permanently closed yet, though it appears highly unlikely they will ever operate again. Thus they are no longer listed as operating, nor are they listed as being closed.

11. "France EDF to Start New Nuclear Reactor by January," *Reuters*, 30 December 1997.

12. Worldwatch Institute database, op. cit. note 1.

13. "Sweden Committed to Phasing Out Its Nuclear Reactors," *Agence France Presse*, 3 February 1998.

14. "New Japanese Nuclear Reactor On-Line," *Reuters*, 15 July 1997.

15. "Profile of Japan's Troubled Nuclear Corporation," *Reuters*, 26 August 1997.

16. Vladimer Sliviak, Socio-Ecological Union, Moscow, e-mail to author, 11 January 1998.

17. "Russia Nuclear Workers to Stage Protest," *Reuters*, 2 July 1997; "Ukraine PM Orders Completion of Nuclear Reactors," *Reuters*, 5 January 1998.

18. "Czech Nuclear Plant to Open Despite Delays," *Reuters*, 6 January 1998.

19. Worldwatch Institute database, op. cit. note 1.

20. "Nuclear Winter," *The Economist*, 10 January 1998.

21. "Indonesia's Habibie Says Nuclear Power Last Option," *Reuters*, 19 March 1997.

22. "Nuclear Winter," op. cit. note 20.

23. Ibid.

24. "Bidding Prices on Turkish Nuclear Power Plant Construction Made Public," *Nuke Info Tokyo*, November/December 1997.

HYDROELECTRIC POWER UP SLIGHTLY (pages 56–57)

1. Figure for 1996 is Worldwatch estimate based on United Nations, *Energy Statistics Yearbook 1995* (New York: 1997), and on British Petroleum (BP), *BP Statistical Review of World Energy 1997* (London: Group Media & Publications, 1997).

2. Data for 1950–74 from United Nations, *World Energy Supplies, 1950–74* (New York: 1976); 1975–95 figures from United Nations, *Energy Statistics Yearbook* (New York: various years); Worldwatch estimate based on BP, op. cit. note 1.

3. Worldwatch estimate based on United Nations, op. cit. note 1.

4. Ibid.

5. David A. Malakoff, "Agency Says Dam Should Come Down," *Science*, 8 August 1997; "Victory for the Fishes," *Economist*, 6 December 1997; Blaine Harden, "U.S. Orders Maine Dam Destroyed," *Washington Post*, 26 November 1997; Carey Goldberg, "Fish Are Victorious Over Dam As U.S. Agency Orders Shutdown," *New York Times*, 26 November 1997.

6. Neil Ulman, "U.S. May Order Removal of Maine Hydro-Electric Dam," *Washington Post*, 25 November 1997; Daniel P. Beard, "Dams Aren't Forever," *New York Times*, 6 October 1997; Tom Kenworthy, "A Voice in the Wilderness," *Washington Post Magazine*, 1 June 1997.

7. Patrick McCully, *Silenced Rivers* (London: Zed Books, 1996).

8. Ibid.; Stephanie Joyce, "Is it Worth A Dam?" *Environmental Health Perspectives*, October 1997.

9. World Bank, *World Bank Lending for Large Dams: A Preliminary Review of Impacts*, OED Precis No. 125 (Washington, DC: 1996); World Conservation Union (IUCN) and World Bank, *Large Dams: Learning from the Past, Looking at the Future*, Workshop Proceedings (Washington, DC: July 1997); Leyla Boulton, "Ecologists Square Up for Dam Debate," *Financial Times*, 11 April 1997; Stephanie Flanders, "Truce Called in Battle of the Dams," *Financial Times*, 14 April 1997.

10. Joyce, op. cit. note 8; IUCN and World Bank, op. cit. note 9.

11. "Dammed if They Do," *Economist*, 30 August 1997; Lily Dizon, "Why World Bank Gave Its Nod to a Giant Dam," *Christian Science Monitor*, 3 December 1997.

12. Leslie Crawford, "Chile Dam Row Shows IFC's Problems with Projects," *Financial Times*, 8 August 1997; Glenn Switkes, "Dispute over Chilean Dam Heightens Debate on Public Financing of Private Sector Projects," *Ecological Economics Bulletin*, Fourth Quarter 1997.

13. Glenn Switkes, "A River Runs Private," *Multinational Monitor*, October 1997.

14. Tony Walker, "Contest Hots Up for Huge Yangtze Power Contracts," *Financial Times*, 25 July 1997; Richard Tomlinson, "Dam! America Misses Out on the World's Biggest Construction Project," *Fortune*, 10 November 1997.

15. Seth Faison, "Set to Build Dam, China Diverts Yangtze While Crowing About It," *New York Times*, 9 November 1997; Dai Qing, *The River Dragon is Coming!* (New York: M.E. Sharpe, 1997).

16. Stephen Bocking, "The Power Elite," *Alternatives Journal*, Spring 1997; David Malin Roodman, "Giant Dam Postponed Indefinitely," *World Watch*, November/December 1997.

17. Bocking, op. cit. note 16.

18. Peter Fraenkel, "Future Development Potential for Small Scale Hydro Power," in *The World Directory of Renewable Energy Suppliers and Services 1996* (London: James & James Ltd., 1996).

19. Sandy L. Beggs, "Fulfilling Small Hydro's Worldwide Potential," in *World Directory*, op. cit. note 18.

20. "Dam! Dam! Dam!" *Financial Times Energy World*, Spring 1997.

21. Jose Roberto Moreira and Alan Douglas Poole, "Hydropower and Its Constraints," in Thomas B. Johansson et al., *Renewable Energy: Sources for Fuels and Electricity* (Washington, DC: Island Press, 1993); Peter N. Spotts, "Dams Disrupt a Key Balance in Sea," *Christian Science Monitor*, 27 March 1997; Philip M. Fearnside, "Greenhouse-Gas Emissions from Amazonian Hydroelectric Reservoirs: The Example of Brazil's Tucurui Dam as Compared to Fossil Fuel Alternatives," *Environmental Conservation*, 7 April 1997.

WIND POWER SETS RECORDS
(pages 58–59)

1. Estimates based on Birger Madsen, BTM Consult, Ringkobing, Denmark, letter to author, 10 February 1998, and on BTM Consult, *International Wind Energy Development: World Market Update 1996* (Ringkobing, Denmark: March 1997).

2. Madsen, op. cit. note 1; the total installed capacity for the end of 1997 reflects both the 1,566 megawatts of turbines added during the year and the turbines abandoned or dismantled.

3. Andrea Wagner, Bundesverband WindEnergie e.V., Bonn, Germany, letter to author, 21 January 1998.

4. Sara Knight, "Bonn Brought to Standstill," *Windpower Monthly*, October 1997.

5. Sara Knight, "Liberalisation Law Puts Cap on Wind Output," *Windpower Monthly*, December 1997; Andrea Wagner, Bundesverband WindEnergie e.V., Bonn, Germany, letter to author, 26 February 1998.

6. Madsen, op. cit. note 1.

7. Preben Maegaard, Folkcenter for Renewable Energy, Hurup Thy, Denmark, discussion with author, Tokyo, 3 November 1997.

8. Ibid.

9. Madsen, op. cit. note 1.

10. Ibid.

11. Ibid.

12. "Germans Plan Big Wind Farm South of Barcelona," *Windpower Monthly*, December 1997.

13. Madsen op. cit. note 1; Crispin Aubrey, "Confidence Returns After Uncertain Year," *Wind Directions*, April 1997.

14. Madsen, op. cit. note 1.

15. Ibid.
16. Zhang Dan, "China Eases the Way for Steady Progress," *Windpower Monthly*, November 1997.
17. Ibid.
18. Ros Davidson, "Wind to Charge Zero Emission Car Fleet," *Windpower Monthly*, November 1997.
19. Ibid.; Madsen, op. cit. note 1.
20. *Wind Energy Weekly*, 26 January 1998.
21. Ros Davidson and Sara Knight, "American Giant Moves into European Market," *Windpower Monthly*, November 1997.
22. Kent Dahl, "Japanese Firm Makes Solid Commitment," *Windpower Monthly*, June 1997.
23. "Government Urged to Boost UK Solar Energy Industry," *ENDS Report 274*, November 1997.
24. David Milborrow, independent energy consultant, presentation at European Wind Energy Association Conference, Dublin, Ireland, 6 October 1997.

SOLAR CELL SHIPMENTS HIT NEW HIGH (pages 60–61)

1. Paul Maycock, "1997 World Cell/Module Shipments," *PV News*, February 1998.
2. Paul Maycock, *PV News*, various issues.
3. Ibid.
4. Paul Maycock, "Japanese FY 1998 PV Budget up 32%, Despite Financial Uncertainty," *PV News*, February 1998.
5. "Government Boosts Incentives for Solar Power," *COMLINE Daily News Tokyo Financial Wire*, 20 November 1997.
6. Maycock, op. cit. note 1.
7. Allan L. Frank, "Kyocera Explains Japan's Roof Program," *The Solar Letter*, 21 November 1997; Solar Energy Industries Association, "Country Briefing—Japan Photovoltaic Promotion Programs," as posted at < http://www.seia.org/mrjapan.htm >, viewed 16 December 1997.
8. Suvendrini Kakuchi, "Environment-Japan: Solar Power vs. Global Warming," *InterPress Service,* 29 November 1997.
9. Philip Cohen, "Cheap Solar Cells Have Their Day in the Sun," *New Scientist*, 12 April 1997.
10. Paul Maycock, Photovoltaic Energy Systems, Inc., Warrenton, VA, discussion with author, 29 January 1997. The price estimate is a best guess based on discussions with manufacturers.
11. Maycock, op. cit. note 1.
12. Seth Dunn, "Power of Choice," *World Watch*, September/October 1997; Matthew L. Wald, "An Industry Relishes Its Day in the Sun; But U.S. Solar Cell Makers See Clouds Rolling in from Overseas," *New York Times*, 16 August 1997.
13. Sacramento Municipal Utility District, "PV Pioneer Program," as posted at < http://www.smud.org/energy/solar/index.html >, viewed 16 December 1997; Robert Masullo, "SMUD Solar Programs Signal Dawning of Next Age in Electricity," *Sacramento Bee*, 5 October 1997.
14. Brenda Biondo, "Pushing Solar Energy Through the Roof," *Solar Industry Journal*, Second Quarter 1997.
15. Maycock, op. cit. note 1.
16. Douglas Sutton, "Experts Ask: Is Europe Paying Only Lip Service to Solar Power?" *Deutsche Presse-Agentur*, 28 October 1997; Paul Maycock, "European Module Shipment Flat for the First Time Ever!" *PV News*, February 1996; Paul Maycock, "European Cell/Module Shipments Decrease," *PV News*, February 1997.
17. Peter Norman, "Germany Backs Solar Energy," *Financial Times,* 5 November 1997; Robert Koenig, "Two New Plants Could Make Germany World's Top Solar-Energy-Cell Exporter," *Journal of Commerce*, 12 November 1997.
18. Paul Maycock, "Royal Dutch Shell, Pilkington Solar to Build the World's Largest PV Cell Manufacturing Plant," *PV News*, December 1997.
19. World Bank, *Rural Energy and Development: Improving Energy Supplies for Two Billion People* (Washington, DC: 1996); Mark Crawford, "PV Makers See Potential, Profit in Third World Markets," *Energy Daily*, 23 July 1997.
20. Christopher Flavin and Molly O'Meara, "Shining Examples," *World Watch*, May/June 1997; Jenniy Gregory et al., Intermediate Technology Publications in association with the Stockholm Environment Institute, *Financing Renewable Energy Projects: A Guide for Development Workers* (Nottingham, U.K.: The Russell Press, 1997); Michael Northrup, "Selling Solar: Financing Household Solar Energy in the Developing World," *Solar Today*, January/February 1997.
21. Solar Electric Light Company, "International Solar Energy Company Launched To Provide Solar Electricity to Developing Countries," press release (Washington, DC: 1 October 1997).
22. Richard Hansen, Soluz, Inc., North Chelmsford, MA, discussion with author, 18 February 1997; John Rogers, Soluz, Inc., North Chelmsford, MA, e-mail to author, 26 January 1998.
23. Sunlight Power International, "Sunlight Power

International Expands Operations with $2 Million Investment," press release (Washington, DC: 22 April 1997); Paul Maycock, "Sunlight Power Gains Further Finance," *PV News*, August 1997.

24. Atiya Hussain, "Big Players Target Growing Solar Industry in U.S.," *Reuters*, 16 January 1998.

25. John Browne, Group Chief Executive, British Petroleum, "Creating the Sustainable Company," presentation to the Andersen Consulting World Forum on Change, 6 June 1997; Jeroen van der Veer, Group Managing Director, Royal Dutch/Shell Group, "Shell International Renewables—Bringing Together the Group's Activities in Solar Power, Biomass, and Forestry," press conference, London, 6 October 1997.

SALES OF COMPACT FLUORESCENTS SURGE (pages 62–63)

1. Nils Borg, "Global CFL Boom," *IAEEL Newsletter* (International Association for Energy Efficient Lighting), March–April 1998.

2. Data for 1988–89 from Evan Mills, Lawrence Berkeley Laboratory, Berkeley, CA, letter to Worldwatch, 3 February 1993; 1990–97 from Borg, op. cit. note 1.

3. Worldwatch estimate based on 15-percent decay in existing CFL stock per year and the same amount of light from 15-watt CFLs and 60-watt incandescents.

4. Worldwatch estimate based on 15-percent decay in existing CFL stock per year, 15-watt CFLs replacing 60-watt incandescents, 4 hours of lighting per day, and 0.17 tons of carbon and 0.0037 tons of sulfur dioxide per 1,000 kilowatt-hours of electricity consumed in the United States. While the estimate expresses the savings from installing CFLs instead of incandescents, it is difficult to determine how many CFLs are literally used in place of incandescents. Electricity consumption and carbon emissions from U.S. Department of Energy (DOE), Energy Information Administration, *Annual Energy Outlook 1998 with Projections Through 2020* (Washington, DC: U.S. Government Printing Office, 1997); sulfur dioxide emissions from U.S. Environmental Protection Agency, *National Air Pollutant Emission Trends Report*, 1900–1996 (Washington, DC: U.S. Government Printing Office, 1997).

5. Nils Borg, IAEEL, Berkeley, CA, e-mail to author, 17 February 1998.

6. Worldwatch estimate based on Borg, op. cit. note 1, and on Borg, op. cit. note 5. Although the estimate assumes that 15-watt CFLs have a 10,000-hour life, some poorer quality CFLs may not last that long.

7. Solstice, "Light Sources: Compact Fluorescent Lamps," < http://solstice.crest.org/environment/ gotwh/general/light-sources/ >, viewed 14 January 1998.

8. Worldwatch estimate of the net present value of the payback from replacing a 75¢, 60-watt, 1,000-hour incandescent bulb with a $10, 15-watt, 10,000-hour CFL, assuming 4 hours of lighting a day, a 3.5-percent annual rate of return on five-year savings, and an electricity price of 8.4¢ per kilowatt-hour. Electricity price from DOE, op. cit. note 4.

9. Borg, op. cit. note 1.

10. Ibid.

11. Ibid.

12. Ming Yang and Peter du Pont, "The Green Lights of China," *E-Notes* (International Institute for Energy Conservation), March 1997.

13. Nils Borg, IAEEL, Berkeley, CA, e-mail to author, 12 February 1998; Steven Nadel et al., *Lighting Efficiency in China: Current Status, Future Directions* (Washington, DC: American Council for an Energy-Efficient Economy, May 1997).

14. Nils Borg, IAEEL, Berkeley, CA, e-mail to author, 13 February 1998.

15. Nils Borg, IAEEL, Berkeley, CA, discussion with author, 13 February 1998.

16. Fredrik Lundberg, "IKEA Gives Away 25 MW," *IAEEL Newsletter*, March–April 1998.

17. Peter Tulej, "A Bright Light in Poland," *E-Notes* (International Institute for Energy Conservation), August 1997.

18. Chris Granda, Ecos Consulting, discussion with author, 22 January 1998.

19. Dana Younger, International Finance Corporation, e-mail to author, 20 January 1998.

20. Borg, op. cit. note 15.

21. Nils Borg, "Metal-Halide Lamps Use More Ceramics," *IAEEL Newsletter*, February 1997; Evan Mills and Diana Vorsatz, "Compact Fluorescents Face Tough Competition," *IAEEL Newsletter*, March–April 1998.

22. Chris Calwell, "Halogen Torchieres: Cold Facts and Hot Ceilings," *E-Source Tech Update*, September 1996.

23. Chris Calwell and Evan Mills, "Halogen Torchieres: A Look at Market Transformation in Progress," 3 September 1997, presented at the

4th European Conference on Energy-Efficient Lighting, Copenhagen, Denmark, 19–21 November 1997.

24. Calwell, op. cit. note 22.

25. Ibid.

26. Chris Calwell, "Energy Saving Torchieres Coming to a Store Near You," *E-Source Tech Update*, July 1997; Evan Ramstad, "Prospects Dim for Hot, Costly Halogens," *Wall Street Journal*, 10 March 1997.

CARBON EMISSIONS RESUME RISE (pages 66–67)

1. Figure for 1997 is Worldwatch estimate based on G. Marland et al., "Global, Regional, and National CO_2 Emission Estimates from Fossil Fuel Burning, Cement Production, and Gas Flaring: 1751–1995 (revised January 1998)," Oak Ridge National Laboratory, < http://cdiac.esd.ornl.gov/ >, viewed 21 January 1998, on British Petroleum (BP), *BP Statistical Review of World Energy 1997* (London: Group Media & Publications, 1997), on U.S. Department of Energy (DOE), Energy Information Administration (EIA), *Monthly Energy Review*, January 1998 (Washington, DC: 1998), on European Commission, *The Market for Solid Fuels in the Community in 1996 and the Outlook for 1997*, Revision of Commission Report SEC (97) (Brussels: 3 October 1997), on J. Perez Martin, European Commission, Energy Directorate, letter to author, 19 January 1998, on PlanEcon Inc., *PlanEcon Energy Outlook, Regional Energy Update for 1996–97* (Washington, DC: 1997), and on P.T. Bangsberg, *Journal of Commerce*, letter to author, 26 January 1998.

2. Worldwatch estimate based on sources cited in note 1.

3. Figure for 1996 is Worldwatch estimate based on Marland et al., op. cit. note 1, and on BP, op. cit. note 1; 1950–95 figures are Worldwatch estimates based on Marland et al., op. cit. note 1.

4. Worldwatch estimate based on Marland et al., op. cit. note 1, and on BP, op. cit. note 1.

5. Worldwatch estimate based on Marland et al., op. cit. note 1, and on BP, op. cit. note 1.

6. Worldwatch estimate based on BP, op. cit. note 1; DOE, EIA, *Emissions of Greenhouse Gases in the United States 1996* (Washington, DC: October 1997).

7. Worldwatch estimate based on BP, op. cit. note 1.

8. Ibid.

9. Worldwatch estimate based on Marland et al., op. cit. note 1, and on BP, op. cit. note 1.

10. Worldwatch estimate based on Marland et al., op. cit. note 1, and on BP, op. cit. note 1.

11. Worldwatch estimate based on Marland et al., op. cit. note 1, and on BP, op. cit. note 1.

12. Worldwatch estimate based on Marland et al., op. cit. note 1, and on BP, op. cit. note 1.

13. Worldwatch estimate based on Marland et al., op. cit. note 1, and on BP, op. cit. note 1.

14. Worldwatch estimate based on BP, op. cit. note 1, and on Population Reference Bureau, "1997 Population Data Sheet," wallchart (Washington, DC: May 1997).

15. Worldwatch estimate based on BP, op. cit. note 1.

16. J.T. Houghton et al., eds., *Climate Change 1995: The Science of Climate Change*, Contribution of Working Group I to the Second Assessment Report of the Intergovernmental Panel on Climate Change (IPCC) (Cambridge, U.K.: Cambridge University Press, 1996).

17. Timothy Whorf and C.D. Keeling, Scripps Institution of Oceanography, La Jolla, CA, letter to author, 2 February 1998; Houghton et al., op. cit. note 16.

18. Houghton et al., op. cit. note 16.

19. Robert T. Watson, Marufu Zinyowera, and Richard H. Moss, eds., *Climate Change 1995: Impacts, Adaptation, and Mitigation*, Contribution of Working Group II to the Second Assessment Report of the IPCC (Cambridge, U.K.: Cambridge University Press, 1996).

20. John T. Houghton et al., eds., *Stabilization of Atmospheric Greenhouse Gases: Physical, Biological and Socio-economic Implications*, IPCC Technical Paper 3 (Geneva: February 1997); Christian Azar and Henning Rodhe, "Targets for Stabilization of Atmospheric CO_2," *Science*, 20 June 1997.

21. U.N. Framework Convention on Climate Change, "Kyoto Protocol to the United Nations Framework Convention on Climate Change," 10 December 1997; "Report of the Third Conference of the Parties to the United Nations Framework Convention on Climate Change: 1–11 December 1997," *Earth Negotiations Bulletin*, 13 December 1997.

22. Worldwatch estimate based on Marland et al., op. cit. note 1, and on BP, op. cit. note 1.

23. Greenpeace International, "The Kyoto Protocol: Key Issues," Greenpeace Briefing Paper, Third Conference to the Parties to the UN Framework Convention on Climate Change, 1–10

December 1997, Kyoto, Japan.

24. "Report of the Third Conference," op. cit. note 21.

GLOBAL TEMPERATURE REACHES RECORD HIGH
(pages 68–69)

1. James Hansen et al., Goddard Institute for Space Studies, Surface Air Temperature Analyses, "Global Land-Ocean Temperature Index," as posted at < http://www.giss.nasa.gov/Data/GISTEMP >, viewed 14 January 1998.

2. The importance of Figure 1 is the change in temperature over time, as the Goddard Institute analyzes temperature change rather than absolute temperature. In earlier versions of *Vital Signs,* Worldwatch added the temperature change reported by the Goddard Institute to an estimated global temperature of 15 degrees Celsius, but the institute has since informed Worldwatch that a better base number would be 14 degrees Celsius. James Hansen, Goddard Institute for Space Studies, New York, e-mail to author, 18 January 1998.

3. "World Warms Into Record Books," (London) *Daily Telegraph,* 28 November 1997; National Climatic Data Center (NCDC), National Oceanic and Atmospheric Administration (NOAA), "The Climate of 1997," as posted at < http://www.ncdc.noaa.gov/pw/cg/ghcn/ghcn_sst/ >, viewed 12 January 1998.

4. Hansen et al., op. cit. note 1; J.T. Houghton et al., eds., *Climate Change 1995: The Science of Climate Change,* Contribution of Working Group I to the Second Assessment Report of the Intergovernmental Panel on Climate Change (Cambridge, U.K.: Cambridge University Press, 1996).

5. Houghton et al., op. cit. note 4.

6. R.B. Myeni et al., "Increased Plant Growth in the Northern High Latitudes from 1981 to 1991," *Nature,* 17 April 1997; David Thomson, "The Seasons, Global Temperature, and Precession," *Science,* 7 July 1995.

7. L.G. Thompson et al., "Late Glacial Stage and Holocene Tropical Ice Core Records from Huascaran," *Science,* 7 July 1995; W. Haeberli and M. Hoelzle, "Application of Inventory Data for Estimating Characteristics of and Regional Climate Change Effects on Mountain Glaciers— A Pilot Study with the European Alps," *Annals of Glaciology,* vol. 21, pp. 206–12, 1995.

8. E.J. Rignot et al., "North and Northeast Greenland Ice Discharge from Satellite Radar Interferometry," *Science,* 9 May 1997.

9. William K. de la Mare, "Abrupt Mid-Twentieth-Century Decline in Antarctic Sea-Ice Extent from Whaling Records," *Nature,* 4 September 1997.

10. Houghton et al., op. cit., note 4.

11. NOAA, "1997 Warmest Year of Century, NOAA Reports," press release (Washington, DC: 8 January 1998).

12. Ibid.

13. B.D. Santer et al., "Detection of Climate Change and Attribution of Causes," in Houghton et al., op. cit. note 4; B.D. Santer et al., "A Search for Human Influences on the Thermal Structure of the Atmosphere," *Nature,* 4 July 1996; Robert Kaufmann and David Stern, "Evidence for Human Influence on Climate from Hemispheric Temperature Relations," *Nature,* 3 July 1997.

14. James Hansen et al., Goddard Institute for Space Studies, Surface Air Temperature Analyses, "1997 Temperature Observations," as posted at < http://www.giss.nasa.gov/research/observe/ >, viewed 14 January 1998; National Center for Atmospheric Research, "Quick Rise in Temperatures Suggests a Blockbuster El Niño for the Late Nineties; NCAR El Niño Colloquium This Month," press release (Boulder, CO: 17 July 1997).

15. NOAA, El Niño Theme Page, as posted at < http://www.pmel.noaa.gov/toga-tao/ >, viewed 15 December 1997.

16. Rob Qualyle and Catherine Godfrey, NCDC, NOAA, e-mail to author, 12 February 1998.

17. De-Zheng Sun, "El Niño: A Coupled Response to Radiative Heating?" *Geophysical Research Letters,* 15 August 1997; Kevin Trenberth and Timothy Hoar, "The 1990–1995 El Niño-Southern Oscillation Event: Longest on Record," *Geophysical Research Letters,* 1 January 1997.

18. R.T. Watson et al., eds., *Climate Change 1995: Impacts, Adaptations, and Mitigation,* Contribution of Working Group II to the Second Assessment Report of the Intergovernmental Panel on Climate Change (Cambridge, U.K.: Cambridge University Press, 1996).

19. Norman Myers, "Environmental Unknowns," *Science,* 21 July 1995; Stephen Schneider, *Laboratory Earth: The Planetary Gamble We Can't Afford to Lose* (New York: Basic Books, 1997).

20. Norman Myers, "Two Key Challenges for Biodiversity: Discontinuities and Synergisms," *Biodiversity and Conservation,* vol. 5, pp.

1025–34, 1996.

21. S. Manabe and R. Stouffer, "Multiple Century Response of a Coupled Ocean-Atmosphere Model to an Increase of Atmospheric Carbon Dioxide," *Journal of Climate*, January 1994; Thomas F. Stocker and Andreas Schmittner, "Influence of CO_2 Emission Rates on the Stability of the Thermohaline Circulation," *Nature*, 28 August 1997.

22. Wallace S. Broecker, "Thermohaline Circulation, the Achilles Heel of Our Climate System: Will Man-Made CO_2 Upset the Current Balance?" *Science*, 28 November 1997.

CFC PRODUCTION CONTINUES TO PLUMMET (pages 70–71)

1. Figures for 1950 and 1955 are Worldwatch estimates based on Fluorocarbon Program Panel, "Production, Sales, and Calculated Related Release of CFC-11 and CFC-12" (Washington, DC: Chemical Manufacturers Association, December 1990); 1960–95 from Sharon Getamal, DuPont, Wilmington, DE, letter to Worldwatch, 15 February 1996; 1996 Worldwatch estimate based on United Nations Environment Programme (UNEP), "1996 Data for Article 5 Parties" and "1996 Data for Non Article 5 Parties," as of 4 February 1998. For an analysis of the quality of the data reported to UNEP, see Sebastian Oberthur, *Production and Consumption of Ozone-Depleting Substances, 1986–1995: The Data Reporting System under the Montreal Protocol* (Berlin: Deutshce Gesellschaft fur Technisce Zusammenarbeit, 1997).

2. Hilary F. French, "Learning from the Ozone Experience," in Lester Brown et al., *State of the World 1997* (New York: W.W. Norton & Company, 1997); Richard Benedick, *Ozone Diplomacy* (Cambridge, MA: Harvard University Press, 1991).

3. UNEP, Ozone Secretariat, *Production and Consumption of Ozone Depleting Substances 1986–1995* (Montreal: September 1997).

4. UNEP, op. cit. note 1; UNEP op. cit. note 3.

5. J.C. Farman et al., "Large Losses of Total Ozone in Antarctica Reveal Seasonal ClO_x/NO_x Interaction," *Nature*, 16 May 1985; World Meteorological Organization (WMO), *Scientific Assessment of Ozone Depletion: 1994*, Report No. 37 (Geneva: 1995).

6. WMO, op. cit. note 5.

7. National Oceanic and Atmospheric Administration (NOAA), "Southern Hemisphere Winter Summary 1997," December 1997, < http://nic.fb4.noaa.gov/products/stratosphere/winter_bulletins/sh_97/ >, viewed 5 January 1998; "Antarctic Ozone Hole as Large as Ever," *Global Environmental Change Report*, 24 October 1997.

8. Rolf Muller et al., "Severe Chemical Ozone Loss in the Arctic during the Winter of 1995–1996," *Nature*, 16 October 1997; Richard Stolarski, "A Bad Winter for Arctic Ozone," and Markus Rex et al., "Prolonged Stratospheric Ozone Loss in the 1995–1996 Winter," both in *Nature*, 23 October 1997; "International Program Finds Evidence of Holes in Ozone Layer above Arctic Region," *International Environment Reporter*, 11 June 1997; Environment Canada, "Unprecedented Low Ozone Values Recorded Over Canadian Arctic," press release (Ottawa: 7 April 1997).

9. J.R. Herman et al., "UV-B Increases (1979–1992) from Decreases in Total Ozone," *Geophysical Research Letters*, 1 August 1996; NOAA, annual winter bulletins through 1997, < http://nic.fb4.noaa.gov/products/stratosphere/winter_bulletins/ >, viewed 5 January 1998.

10. UNEP, *Environmental Effects of Ozone Depletion: 1994 Assessment* (Nairobi: November 1994); UNEP, *Environmental Effects of Ozone Depletion: Interim Summary, September 1997*, < http://sedac.ciesin.org/ozone/unep/unep97summary.html >, viewed 10 October 1997.

11. Applied Research Consultants for Environment Canada, *Global Benefits and Costs of the Montreal Protocol on Substances that Deplete the Ozone Layer*, September 1997, < http://www.doe.ca/ozone/choices/ >, viewed 29 December 1997. See also Harry Slaper et al., "Estimates of Ozone Depletion and Skin Cancer Incidence to Examine the Vienna Convention Achievements," *Nature*, 21 November 1996.

12. Environment Canada, op. cit. note 8; UNEP, *1994 Report of the Technology and Economics Assessment Panel for the 1995 Assessment of the Montreal Protocol on Substances that Deplete the Ozone Layer* (Nairobi: 1994).

13. "Early Phaseout of Aerosol CFCs Largely Unheralded," *Ozone Depletion Network Online Today* (Environmental Information Network, Inc.), 5 February 1996.

14. Oberthur, op. cit. note 1.

15. Vallette, op. cit. note 1; WMO, op. cit. note 5.

16. Eduardo Ganem, Multilateral Fund Secretariat, e-mail to author, 13 February 1998.

17. Duncan Brack, *International Trade and the*

175

Montreal Protocol (London: Earthscan, for the Royal Institute of International Affairs, 1996); Joby Warrick, "CFC Smuggling, Production Cool Optimism," *Washington Post*, 16 September 1997.

18. Jim Vallette, International Trade Information Service, *Allied Signal, Quimbasicos and the Frio Banditos: A Case Study of the Black Market in CFCs* (Washington, DC: Ozone Action, Inc., 1996); Gavin Hayman, Julian Newman, and Steve Trent, *Chilling Facts About a Burning Issue: CFC Smuggling in the European Union* (London: Environmental Investigation Agency, September 1997).

19. UNEP, op. cit. note 3.

20. World Bank, "Russian Federation Ozone Depleting Substance Consumption Phase-Out Project," Report No. 15326-RU, Project Document, May 1996; Fred Pearce, "The Hole That Will Not Mend," *New Scientist*, 30 August 1997.

21. UNEP, op. cit. note 21; "Developing Countries to Phase Out Methyl Bromide," *Global Environmental Change Report*, 26 September 1997; Fred Pearce, "Promising the Earth: Every Move to Rid the World of Ozone-Eaters Ends Up with Cries of Dirty Dealing," *New Scientist*, 30 August 1997; Leyla Boulton, "Accord on Ozone-Depleting Chemicals," *Financial Times*, 19 September 1997.

WORLD ECONOMY CONTINUES RAPID EXPANSION (pages 74–75)

1. International Monetary Fund (IMF), *World Economic Outlook, Interim Supplement*, December 1997 (Washington, DC: 1997).

2. U.S. Bureau of the Census, *International Data Base*, electronic database, Suitland, MD, updated 10 October 1997.

3. IMF, *World Economic Outlook*, October 1997 (Washington, DC: 1997).

4. Ibid.
5. Ibid.
6. Ibid.
7. Ibid.
8. Ibid.
9. Ibid.
10. Ibid.
11. Ibid.
12. Ibid.
13. IMF, op. cit. note 1.
14. IMF, op. cit. note 3.
15. Ibid.
16. Ibid.
17. Ibid.
18. Ibid.
19. Ibid.
20. Ibid.
21. Ibid.
22. Ibid.; Population Reference Bureau, "1997 World Population Data Sheet," wallchart (Washington, DC: May 1997).
23. IMF, op. cit. note 3.
24. Ibid.
25. IMF, op. cit. note 1; IMF, op. cit. note 3; Vicki Barnett, "Asian Crisis Will Cut Back World Growth, IMF Warns," *Financial Times*, London, 22 December 1997.

TRADE REMAINS STRONG (pages 76–77)

1. Figures for 1950–67 calculated from data in International Monetary Fund (IMF), *World Economic Outlook October 1997* (Washington, DC: 1997); 1968–91 figures and deflators from IMF, *Financial Statistics Yearbook*, November 1997; 1992–97 figures calculated from IMF, *International Financial Statistics*, January 1998, with export unit value indexes supplied by Olga Laveda, Statistician, IMF Statistics Division. Note that preliminary estimates are based on extrapolations for the fourth quarter of 1997, and may not adequately reflect the effects of the crises in Asian currencies markets.

2. "Schools Brief: One World?" *The Economist*, 18 October 1997.

3. IMF, *International Financial Statistics*, op. cit. note 1.

4. Narendra Aggarwal, citing a World Trade Organisation (WTO) study on trade, "Exports of Developing Countries Surge," *Singapore Straits Times*, 10 January 1998.

5. Ibid.

6. World Bank cited in Robert Chote and Mark Suzman, "Developing World to Double Output Share," *Financial Times*, 10 September 1997.

7. Ibid.

8. Milan Brahmbhatt et al., *Global Economic Prospects and the Developing Countries 1997* (Washington, DC: World Bank, 1997).

9. Ibid.

10. "Not Much on the Trade Front, But No Big Setbacks Either," *Latin American Newsletters*, 7

October 1997.

11. Partners or Just Neighbours?" *The Economist*, 11 October 1997.

12. Gerard Baker and Guy de Jonquières, "Clinton Team Wins Most of APEC Tricks," *Financial Times*, 11 November 1997.

13. U.S. International Trade Commission, *Impact of the North American Free Trade Agreement on the U.S. Economy and Industries: A Three Year Review* (Washington, DC: July 1997).

14. Fred Bergsten, Director, and Jeffrey Schott, Senior Fellow, Institute for International Economics, prepared remarks before the Subcommittee on Trade, House Ways and Means Committee, U.S. Congress, Washington, DC, 11 September 1997.

15. Christine Stewart, Canada's Minster for the Environment, State Department briefing at the National Press Club, 22 January 1998.

16. "Dealing for Dollars," *The Economist*, 6 December 1997.

17. Jeffrey Lang, Deputy U.S. Trade Representative, Remarks at the Coalition of Service Industries briefing, *Federal News Service*, 13 January 1998.

18. "Chinese Traders at the Door," *The Economist*, 11 October 1997.

19. John Ridding, "The Going Gets More Difficult," *Financial Times*, 8 December 1997.

20. "Odd Capitol Couplings," *The Village Voice*, 25 November 1997.

21. "US Slammed for Extra-Territorial Policy," *European Report*, 18 February 1998.

PAPER PRODUCTION REMAINS HIGH (pages 78–79)

1. Estimate for 1996 from U.N. Food and Agriculture Organization (FAO), FAOSTAT Statistics Database, < http://apps.fao.org/ >, viewed 16 December 1997; 1995 from Susan Braatz, FAO, e-mail to author, 13 February 1997.

2. FAO, op. cit. note 1; U.S. Bureau of the Census, *International Data Base*, Suitland, MD, updated 10 October 1997.

3. FAO, *State of the World's Forests 1997* (Oxford, U.K.: 1997).

4. Ibid.

5. Ibid.

6. Pulp and Paper International (PPI), *International Fact and Price Book 1997* (San Francisco, CA: Miller Freeman Inc., 1996).

7. Ibid.

8. Ibid.; population numbers from Bureau of the Census, op. cit. note 2.

9. International Institute for Environment and Development (IIED), *Towards a Sustainable Paper Cycle* (London: 1996).

10. FAO op. cit. note 1; Bureau of the Census, op. cit. note 2.

11. IIED, op. cit. note 9.

12. Gary Mead, "Tough Year Ahead For Pulp and Paper," *Financial Times*, 30 January 1998.

13. Ibid.

14. Ibid.

15. FAO, op. cit. note 1.

16. Ibid.

17. Sarah Roberts, *The Potential of the Non-wood Fibre Paper Sector* (London: IIED, December 1996).

18. FAO, op. cit. note 1; Maureen Smith, *The U.S. Paper Industry and Sustainable Production* (Cambridge, MA: The MIT Press, 1997).

19. "China Pulp Projects Abound," *Pulp and Paper Week*, 17 March 1997.

20. Wood Resources International Ltd., *Fiber Sourcing Analysis for the Global Pulp and Paper Industry* (London: IIED, September 1996). IIED reported that 1993 wood pulp production required approximately 618 million cubic meters of wood—equal to 40.39 percent of total industrial wood harvest; IIED, op. cit. note 9.

21. Wood Resources International, op. cit. note 20, reported that 63 percent of the 618 million cubic meters was from the roundwood pulpwood supply and 37 percent was from manufacturing residues and off-site chipping operations.

22. Smith, op. cit. note 18.

WEATHER DAMAGES EASE (pages 80–81)

1. Gerhard A. Berz, Munchener Ruckversicherungs-Gesellschaff, press release (Munich, Germany: 29 December 1997).

2. Ibid.

3. Peter J. Webster and Timothy N. Palmer, "The Past and the Future of El Niño," *Nature*, 11 December 1997.

4. Lowe's Storm97 Hurricane Central, cosponsored by FEMA, "1997 Season Summary," < http://www.storm97.com/index.html >, viewed 12 February 1998.

5. Ibid.

6. John Ward Anderson, "Storms' Double Whammy: Second Hurricane to Hit Mexican Coast Causes Great Damage, But No Deaths," *Washington Post*, 12 November 1997.

7. "New Bushfire Warning in Australia," *BBC News*, 4 December 1997.

8. "Indonesian Forest Fires Said Worst Crisis for Atmosphere Since 1991 Gulf War Oil Fires," *International Environment Reporter*, 29 October 1997.

9. Ibid.

10. World Wide Fund for Nature, *The Year the World Caught Fire* (Gland, Switzerland: December 1997).

11. Ibid.

12. Ibid.

13. "Amazon Burning Worst in Memory, Another Casualty of El Niño," *Associated Press*, 9 October 1997.

14. Stephen Buckley, "Deadly African Floods Expected to Continue," *Washington Post*, 21 November 1997; Nicolo Sarno, "Floods Bring Misery and Chaos to Southern Somalia," *Inter Press Service*, 11 December 1997.

15. Robert Koenig, "Floods Wreak Destruction in Eastern Europe," *Journal of Commerce*, 23 July 1997.

16. Berz, op. cit. note 1.

17. Ibid.

18. Ibid.

19. Rong-Hua Zhang, Lewis M. Rothstein, and Antonio J. Busalacchi, "Origins of Upper-Ocean Warming and El Niño Change on Decadal Scales in the Tropical Pacific Ocean," *Nature*, 26 February 1998.

20. United Nations Environment Programme, "Insurers Call for Cuts in Greenhouse Gas Emissions," press release (Kyoto, Japan: 5 December 1997).

U.N. FINANCES STILL CONSTRAINED (pages 82–83)

1. U.N. General Assembly, "Budgetary and Financial Situation of Organizations of the United Nations System. Statistical Report by the Administrative Committee on Coordination," A/51/505 (New York: 18 October 1996), Table 1; "Assessed Payments to the Regular Budget and Specialized Agencies: 1971–1995," in Tables and Charts, Global Policy Forum, <http://www.globalpolicy.org/finance/>, viewed 21 October 1997.

2. U.N. Department of Public Information, "Setting the Record Straight: Some Facts About the United Nations" (New York: August 1997).

3. "Total UN System Expenditures: 1986–1996," Global Policy Forum, op. cit. note 1.

4. The data presented here were compiled by the Global Policy Forum, a nongovernmental organization in New York. They appear not to include budgets for the International Fund for Agricultural Development (IFAD), the U.N. International Drug Control Programme, the Centre for Human Rights, the International Research and Training Institute for the Advancement of Women, the U.N. Institute for Disarmament Research, the U.N. Research Institute for Social Development, the U.N. Development Fund for Women, or the World Tourism Organization. IFAD has an administrative budget of about $50 million and invests about $320 million per year in loans and grants for projects. The other organs just mentioned together have a budget of roughly $130 million. See U.N. Department of Public Information, *A Guide to Information at the United Nations* (New York: February 1995), and New Zealand Ministry of Foreign Affairs, *1993 United Nations Handbook* (Wellington, New Zealand: 1993). The World Bank Group, the International Monetary Fund, and the World Trade Organization are nominally part of the U.N. system, but for all intents and purposes are separate from it in their decisionmaking, their voting structures, and often their philosophy and goals. They are therefore not included here. For peacekeeping expenditures, see pages 118–19.

5. Because U.N. activities take place across the world, the buying power of U.N. monetary resources—and the inflation eating into that buying power—cannot be captured in a single deflator index needed to express U.N. budgets in constant dollars.

6. Zarrín Caldwell, *U.S. Policy and U.N. Reform: Past, Present, and Future* (Washington, DC: United Nations Association of the United States of America (UNA-USA), 1997).

7. Ibid.

8. "Assessments of Specialized Agencies 1971–1995" and "Expenditures of U.N. Specialized Agencies' Voluntarily-Financed Activities: 1971–1995," Global Policy Forum, op. cit. note 1, viewed 10 October 1997.

9. Calculated from U.N. General Assembly, op. cit. note 1.

10. "Total UN System Expenditures: 1986–1996," op. cit. note 3.

11. U.N. Development Programme, *UNDP 1996/1997 Annual Report* (New York: October 1997).

12. Ibid. In addition to core programs, there are UNDP-administered funds, trust funds, cost-sharing arrangements, and government cash counterpart contributions.

13. "Expenditures of Special Organs," Global Policy Forum, op. cit. note 1, revised October 1997.

14. Falling food aid from Gary Gardner, "Food Aid Falls Sharply," in Lester R. Brown, Michael Renner, and Christopher Flavin, *Vital Signs 1997* (New York: W.W. Norton & Company, 1997); WFP budget from "Expenditures of Special Organs," op. cit. note 13.

15. Refugee trends from Jennifer D. Mitchell, "Refugee Flows Drop Steeply," in this volume; UNHCR budget from "UNHCR by Numbers," < http://www.unhcr.ch/un&ref/numbers/ numbers.htm >, current as of July 1997. The 1997 figure is preliminary.

16. This represents half the $218-million budget for the 1996–97 biennium, based on contributions received by 31 August 1997. The Multilateral Fund for the Implementation of the Montreal Protocol, administered by the U.N. Environment Programme (UNEP), received $140 million in 1997; UNEP, *UNEP Biennial Report 1996–97* (London: December 1997).

17. "Outstanding Debts to the UN Regular Budget at Yearend: 1971–1996," Global Policy Forum, op. cit. note 1. Comparison of arrears to budget in 1995 is a Worldwatch calculation.

18. "Outstanding Debts," op. cit. note 17; "Outstanding Contributions to the Regular Budget, International Tribunals and Peace-keeping Operations as of 31 December 1997," Office of the Spokesman for the Secretary-General, United Nations, New York.

19. Caldwell, op. cit. note 6.

20. Ibid.

21. The deal to pay off past dues, with some three dozen conditions attached, was known as the Helms-Biden agreement; it may be revived in 1998. See "The Year in Review: US Legislation and the UN System," *Washington Weekly Report* (UNA-USA), Special Issue, 12 December 1997.

22. Barbara Crossette, "U.S. Effort to Cut its Dues Dies at an Angry U.N.," *New York Times*, 19 December 1997; "U.N. Rejects U.S. Plea for a Decrease in Dues," *New York Times*, 24 December 1997.

23. Barbara Crossette, "Some Win in Lottery at U.N. Over Dues," *New York Times*, 29 December 1997.

24. Among the top 15 contributors to the U.N. regular budget, only the United States, Brazil, and Ukraine were in arrears on their payments—Brazil with $17 million, Ukraine with $12 million; "Outstanding Contributions," op. cit. note 18.

AUTOMOBILE PRODUCTION SETS RECORD (pages 86–87)

1. Production numbers for 1996–97 are Worldwatch estimates based on American Automobile Manufacturers Association (AAMA), *Motor Vehicle Facts and Figures 1997* (Detroit, MI: 1997), and on Standard & Poor's DRI, *World Car Industry Forecast Report, February 1998* (London: 1998); 1950–55 production figures are from AAMA, *World Motor Vehicle Data, 1996 ed.* (Detroit, MI: 1996); 1955–95 production data are from AAMA, *World Motor Vehicle Data, 1997 ed.* (Detroit, MI: 1997).

2. Fleet numbers for 1996–97 are Worldwatch estimates based on AAMA, *World Data, 1997 ed.* op. cit. note 1, and on Standard & Poor's DRI, op. cit. note 1; 1950–95 fleet figures are from AAMA, *World Data, 1997 ed.*, op. cit. note 1.

3. Worldwatch estimate based on AAMA, *World Data, 1997 ed.*, op. cit. note 1, and on Standard & Poor's DRI, op. cit. note 1; population numbers from U.S. Bureau of the Census, *International Data Base*, Suitland, MD, updated 10 October 1997.

4. Michael S. Lelyveld, "Carmakers Drive Rocky Road in Global Overproduction," *Journal of Commerce*, 25 July 1997; Michael P. Walsh, "World Car Makers Seen Facing Years of Overcapacity," *Car Lines*, June 1997.

5. AAMA, *Facts and Figures 1997*, op. cit. note 1; Standard and Poor's DRI, op. cit. note 1; Keith Bradsher, "Light Trucks Increase Profits But Foul Air More Than Cars," *New York Times*, 30 November 1997.

6. Matthew L. Wald, "Number of Cars Is Growing Faster Than Human Population," *New York Times*, 21 September 1997.

7. AAMA, *Facts and Figures 1997*, op. cit. note 1; "Auto Output Surges in Japan And Is Expected to Stay Strong," *New York Times*, 27 May 1997; Standard & Poor's DRI, op. cit. note 1.

8. AAMA, *Facts and Figures 1997*, op. cit. note 1.

9. Standard & Poor's DRI, op. cit. note 1.

10. John Barham, "Car Makers Gear Up for Drive into Turkey," *Financial Times*, 28 October 1997; Standard & Poor's DRI, op. cit. note 1.

11. "Mir on Earth," *The Economist*, 23 August 1997; Standard & Poor's DRI, op. cit. note 1.

12. Keith Bradsher, "In the Biggest, Booming Cities, A Car Population Problem," *New York Times*, 11 May 1997.

13. Standard & Poor's DRI, op. cit. note 1.

14. Charles W. Thurston, "Global Automakers Augment Brazil's Own Investment Effort," *Journal of Commerce*, 11 August 1997; Standard & Poor's DRI, op. cit. note 1.

15. Haig Simonian, "GM Plans to Develop Car in Brazil," *Financial Times*, 3 June 1997; Standard & Poor's DRI, op. cit. note 1.

16. AAMA, *Facts and Figures 1997*, op. cit. note 1; Alex Taylor III, "Danger: Rough Road Ahead," *Fortune*, 17 March 1997.

17. Standard & Poor's DRI, op. cit. note 1; Steven Mufson, "Car Maker Symbolizes Korean Crisis," *Washington Post*, 18 December 1997; Michael Shuman and Valerie Reitman, "A World-Wide Glut Doesn't Sway Samsung From Auto Business," *Wall Street Journal*, 25 August 1997.

18. Haig Simonian, "Tigers Fill Up Their Tanks," *Financial Times*, 10 June 1997; Standard & Poor's DRI, op. cit. note 1; Paul Blustein, "GM's New Factory in Thailand Rises As Car Sales Fall," *Washington Post*, 10 November 1997; Sandra Sugawara, "Toyota Halts Output in Thailand, Reflecting Region's Overcapacity," *Washington Post*, 6 November 1997.

19. Keith B. Richburg, "Haze Compounds Malaysia's Air Problems," *Washington Post*, 5 October 1997; Standard & Poor's DRI, op. cit. note 1.

20. Standard & Poor's DRI, op. cit. note 1; N. Vasuki Rao, "India Ignites the Interest of Global Auto Industry," *Journal of Commerce*, 3 March 1997; Standard & Poor's DRI, op. cit. note 1.

21. Standard & Poor's DRI, op. cit. note 1; Wayne W.J. Xing, "Shifting Gears," *The China Business Review*, November-December 1997; P.T. Bangsberg, "GM's Midsize Car Venture Finds First Gear in China," *Journal of Commerce*, 11 March 1997.

22. Rebecca Blumenstein, "Global Strategy: GM Is Building Plants in Developing Nations to Woo New Markets," *Wall Street Journal*, 4 August 1997.

23. Robyn Meredith, "The Brave New World of General Motors," *New York Times*, 26 October 1997.

24. Emily Thornton, "Toyota's Green Machine," *Business Week*, 15 December 1997; Keith Bradsher, "U.S. Auto Makers Showing Interest in Fuel Efficiency," *New York Times*, 5 January 1998.

25. International Energy Agency (IEA), *Transport, Energy and Climate Change* (Paris: Organisation for Economic Co-operation and Development/ IEA, 1997); Jane Holtz Kay, "Cars Cloud Kyoto," *Nation*, 8 December 1997.

26. "GM Wants Clean Vehicles, But China Car Lacks Catalyst," *Reuters*, 12 January 1998.

MOTORBIKE PRODUCTION ACCELERATING (pages 88–89)

1. Production data compiled from United Nations, *Industrial Commodity Statistics Yearbook: Production Statistics* (New York: Department for Economic and Social Information and Policy Analysis, Statistical Division, various years), from International Motorcycle Manufacturers Association (IMMA), *Statistics, Production, Sales, PARC, 1997* (Geneva: 1998), and from International Road Federation (IRF), *World Road Statistics 1991–1995* (Geneva: 1996).

2. Production data compiled from United Nations, op. cit. note 1, from IMMA, op. cit. note 1, and from IRF, op. cit. note 1.

3. Production data compiled from United Nations, op. cit. note 1, from IMMA, op. cit. note 1, and from IRF, op. cit. note 1.

4. Production data compiled from United Nations, op. cit. note 1, from IMMA, op. cit. note 1, and from IRF, op. cit. note 1.

5. Production data compiled from United Nations, op. cit. note 1, from IMMA, op. cit. note 1, and from IRF, op. cit. note 1.

6. Production data compiled from United Nations, op. cit. note 1, from IMMA, op. cit. note 1, and from IRF, op. cit. note 1.

7. Kenneth J. Cooper, "The Land of the Family Scooter," *Washington Post*, 23 December 1996.

8. Stephen Stares and Liu Zhi, "Theme Paper 1: Motorization in Chinese Cities: Issues and Actions," in Stephen Stares and Liu Zhi, eds., *China's Urban Transport Development Strategy: Proceedings of a Symposium in Beijing, November 8–10 1995*, World Bank Discussion Paper No. 352 (Washington, DC: World Bank, 1996).

9. Charles L. Wright, *Fast Wheels, Slow Traffic:*

Urban Transport Services (Philadelphia, PA: Temple University Press, 1992).

10. Todd Litman, *Transportation Cost Analysis: Techniques, Estimates, and Implications* (Victoria, BC, Canada: Victoria Transport Policy Institute, 20 January 1998).

11. K.V. Gopalakrishnan, "Should It Be Discarded?" *The Hindu* (Chennai, India), 28 February 1997.

12. Michael P. Walsh, "Theme Paper 2: Motor Vehicle Pollution Control in China: An Urban Challenge," in Stares and Liu, op. cit. note 8.

13. William J. Cook, "Nothing But Blue Skies Over Jakarta? They're Just an Electric Scooter Ride Away," *U.S. News and World Report*, 30 December 1996/6 January 1997.

14. Ibid.

15. Stares and Liu, op. cit. note 8.

16. "ZAP Electric Bikes Have Bright Future in China," *Electric Vehicles Energy Network Online Today*, 1 May 1997.

17. Asif Faiz, Christopher S. Weaver, and Michael P. Walsh, *Air Pollution from Motor Vehicles: Standards and Technologies for Controlling Emissions* (Washington, DC: World Bank, 1996).

18. Technologies from Walsh, op. cit. note 12; expense from Gopalakrishnan, op. cit. note 11.

19. Cook, op. cit. note 13.

20. "Taiwan Seeking to Corner Electric Bike," Nautilus Institute, e-mail to author, 23 January 1998.

BICYCLE PRODUCTION DECLINES (pages 90–91)

1. "Focus on Foreign Markets," *1998 Interbike Directory* (Laguna Beach, CA: Miller-Freeman, 1998).

2. Ibid.

3. Worldwatch calculation based on data in *1998 Interbike Directory* (Laguna Beach, CA: Miller-Freeman, 1998).

4. Ibid.

5. "Focus on Foreign Markets," op. cit. note 1.

6. Worldwatch calculation based on data in *1998 Interbike Directory*, op. cit. note 3.

7. Energy use from Marcia D. Lowe, *The Bicycle: Vehicle for a Small Planet*, Worldwatch Paper 90 (Washington, DC: Worldwatch Institute, September 1989); cost is a Worldwatch calculation based on a purchase price of $500 for a bicycle and $15,000–25,000 for a car.

8. Anton G. Welleman, Cees J. Louisse, and Dirk M. Ligtermoet, "Theme Paper 5: Bicycles in Cities," in Stephen Stares and Liu Zhi, eds., *China's Urban Transport Development Strategy; Proceedings of a Symposium in Beijing, November 8–10 1995*, World Bank Discussion Paper no. 352 (Washington, DC: World Bank, 1996).

9. Frank Jamerson, Electric Battery Bicycle Company, Naples, FL, discussion with author, 19 January 1998.

10. Ibid.

11. "ZAP Electric Bikes Have Bright Future in China," *Electric Vehicles Energy Network Online Today*, 1 May 1997; "ZAP Expanding Into Overseas Markets," *Bicycle Retailer and Industry News*, 1 August 1997; Ben Edwards, "Electric Bikes: Are They a Promising Niche for Retailers?" *Bicycle Retailer and Industry News*, 1 September 1997.

12. Frank Jamerson, "Electric Bikes Worldwide 96: China Exhibition Shanghai/Interbike Anaheim," booklet (Naples, FL: Electric Battery Bicycle Company, 20 January 1997).

13. Ben Edwards, "Electric Bike Firm Ready to Ship, Retail, and Roll," *Bicycle Retailer and Industry News*, 1 August 1997.

14. "ZAP Electric Bikes Have Bright Future in China," op. cit. note 11.

15. John Pucher, "Bicycling Boom in Germany: A Revival Engineered by Public Policy," *Transportation Quarterly*, Fall 1997.

16. Ibid.

17. Ibid.

18. Ibid.

19. Ibid.

20. Susan Wallis, "La Route Verte: 3000 Canadian Kilometers for Cyclist," *The Bicycle News Agency*, < http://webhotel.uni-c.dk/dcf/agency/2497.htm >, viewed 22 December 1997.

21. Welleman, Louisse, and Ligtermoet, op. cit. note 8.

SATELLITE LAUNCHES REBOUND (pages 94–95)

1. Jos Heyman, *Spacecraft Tables 1957–1990* (San Diego, CA: Univelt, 1991); Jos Heyman *Spacecraft Tables 1957–1995*, computer diskette, Univelt, San Diego, CA, 1996; update for 1996 and 1997 from Jos Heyman, Astronautical Society of Western Australia, letters to author, 27 November 1997 and 11 February 1998.

2. The total does not include crewed, interplane-

tary, or lunar spacecraft.

3. Arthur C. Clarke, "Extra-Terrestrial Relays: Can Rocket Stations Give Worldwide Radio Coverage?" *Wireless World*, October 1945, reprinted in Arthur C. Clarke, *How the World Was One* (New York: Bantam Books, 1992).

4. Anthony Michaelis, *From Semaphore to Satellite* (Geneva: International Telecommunication Union, 1965).

5. Heyman, *Spacecraft Tables 1957–1990*, op. cit. note 1.

6. Ibid.; Heyman, letter to author, op. cit. note 1.

7. Heyman, letter to author, op. cit. note 1.

8. Heyman, *Spacecraft Tables 1957–1990*, op. cit. note 1.

9. Heyman, letter to author, op. cit. note 1.

10. Heather E. Hudson, *Communication Satellites: Their Development and Impact* (New York: The Free Press, 1990); Intelsat, "About Intelsat," 3 November 1997, < http://www.intelsat.int/cmc/ info/intelsat.htm >, viewed 16 January 1998.

11. John Bray, *The Communications Miracle: The Telecommunication Pioneers from Morse to the Information Superhighway* (London: Plenum Press, 1995).

12. Mike May, "High Hopes for Low Satellites," *Technology Review*, October 1997; Eric Schine et al., "The Satellite Biz Blasts Off," *Business Week*, 27 January 1997.

13. Mike Mills, "Orbit Wars," *Washington Post Magazine*, 3 August 1997.

14. Schine et al., op. cit. note 12.

15. This venture is backed by cellular phone pioneer Craig McGaw, Microsoft Chairman Bill Gates, and the Boeing Company; Kristi Coale, "Teledesic Mounts Lead in New Space Race," *Wired*, 14 October 1997; Teledesic Corporation, "Boeing to Build Teledesic's Internet-In-The-Sky," press release, Seattle, WA, 29 April 1997.

16. Jonathan Ball et al., "Positioning and Navigation with GPS," < http://www.comlinks.com/ satcom/pangps.htm >, viewed 11 January 1998.

17. Kevin Corbley, "Remote Sensing Skies Filling with Satellite Plans," *EOM* (Earth Observation Magazine), October 1996; "Spy-Quality Satellite Ready to Sell Images," *Reuters*, 25 December 1997.

18. Consortium for International Earth Science Information Network (CIESIN),"The Use of Satellite Remote Sensing to Study the Human Dimensions of Global Environmental Change," < http://www.ciesin.org/TG/RS/RS-home. html>, viewed 17 July 1997; William Acevedo, Timothy Foresman, and Janis Buchanan,

"Human Transformation Processes: Origins and Philosophy of a Temporal Database," *Sistema Terra: Remote Sensing and the Earth*, December 1996.

19. William K. Stevens, "NASA Readies a 'Mission to Planet Earth,'" *New York Times*, 17 February 1998.

20. Tony Reichhardt, "Environmental GIS: The World in a Computer," *Environmental Science and Technology*, vol. 30, no. 8, 1996.

21. "Newest Farm Implements: Satellites," *Environmental News Network*, 29 December 1997; S.J. O'Connor et al., "The Use of Low-Cost Remote Sensing and GIS for Identifying and Monitoring the Environmental Factors Associated with Vector-Borne Disease Transmission," in Don de Savigny and Pardu Wijeyaratne, International Development Research Centre, eds., *GIS for Health and the Environment* (Ottawa, Canada: Renouf Publishing, 1995); Dana Mackenzie, "Ocean Floor Is Laid Bare by New Satellite Data," and Walter H.F. Smith and David T. Sandwell, "Global Sea Floor Topography from Satellite Altimetry and Ship Depth Soundings," both in *Science*, 26 September 1997.

22. Kristi Coale, "Small Satellites Push for Elbow Room," *Wired*, 14 October 1997; Craig Bicknell, "Welcome to the Celestial Junkyard," *Wired*, 17 October 1997.

TELEPHONE NETWORK EXPANDS
(pages 96–97)

1. International Telecommunication Union (ITU), *World Telecommunication Indicators on Diskette* (Geneva: 1996); 1996 from ITU, *Challenges to the Network: Telecoms and the Internet* (Geneva: September 1997). The ITU collects information on telephone "main lines." These can be either exclusive or shared, so the number of telephone subscribers exceeds the number of lines. They can be used not only for telephone sets but also for fax machines or personal computers.

2. ITU, *Indicators on Diskette*, op. cit. note 1; ITU, *Challenges to the Network*, op. cit. note 1.

3. U.S. Bureau of the Census, *International Data Base*, electronic database, Suitland, MD, updated 10 October 1997; ITU, *Indicators on Diskette*, op. cit. note 1; ITU, *Challenges to the Network*, op. cit. note 1.

4. Colin Cherry, "The Telephone System: Creator

of Mobility and Social Change," in Ithiel de Sola Pool, ed., *The Social Impact of the Telephone* (Cambridge, MA: The MIT Press, 1977).

5. John R. Pierce, "The Telephone and Society in the Past 100 Years," in Pool, op. cit. note 4; Frances Cairncross, *The Death of Distance: How the Communications Revolution Will Change Our Lives* (Boston, MA: Harvard Business School Press, 1997); Wilson Dizard Jr., *Meganet: How the Global Communications Network Will Connect Everyone on Earth* (Boulder, CO: Westview Press, 1997).

6. Pool, op. cit. note 4; Heather E. Hudson, *When Telephones Reach the Village: The Role of Telecommunications in Rural Development* (Norwood, NJ: Ablex, 1984).

7. Gregory Staple, "The Next Generation of Undersea Mega-Cables," in Gregory Staple, ed., *Telegeography 1997/98: Global Telecommunications Traffic Statistics and Commentary* (Washington, DC: Telegeography, Inc., 1997); Jeff Hecht, "Add Oxygen," *New Scientist*, 3 January 1998; ITU, *Indicators on Diskette*, op. cit. note 1.

8. ITU, *Indicators on Diskette*, op. cit. note 1; Organisation for Economic Cooperation and Development, *Communications Outlook 1997* (Paris: 1997).

9. ITU, *Indicators on Diskette*, op. cit. note 1.

10. Ibid.

11. J. Warren Stehman, *The Financial History of the American Telephone and Telegraph Company* (Boston, MA: Houghton Mifflin Co., The Riverside Press, 1925).

12. World Trade Organization, "Ruggiero Congratulates Governments on Landmark Telecommunications Agreement," press release (Geneva: 17 February 1997); Alex Arena, "The WTO Telecommunications Agreement: Some Personal Reflections," in Staple, op. cit. note 7.

13. Douglas P.E. Smith, *Convergence: Telephones, Mobile Phones and the Internet* (New York: Salomon Brothers, 5 September 1997).

14. ITU, *Indicators on Diskette*, op. cit. note 1; ITU, *Challenges to the Network*, op. cit. note 1.

15. Rogati Kayani and Andrew Dymond, *Options for Rural Telecommunications Development* (Washington, DC: World Bank, 1997).

16. Rachel Schwartz, *Wireless Communications in Developing Countries: Cellular and Satellite Systems* (Boston, MA: Artech House, 1996); Lisa Sykes, "Hanging on for the Phone," *New Scientist*, 14 June 1997; S. Kamaluddin, "Calling Countryfolk," *Far Eastern Economic Review*, 24

April 1997; N. Vasuki Rao, "Bangladeshi Officials Pitch Nation as Perfect for Telecom Investment," *Journal of Commerce*, 9 October 1997.

17. ITU, *Asia-Pacific Telecommunication Indicators: New Telecommunication Operators* (Geneva: 1997).

18. ITU, *Challenge to the Network*, op. cit. note 1; Larry Armstrong, Neal Sandler, and Peter Elstrom, "You're Coming Over Loud—And Almost Clear," *Business Week*, 27 October 1997.

19. Pool, op. cit. note 4.

20. Jean Gottman, "Megalopolois and Antipolis: The Telephone and the Structure of the City," and J. Alan Moyer, "Urban Growth and the Telephone: Some Relationships at the Turn of the Century," both in Pool, op. cit. note 4; Patricia Mokhtarian, "Now That Travel Can be Virtual, Will Congestion Virtually Disappear?" *Scientific American*, October 1997.

21. Ithiel de Sola Pool, *Technologies Without Boundaries: On Telecommunications in a Global Age* (Cambridge, MA: Harvard University, 1990).

22. Ibid.; ITU, *Telecommunication and the Environment: The Way to Sustainable Development*, <http://www.itu.int/PPI/projects/environ/environ.html>, viewed 29 September 1997.

INTERNET USE GROWS EXPONENTIALLY (pages 98–99)

1. International Telecommunication Union (ITU), *Challenges to the Network: Telecoms and the Internet* (Geneva: September 1997).

2. Host computers from Network Wizards, "Internet Domain Surveys, 1981–1998," <http://www.nw.com>, viewed 6 February 1998; users from Nua Ltd., "Internet Surveys, November 1997 and January 1998," <http://www.nua.ie/>, viewed 13 November 1997 and 1 February 1998. On average, a host computer serves between three and six users, but this number can vary.

3. ITU, op. cit. note 1. For instance, America Online has a million hosts and 10 million users; Mark Lottor, Network Wizards, California, discussion with author, 12 February 1998; Nicholas Denton, "AOL: US Online Service Hits the Big Time," *Financial Times*, 12 January 1998.

4. Frances Cairncross, *The Death of Distance: How the Communications Revolution Will Change Our*

Lives (Boston, MA: Harvard Business School Press, 1997); Wilson Dizard Jr., *Meganet: How the Global Communications Network Will Connect Everyone on Earth* (Boulder, CO: Westview Press, 1997); ITU, op. cit. note 1.

5. Nua, op. cit. note 2. Figures 2 and 3 based on Network Wizards, op. cit. note 2, on ITU, op. cit. note 1, on ITU, *World Telecommunications Indictors on Diskette* (Geneva: 1996), on Network Solutions, Inc., "Network Solutions Reports Record Growth of International Domain Name Registrations," press release (Herndon, VA: 4 February 1998), and on United Nations Population Fund (UNFPA), *The State of World Population* (New York: various years). Additional methodology from Laura Mannisto, ITU, Geneva, e-mails to and discussions with author, 20 and 23 February 1998.

6. Nua, op. cit. note 2; U.S. figure from IntelliQuest, "Latest IntelliQuest Survey Reports 62 Million American Adults Access The Internet/Online Services," press release (Austin, TX: 5 February 1998). Estimates of the number of Internet users vary significantly. For instance, estimates of the U.S. online population in 1997 range from 36 million (FIND/SVP, *1997 American Internet User Survey* (New York: 1997)) to 62 million (Intelliquest, op. cit. this note); for the global population online, the numbers range from 57 million (John S. Quarterman, Matrix Information and Directory Services, "1997 Users and Hosts of the Internet and the Matrix," < http://www.mids.org/press/ >, January 1997) to 107 million (Nua, op. cit. note 2). The host computer approach has a much smaller margin of variability and is hence a more accurate indicator of Internet growth.

7. Nua, op. cit. note 2; population from UNFPA, op. cit. note 5.

8. Africa based on Network Wizards, op. cit. note 2, and on UNFPA, op. cit. note 5; Finland based on ibid, on Mannisto, op. cit. note 5, and on Youssef M. Ibrahim, "As Most Wired Nation, Finland Has Jump on 21st Century," *New York Times*, 20 January 1997.

9. Dizard, op. cit. note 4; Barbara F. Grimes, ed., *Ethnologue: Languages of the World*, 13th ed. (Dallas, TX: Summer Institute of Linguistics, Inc., 1996).

10. ITU, op. cit. note 1.

11. Based on ibid., on Network Wizards, op. cit. note 1, and on UNFPA, op. cit. note 5.

12. China from "China Prepares for Internet," *USA Today*, 17 November 1997, and from "China and the Internet: The Great Wall Wired," *The Economist*, 7 February 1998; India from "1.5 Million Internet Users in India by 2000," *Reuters*, 8 July 1997; "India Opens Up to Private ISPs," *Wired News*, 16 September 1997.

13. Howard French, "In Africa, the Reality of Technology Falls Short," *New York Times*, 26 January 1998.

14. Dewang Mehta, Executive Director, National Association of Software and Service Companies, India, e-mail to author, 14 February 1998; Allen R. Myerson, "Need Software Programmers? Surf Abroad," *New York Times*, 18 January 1998; John Stremlau, "Dateline Bangalore: Third World Technopolis," *Foreign Policy*, Spring 1996.

15. Guillermo Delgado-P. and Marc Becker, "Latin America: The Internet and Indigenous Texts," *Cultural Survival Quarterly*, Winter 1998; Albert Gabrial, "Assyrians: "3,000 Years of History, Yet the Internet is Our Only Home," *Cultural Survival Quarterly*, Winter 1998; Aanta Forsgren, "Use of Internet Communication Among the Sami People," *Cultural Survival Quarterly*, Winter 1998.

16. Mary Oakes Smith, "Results on the Ground," HDDFLASH online newsletter, Human Development Department, World Bank, December 1997; David Wright and Leonid Androuchko, "Telemedicine and Developing Countries," *Journal of Telemedicine and Telecare*, vol. 2, no. 2, 1996; Dr. James Nelson, International TeleMedicine Associates, Inc., Scripps Medical Center, California, discussion with author, 23 February 1998.

17. Paul Constance, "Going Digital," *IDB America* (magazine of the Inter-American Development Bank), November 1997.

18. Heather Bourbeau, "Net Gains for the Rural Poor," *Financial Times*, 12 August 1997.

19. Matthew McAllester, "Democracy of Internet Threatens Some Nations: In Burma, Net Access Can Be a Path to Prison. But Some Take the Risk," *Philadelphia Inquirer*, 20 November 1997; "Unstoppable Internet Will Defy Controls," *Reuters' European Business Report*, 16 January 1997; "Why the Net Should Grow Up," *The Economist*, 19 October 1996.

20. Arthur C. Clarke quoted in Cairncross, op. cit. note 4.

21. Jane Holtz Kay, *Asphalt Nation: How the Automobile Took Over America and How We Can Take It Back* (New York: Crown Publishers, 1997); James J. Flink, *The Car Culture* (Cambridge, MA: The MIT Press, 1975).

22. Paul Taylor, "Internet Users 'Likely to Reach 500m by 2000'," *Financial Times*, 13 May 1996, and based on data supplied by Mannisto, op. cit. note 5.

POPULATION GROWTH CONTINUES (pages 102–03)

1. U.S. Bureau of the Census, *International Data Base*, electronic database, Suitland, MD, updated 10 October 1997.
2. United Nations, *World Population Prospects: The 1996 Revision* (New York: draft, 24 October 1996).
3. Ibid.
4. Bureau of the Census, op. cit. note 1.
5. Ibid.
6. Ibid.
7. Macro International, *Bangladesh Demographic and Health Survey, 1996–97*, Preliminary Report (Calverton, MD: June 1997).
8. Carl Haub, Demographer, Population Reference Bureau, Washington, DC, discussion with author, 23 December 1997; Office of the Registrar General, India, *Registrar General's News Letter*, January–June 1997; United Nations, op. cit. note 2.
9. United Nations, op. cit. note 2.
10. Ibid.
11. Ibid.
12. Ibid.
13. Ibid.
14. Ibid.; Bureau of the Census, op. cit. note 1.
15. "The ICPD Programme of Action," *Populi*, October 1994.
16. "Zambia: New Family Planning Policy Applauded," *Comtex Newswire*, 6 October 1997.
17. Barbara Shane, *Family Planning Saves Lives* (Washington, DC: Population Reference Bureau, January 1997).
18. United Nations Population Fund (UNFPA), "Meeting The Goals of The ICPD: Consequences of Resource Shortfalls up to the Year 2000," paper presented to the Executive Board of the U.N. Development Programme and the UNFPA, New York, 12–23 May 1997.
19. Jörn Brömmelhörster, "Editorial," *Bonn International Center for Conversion's On-line MILEX Newsletter: News, Discussions, and Networking*, <http://www.bicc.uni-bonn.de/milex>, viewed 24 September 1997.
20. UNFPA, op. cit. note 19.

21. Ibid.
22. Michael Vlassoff, UNFPA, New York, discussion with author, 28 October 1997.
23. Ibid.
24. Steven A. Holmes, "U.S. Aid to World Birth-Control Efforts Faces Cuts," *New York Times*, 12 September 1996; Alan Fram, "GOP Compromises, House OKs Aid Bill," *Associated Press*, 13 November 1997.

REFUGEE FLOWS DROP STEEPLY (pages 104–05)

1. U.N. High Commissioner for Refugees (UNHCR), *The State of the World's Refugees 1997–1998* (New York: Oxford University Press, 1997).
2. Ibid.
3. Ibid.
4. Ibid.
5. Ibid.
6. Ibid.
7. Ibid.
8. Ibid.
9. Ibid.
10. Ibid.
11. Ibid.
12. Ibid.
13. Frances Williams, "More Refugees Have Nowhere to Run," *Financial Times*, 9 December 1997.
14. UNHCR, op. cit. note 1.
15. Ibid.
16. "U.N. Reports Rise in Refugees Rate," *Associated Press*, 8 December 1997.
17. U.S. Committee for Refugees, *World Refugee Survey 1997* (Washington, DC: 1997); Williams, op. cit. note 13.
18. "U.N. Reports Rise," op. cit. note 16.
19. Geoff Kitney, "Rich Countries Threatened by Tide of the Poor," *Sydney Morning Herald*, 10 January 1998.
20. "U.N. Reports Rise," op. cit. note 16.
21. Curtis Runyan, "No Asylum for Refugees," *World Watch*, November/December 1997.
22. "Germany's Forced Return of Bosnians," *The Forced Migration Monitor* (Open Society Institute, New York), September 1997.
23. Runyan, op. cit. note 21; U.S. Committee for Refugees, op. cit. note 17.
24. Runyan, op. cit. note 21; U.S. Committee for Refugees, op. cit. note 17.

25. Runyan, op. cit. note 21; U.S. Committee for Refugees, op. cit. note 17.

HIV/AIDS PANDEMIC FAR FROM OVER (pages 106–07)

1. Joint United Nations Programme on HIV/AIDS (UNAIDS), *Report on the Global HIV/AIDS Epidemic* (Geneva: December 1997).
2. Ibid.
3. AIDS cases in 1997 from Daniel Tarantola, François-Xavier Bagnoud Center for Health and Human Rights, Harvard School of Public Health, Cambridge, MA, discussion with author, 13 February 1998; UNAIDS, op. cit. note 1.
4. UNAIDS, op. cit. note 1.
5. Ibid.
6. Ibid.
7. Monitoring the AIDS Pandemic Network (MAP), "The Status and Trends of the HIV/AIDS/STD Epidemics in Sub-Saharan Africa," Official Satellite Symposium of the 10th International Conference on STD and AIDS in Africa, Abidjan, Côte D'Ivoire, 3–4 December 1997.
8. UNAIDS, op. cit. note 1.
9. MAP, op. cit. note 7.
10. Ibid.
11. Lawrence K. Altman, "AIDS Surge is Forecast for China, India and Eastern Europe," *New York Times*, 4 November 1997.
12. MAP, "The Status and Trends of the HIV/AIDS/STD Epidemics in Asia and the Pacific," prepared for the 4th International Conference on AIDS in Asia and the Pacific, Manila, Philippines, 25–29 October 1997.
13. Ibid.
14. Jonathan Mann and Daniel Tarantola, eds., *AIDS in the World II* (New York: Oxford University Press, 1996).
15. U.S. Centers for Disease Control and Prevention, "HIV/AIDS Surveillance Report, June 1997," Midyear Edition, vol. 9, no. 1, 1997.
16. UNAIDS, op. cit. note 1.
17. Peter Lamptey, "HIV/AIDS Prevention for Youth: The Best Hope for Controlling the Epidemic," issued for World Aids Day 1997 (Arlington, VA: Family Health International, 1 December 1997).
18. Ibid.
19. Ibid.
20. Ibid.
21. Lamptey, op. cit. note 17.
22. UNAIDS, op. cit. note 1.
23. Ibid.; MAP, op. cit. note 7; MAP, op. cit. note 12.
24. World Bank, *Confronting AIDS: Public Priorities in a Global Epidemic* (New York: Oxford University Press, 1997).
25. Feachem quote from Nalia Sattar, "HIV: The Poverty Virus Coming Soon to a Family Near You," *HIMAL South Asia*, May 1996.
26. World Bank , op. cit. note 25.
27. Peter Lamptey and Willard Cates, "Ounce of Prevention Worth a Million Lives," *Network* (Family Health International, Arlington, VA), Winter 1997.

URBAN AREAS SWELL (pages 108–09)

1. United Nations, *World Urbanization Prospects: The 1996 Revision* (New York: draft, 1 May 1997).
2. Ibid.
3. United Nations Population Fund, *Population, Resources and the Environment: The Critical Challenges* (New York: October 1991).
4. United Nations, op. cit. note 1.
5. Ibid.; The Population Institute, "50% of Population To Live in Cities," *The Population Institute Online Newsletter*, November–December 1995, <http://www.webcreations.com/POPLINE>, viewed 2 December 1997.
6. United Nations, op. cit. note 1.
7. Andrew Lees, *Cities Perceived: Urban Society in European and American Thought: 1820–1940* (New York: Columbia University Press, 1985).
8. United Nations, op. cit. note 1.
9. Ibid.
10. Ibid.
11. Ibid.
12. Ibid.
13. Ibid.; Lees, op. cit. note 7.
14. United Nations, op. cit. note 1.
15. Ibid.
16. Ibid.
17. Ibid.; "How The Cities Grow," *People & The Planet*, vol. 5, no. 2, 1996.
18. U.N. Development Programme, *Human Development Report 1997* (New York: Oxford University Press, 1997); Martin Brockerhoff and Ellen Brennan, *The Poverty of Cities in the Developing World* (New York: The Population Council, 1997).
19. Brockerhoff and Brennan, op. cit. note 18.

20. United Nations, op. cit. note 1.
21. "How The Cities Grow," op. cit. note 17.
22. Tata Institute of Fundamental Research, "The Bombay Metropolitan Region," < http://theory.tifr.res.in/bombay/amenities >, updated May 1997, viewed 2 December 1997.
23. Ibid.
24. Asian Development Bank, *Annual Report 1996* (Singapore: 1996).

CIGARETTE PRODUCTION HITS ALL-TIME HIGH (pages 110–11)

1. U.S. Department of Agriculture (USDA), Foreign Agricultural Service (FAS), *World Cigarette Database,* electronic database, Washington, DC, December 1997.
2. Ibid.; U.S. Bureau of the Census, *International Data Base,* electronic database, Suitland, MD, updated 10 October 1997.
3. USDA, op. cit. note 1.
4. Ibid.
5. Ibid.; USDA, FAS, "Tobacco Annual Report for Japan," Attache Report, May 1997.
6. USDA, op. cit. note 1.
7. Ibid.
8. Ibid.; USDA, FAS, "Tobacco Annual Report for Philippines," Attache Report, May 1997.
9. USDA, op. cit. note 1.
10. Ibid.
11. USDA, FAS, "Tobacco Annual Report for Bulgaria," Attache Report, May 1997; Market Tracking International Ltd., *World Tobacco File, 1996* (London: International Trade Publications Ltd., 1996).
12. USDA, op. cit. note 1.
13. Ibid.
14. Solomon Brothers, Tobacco Research Group, unpublished printout, New York, 30 January 1998.
15. World Health Organization (WHO), *Investing in Health Research and Development*, Report of the Ad Hoc Committee on Health Research Relating to Future Intervention Options Convened Under the Auspices of the WHO (Geneva: 1996).
16. Action on Smoking and Health, *ASH Smoking and Health Review*, November-December 1997.
17. A.K. Hackshaw, M. Law, and N.J. Wald, "The Accumulated Evidence on Lung Cancer and Environmental Tobacco Smoke," and "Environmental Tobacco Smoke Exposure and Ischaemic Heart Disease: An Evaluation of the Evidence,"
British Medical Journal, 18 October 1997; Australian National Health and Medical Research Council, *The Health Effects of Passive Smoking* (Canberra, Australia: Australian Government Publishing Service, November 1997).
18. WHO, "Tobacco Epidemic: Health Dimensions," Fact Sheet No. 154 (Geneva: May 1997).
19. Barry Meier, "Tobacco Firms Fire Up Smoking Campaigns in Third World," *New York Times*, 19 January 1998.
20. WHO, op. cit. note 18.
21. WHO, *Tobacco Alert*, "Advisory Kit for World No-Tobacco Day, 31 May 1997" (Geneva: November 1996); "Fireworks Follow Smoke," *Down To Earth*, 30 September 1997.
22. "UNICEF Chief Calls for Global Curbs on Tobacco," press release (New York: 1 May 1997).

MILITARY EXPENDITURES CONTINUE TO DECLINE (pages 114–15)

1. These figures are Worldwatch estimates based on the following sources: Rita Tullberg, "World Military Expenditure," *Bulletin of Peace Proposals*, no. 3–4, 1986; U.S. Arms Control and Disarmament Agency (ACDA), *World Military Expenditures and Arms Transfers 1996* (Washington, DC: U.S. Government Printing Office, July 1997); Bonn International Center for Conversion (BICC), *Conversion Survey 1997. Global Disarmament and Disposal of Surplus Weapons* (New York: Oxford University Press, 1997); International Institute for Strategic Studies (IISS), *The Military Balance 1997/98* (Oxford: Oxford University Press, October 1997).
2. Calculated from gross world product data in Lester R. Brown, "World Economy Expands Faster," in Lester R. Brown, Michael Renner, and Christopher Flavin, *Vital Signs 1997* (New York: W.W. Norton & Company, 1997).
3. Paul George, Agnès Courades Allebeck, and Eva-maria Loose-Weintraub, "Military Expenditures," in Stockholm International Peace Research Institute (SIPRI), *SIPRI Yearbook 1997: Armaments, Disarmament and International Security* (New York: Oxford University Press, 1997).
4. ACDA, op. cit. note 1; IISS, op. cit. note 1; BICC, op. cit. note 1. BICC data are partially derived from ACDA, but "in cases in which sufficient support for deviation from ACDA data

existed," BICC substituted data derived from other sources, including SIPRI, the International Monetary Fund, NATO (for NATO member states), and press clippings.

5. ACDA, op. cit. note 1.
6. Ibid.
7. IISS, op. cit. note 1.
8. BICC, op. cit. note 1.
9. U.S. Department of Defense, Office of the Undersecretary of Defense (Comptroller), *National Defense Budget Estimates for FY 1997* (Springfield, VA: National Technical Information Service, April 1996), Table 7–2. This document expresses outlays in terms of 1987 dollars; here, they are given in 1995 dollars, using deflators reported in Ibid., Table 5–8.
10. Calculated from BICC, op. cit. note 1. BICC reports expenditure data in 1993 dollars; here, the data are expressed in 1995 dollars, using deflators reported in U.S. Department of Defense, op. cit. note 9.
11. BICC, op. cit. note 1.
12. Ibid.
13. Ibid.
14. Ibid.
15. "Economy Dents Thai Defence," *Jane's Defense Weekly*, 10 December 1997; Steven Lee Myers, "Asian Turmoil Putting Brakes On Arms Race," *New York Times*, 13 January 1998.
16. Calculated from BICC, op. cit. note 1.
17. Ibid.
18. Ibid.

ARMED CONFLICTS DIMINISH
(pages 116–17)

1. Klaus Jürgen Gantzel and Torsten Schwinghammer, *Die Kriege nach dem Zweiten Weltkrieg 1945 bis 1992. Daten und Tendenzen* (Münster and Hamburg: Lit Verlag, 1995); Dietrich Jung, Klaus Schlichte, and Jens Siegelberg, *Das Kriegsgeschehen 1995. Daten und Tendenzen der Kriege und bewaffneten Konflikte im Jahr 1995* (Bonn: Stiftung Entwicklung und Frieden, 1996); Thomas Rabehl, Arbeitsgemeinschaft Kriegsursachenforschung (AKUF), Institute for Political Science, University of Hamburg, e-mail to author, 8 January 1998.
2. Margareta Sollenberg, ed., *States in Armed Conflict 1996*, Report No. 46 (Uppsala, Sweden: Uppsala University, Department of Peace and Conflict Research, July 1997); Margareta

Sollenberg, Uppsala Conflict Data Project, Department of Peace and Conflict Research, Uppsala University, Sweden, e-mail to author, 16 January 1998. The 1997 figure is preliminary.
3. Sollenberg, *States in Armed Conflict 1996*, op. cit. note 2.
4. Ibid.
5. Ibid.
6. UNICEF, *The State of the World's Children 1996* (New York: Oxford University Press, 1996).
7. Rachel Brett and Margaret McCallin, *Children: The Invisible Soldiers* (Växjö, Sweden: Rädda Barnen [Swedish Save the Children], 1996).
8. Project Ploughshares, *Armed Conflicts Report 1996* (Waterloo, Canada: Institute of Peace and Conflict Studies, Conrad Grebel College, 1996).
9. Sollenberg, *States in Armed Conflict 1996*, op. cit. note 2.
10. Ibid.
11. Ibid.
12. Ibid.
13. Ibid.
14. Ibid.
15. Ibid.
16. Ibid.
17. Ibid.
18. Ibid.
19. Ibid.
20. Worldwatch calculation, based on Ruth Leger Sivard, *World Military and Social Expenditures 1996* (Washington, DC: World Priorities, 1996).
21. Ibid. Data are presented here in five-year periods because there is no reliable information on the year-by-year death toll. The five-year data have been calculated on the basis of the total number of persons killed in each conflict. Where wars have straddled two or more five-year periods, the total number of deaths was divided on a proportional basis.
22. Sivard, op. cit. note 20.
23. Milton Leitenberg, *Humanitarian Intervention and Other International Initiatives to Enforce Peace* (College Park, MD: Center for International and Security Studies at Maryland, University of Maryland, February 1993). Most of the difference between the Sivard and Leitenberg data arises from Leitenberg's extraordinarily high figures for revolutionary violence within China from the 1940s to the 1970s.
24. Steven Hansch, "An Explosion of Complex Humanitarian Emergencies," *Hunger Notes*, Winter 1996; Sivard, op. cit. note 20.

U.N. PEACEKEEPING CONTRACTS FURTHER (pages 118–19)

1. Data for 1947–96 are documented in Michael Renner, "U.N. Peacekeeping Declines Sharply," in Lester R. Brown, Michael Renner, and Christopher Flavin, *Vital Signs 1997* (New York: W.W. Norton & Company, 1997); figure for 1997 is a Worldwatch estimate based on assessment figures in "Outstanding Contributions to the Regular Budget, International Tribunals and Peace-Keeping Operations as of 31 December 1997," Office of the Spokesman for the Secretary-General, United Nations, New York, and on "Peacekeeping Redux ...But Still Indispensible," <http://www.un.org/Depts/dpko/yir97/peacekp.htm>, viewed 13 March 1998.
2. Calculated from data reported in Peace-keeping Data Tables on the Council, Global Policy Forum, <http://www.globalpolicy.org/security/>, viewed 21 October 1997.
3. Suzanne Daley, "Tensions Threaten Angola's 3-Year Peace," *New York Times*, 1 August 1997; U.N. Security Council Resolution 1149, New York, 27 January 1998.
4. "U.N. Extends Monitoring of Police in Haiti," *New York Times*, 29 November 1997; Larry Rohter, "U.N. Troops to Leave Haiti as Feeble as They Found It," *New York Times*, 4 December 1997; "Haiti—UNTMIH" and "Croatia—UNTAES," listed under Current Missions at U.N. Department of Peacekeeping Operations (DPKO) Web site, <http://www.un.org/Depts/dpko/>, viewed 21 October 1997.
5. "Liberia—UNOMIL" and "Guatemala—MINUGUA," Current Missions, U.N. DPKO Web site, op. cit. note 4.
6. "Croatia—UNTAES," "Croatia—UNMOP," and "Bosnia and Herzegovina—UNMIBH," Current Missions, DPKO Web site, op. cit. note 4; troop size calculated from data in "Size of Individual Peacekeeping Operations by Month: 1997," Peacekeeping Data Tables, op. cit. note 2.
7. U.N. Security Council Resolution 1145, New York, 19 December 1997.
8. "Size of Individual Peacekeeping Operations by Month: 1997," op. cit. note 6.
9. "Current Peacekeeping Operations" and "Completed Peacekeeping Operations," U.N. DPKO Web site, op. cit. note 4.
10. Ibid.
11. Estanislao Angel Zawels, "Specificity in Peacekeeping Operation Mandates: The Evolution of Security Council Methods of Work," in Estanislao Angel Zawels et al., *Managing Arms in Peace Processes: The Issues*, United Nations Institute for Disarmament Research, Disarmament and Conflict Resolution Project (New York: United Nations, 1996); "Changing Patterns in the Use of the Veto in the Security Council," Data Tables on the Council, op. cit. note 2; "List of Matters Considered/Actions Taken by the Security Council in 1997," United Nations, <http://www.un.org/Depts/dhl/resguide/>, updated 19 January 1998.
12. Calculated from Zawels, op. cit. note 11, from Trevor Findlay, "Armed Conflict Prevention, Management and Resolution," in Stockholm International Peace Research Institute, *SIPRI Yearbook 1996: Armaments, Disarmament and International Security* (New York: Oxford University Press, 1996), from "Changing Patterns in the Use of the Veto," op. cit. note 11, and from "List of Matters Considered," op. cit. note 11.
13. Calculated from Zawels, op. cit. note 11, from Findlay, op. cit. note 12, from "Changing Patterns in the Use of the Veto," op. cit. note 11, and from "List of Matters Considered," op. cit. note 11. This excludes 43 vetoes that were used to block nominees for U.N. Secretary-General.
14. Past trend from Renner, op. cit. note 1; 1997 figure from "Outstanding Contributions," op. cit. note 1.
15. For details on congressional action, see *Washington Weekly Report* (United Nations Association of the United States), particularly "The Year in Review: US Legislation and the UN System," Special Issue, 12 December 1997.
16. "US vs. Total Debt to the UN: 1997," in Tables and Charts, Global Policy Forum, <http://www.globalpolicy.org/finance/>, viewed 21 October 1997.
17. James Bennet, "Clinton Calls for Keeping Troops in Bosnia with No New Exit Date," *New York Times*, 19 December 1997.

FOREST DECLINE CONTINUES (pages 124–25)

1. Dirk Bryant, Daniel Nielsen, and Laura Tangley, *The Last Frontier Forests: Ecosystems and Economies on the Edge* (Washington, DC: World Resources Institute, 1997).
2. U.N. Food and Agriculture Organization (FAO), *State of the World's Forests 1997* (Oxford, U.K.: 1997).

3. Ibid.
4. Bryant, Nielson, and Tangley, op. cit. note 1.
5. Ibid.
6. Ibid.
7. Ibid.
8. Nigel Dudley, Jean-Paul Jeanrenaud, and Francis Sullivan, *Bad Harvest? The Timber Trade and the Degradation of the World's Forests* (London: Earthscan Publications Ltd., 1995).
9. FAO, op. cit. note 2.
10. Ibid.
11. Ibid.
12. Ibid.
13. Tropical dry forests from Anil Agarwal, "Dark Truths and Lost Woods," *Down to Earth* (India), 15 June 1997; mangrove forests from Solon Barraclough and Andrea Finger-Stich, *Some Ecological and Social Implications of Commercial Shrimp Farming in Asia*, Discussion Paper 74 (Geneva: United Nations Research Institute for Social Development, March 1996); temperate rainforests in North America from Dominick DellaSala et al., "Protection and Independent Certification: A Shared Vision for North America's Diverse Forests," mapping analysis (Washington, DC: World Wildlife Fund–US and World Wildlife Fund–Canada, 1997), and from Conservation International, Ecotrust, and Pacific GIS, "Coastal Temperate Rain Forests of North America," map (Washington, DC, and Portland, OR: 1995).
14. Bryant, Nielsen, and Tangley, op. cit. note 1; Reed Noss, E.T. LaRoe III, and J.M. Scott, *Endangered Systems of the United States: A Preliminary Assessment of Loss and Degradation* (Washington, DC: U.S. Department of the Interior, National Biological Service., 1995); DellaSala et al., op. cit. note 13.
15. Dudley, Jeanrenaud, and Sullivan, op. cit. note 8.
16. FAO, op. cit. note 2. FAO counts palm oil plantations as agricultural area. If they were included under forest plantation extent, the figure would be much higher; Dudley, Jeanrenaud, and Sullivan, op. cit. note 8.
17. FAO, op. cit. note 2.
18. U.N. Economic Commission for Europe, International Co-operative Programme on Assessment and Monitoring of Air Pollution Effects on Forests, "Forest Condition Report 1996 (Summary)," < http://www.dainet.de/bfh/icpfor/icpfor.htm >, viewed 23 October 1997.
19. Bryant, Nielson, and Tangley, op. cit. note 1.
20. Ibid.
21. Ibid.
22. Ibid.
23. Ibid.
24. Ibid.
25. Ibid.
26. Ibid.
27. World Wide Fund for Nature, *The Year the World Caught Fire* (Gland, Switzerland: December 1997).

TREE PLANTATIONS TAKING ROOT (pages 126–27)

1. U.N. Food and Agriculture Organization (FAO), *State of the World's Forests 1997* (Oxford, U.K.: 1997).
2. Ibid.
3. Ibid.
4. Ibid.
5. FAO, *Forest Resources Assessment 1990: Tropical Countries*, Forestry Paper 112 (Rome: 1992), cited in B. Solberg, ed., *Long-Term Trends and Prospects in World Supply and Demand for Wood and Implications for Sustainable Forest Management* (Joensuu, Finland: European Forest Institute, 1996).
6. FAO, op. cit. note 1.
7. Ibid.
8. Michael D. Bazett, *Industrial Wood, Study No. 3, Shell/World Wide Fund for Nature Tree Plantation Review* (London: Shell Petroleum Company and World Wide Fund for Nature, 1993), cited in Ricardo Carrere and Larry Lohmann, *Pulping the South, Industrial Tree Plantations and the World Paper Economy* (London: Zed Books, Ltd, 1996).
9. Ibid.
10. Ibid.
11. Ibid.
12. Carrere and Lohmann, op. cit. note 8.
13. Ibid.; Anita Kerski, "Pulp, Paper and Power—How an Industry Reshapes its Social Environment," *The Ecologist*, July/August 1995; Charles W. Thurston, "Brazil Upgrading its Pulp Capacity," *Journal of Commerce*, 8 October 1997.
14. Robert W. Hagler, "The Global Wood Fiber Equation—A New World Order?" Proceedings, Third International Pulp and Paper Symposium: What is Determining International Competitiveness in the Global Pulp and Paper Industry? 13–14 September 1994 (Seattle: University of Washington, Center for International Trade in

Forest Products, 1994).

15. Bill Finch, "Eucalyptus: Is This the Tree That Eats Alabama's Lunch?" *Mobile (AL) Register*, 27 October 1996.

16. Carrere and Lohmann, op. cit. note 8.

17. International Institute for Environment and Development (IIED), *Towards a Sustainable Paper Cycle* (London: 1996).

18. Ibid.

19. Ibid.

20. Subsidies from Carerre and Lohmann, op. cit. note 8, from "Government Gives About $18 Million to Private, Commercial Tree Plantations," *International Environment Reporter*, 1 October 1997, and from Kevin G. Hall, "Mexico Spells Out Rules for Forest Subsidy Plan," *Journal of Commerce*, 28 August 1997; foreign investment from "Southern Hemisphere Plantations Turn up Heat on Traditional Northern Woodfiber Suppliers," *Pulp and Paper Week*, 20 December 1993, from "International News," *International Wood Fiber Report*, 1 September 1995, from Stephanie Nall and William Armbruster, "U.S. Forest Products Companies Eye New Zealand," *Journal of Commerce*, 19 May 1997, and from "Changes Ongoing in World Markets," *International Wood Fiber Report*, July 1997.

21. "Outlook for Latin America's Growth Remains Impressive," *International Wood Fiber Report*, March 1997.

22. Figure of 800,000 hectares from Ricardo Carrere, Director of the Instituto del Tercer Mundo, Montevideo, Uruguay, e-mail to author, 5 January 1998; 50,000 hectares from Nigel Dudley, Sue Stolton, and Jean-Paul Jeanrenaud, *Pulp Fact, The Environmental and Social Impacts of the Pulp and Paper Industry* (Gland, Switzerland: World Wide Fund for Nature, 1995).

23. Robert Flynn & Associates, Tacoma, WA, "An Overview of Worldwide Fiber Availability: Today and Tomorrow," presented to the APA Western Technical Division Fall Meeting, 11 October 1995, Kelso, WA.

24. Robert Flynn & Associates, Tacoma, WA, "The Globalization of Forestry: Chile," presented to the Western Forestry Conference, 13 December 1996.

25. IIED, op. cit. note 17.

26. Dr. Robert Bain, Executive Director, "Forest Management to Offset Greenhouse Growth," press release (Kingston, ACT, Australia: National Association of Forest Industries, 30 November 1997).

27. Rowan Taylor and Ian Smith, *The State of New Zealand's Environment 1997* (Wellington, New Zealand: The Ministry for the Environment and GP Publications, 1997).

28. FAO, op. cit. note 1.

29. As discussed in Carrere and Lohmann, op. cit. note 8.

30. Unfortunately, there are no global data that provide information on the land use or natural forests that tree plantations have replaced. FAO does not distinguish between plantations established on previously deforested lands and lands deforested as a prelude to installing plantations.

31. World Wide Fund for Nature, *The Year the World Caught Fire* (Gland, Switzerland: December 1997); up until 1997, 1.4 million hectares of forest had been cleared to establish plantations in Indonesia, according to IIED, op. cit. note 17.

32. IIED, op cit. note 17.

33. William H. McWilliams, John R. Mills, and William Burkman, "The State of the Nation's Forestland," *National Woodlands*, April 1993.

VERTEBRATES SIGNAL BIODIVERSITY LOSSES (pages 128–29)

1. Estimates for total species on Earth reviewed by Nigel Stork, "Measuring Global Biodiversity and Its Decline," in Marjorie L. Reaka-Kudla, Don E. Wilson, and Edward O. Wilson, eds., *Biodiversity II: Understanding and Protecting Our Biological Resources* (Washington, DC: Joseph Henry Press, 1997).

2. Vertebrate species total from Jonathan Baillie and Brian Groombridge, eds., *1996 IUCN Red List of Threatened Animals* (Gland, Switzerland: World Conservation Union (IUCN), 1996).

3. Bird species total rounded from ibid., and from Howard Youth, "Flying Into Trouble," *World Watch*, January/February 1994; mammal species total from Baillie and Groombridge, op. cit. note 2.

4. Reptile species total from Harold G. Cogger, *Reptiles and Amphibians of Australia* (Ithaca, NY: Reed Books/Cornell University Press, 1992); amphibian species total from Darrel R. Frost, ed., *Amphibian Species of the World: A Taxonomic and Geographic Reference* (Lawrence, KS: Allen Press/Association of Systematics Collections, 1985); fish species total from Baillie and Groombridge, op. cit. note 2.

5. Calculated from Baillie and Groombridge, op. cit. note 2.
6. Ibid.
7. Ibid.
8. Calculated from ibid.
9. Ibid.
10. Wayne C. Starnes, "Colorado River Basin Fishes," in National Biological Service, U.S. Department of Interior, *Our Living Resources 1994* (Washington, DC: 1995).
11. Salvador Contreras and M. Lourdes Lozano, "Water, Endangered Fishes, and Development Perspectives in Arid Lands of Mexico," *Conservation Biology*, June 1994.
12. Calculated from Baillie and Groombridge, op. cit. note 2.
13. Ibid.
14. Michael McRae, "Road Kill in Cameroon," *Natural History*, February 1997.
15. Peter Matthiessen, "The Last Wild Tiger," *Audubon*, March-April 1997; Peter Jackson and Elizabeth Kemf, *Tigers in the Wild: A WWF Status Report* (Gland, Switzerland: World Wide Fund for Nature, 1996).
16. Matthiessen, op. cit. note 15.
17. John W. Terborgh, "The Big Things That Run the World—A Sequel to E.O. Wilson," *Conservation Biology*, December 1988.
18. Calculated from Baillie and Groombridge, op. cit. note 2.
19. Chris Bright, "Tracking the Ecology of Climate Change," in Lester R. Brown et al., *State of the World 1997* (New York: W.W. Norton & Company, 1997).
20. Gary Paul Nabhan, *Cultures of Habitat* (Washington, DC: Counterpoint Press, 1997).

ORGANIC WASTE REUSE
SURGING (pages 130–31)

1. Gary Gardner, *Recycling Organic Waste: From Urban Pollutant to Farm Resource*, Worldwatch Paper 135 (Washington, DC: Worldwatch Institute, August 1997).
2. Table 1 based on the following: U.S. examples from Nora Goldstein, "The State of Garbage in America," *Biocycle*, April 1997, from Nora Goldstein, "National Trends in Food Residuals Composting," *Biocycle*, July 1997, and from Nora Goldstein and Dave Block, "Nationwide Inventory of Food Residuals Composting," *Biocycle*, August 1997; Germany from "Biological Waste Treatment," *Warmer Bulletin*, November 1997, and from Glenda Gies, "Developing Compost Standards in Europe," *Biocycle*, October 1997; Hang-Sik Shin, Eung-Ju Hwang, and Chai-Sung Gee, "Food Residuals Management in Korea," *Biocycle*, October 1997;. Maria Kelleher, "Land Diversion—Canadian Specifics," *Warmer Bulletin*, November 1997; Flemish Organisation for the Promotion of Marketing of VFG and Green Waste Compost, *VLACO's Activity Report, '96* (Mechelen, Belgium: March 1997).
3. Goldstein, "State of Garbage," op. cit. note 2.
4. United States from National Research Council (NRC), *Use of Reclaimed Water and Sludge in Food Crop Production* (Washington, DC: National Academy Press, 1996); Europe from Peter Matthews, ed., *A Global Atlas of Wastewater Sludge and Biosolids Use and Disposal* (London: International Association on Water Quality, 1996) and from Peter Matthews, Director of Innovation, Anglian Water, Cambridgeshire, U.K., letter to author, 24 June 1997.
5. Figure of 11 percent is an average of member states' reporting rates for the early 1990s, and is based on data in Organisation for Economic Cooperation and Development (OECD), *Towards Sustainable Agricultural Production: Cleaner Technologies* (Paris: 1994).
6. Gardner, op. cit. note 1.
7. Water pollution from OECD, op. cit. note 5.
8. Goldstein, "State of Garbage," op. cit. note 2.
9. For the United States, see NRC, op. cit. note 4; for Europe, see Cecil LueHing et al., "Sludge Management in Highly Urbanized Areas," in Matthews, *Global Atlas*, op. cit. note 4.
10. Nyle C. Brady and Ray R. Weil, *The Nature and Properties of Soils*, 11th ed. (Upper Saddle River, NJ: Prentice Hall, 1996).
11. H.A.J. Hoitink, A.G. Stone, and D.Y. Han, "Suppression of Plant Diseases by Composts," accepted for publication in *HortScience*, 1997; replacement of methyl bromide from William Quarles and Joel Grossman, "Alternatives to Methyl Bromide in Nurseries—Disease Suppressive Media," *IPM Practitioner*, August 1995.
12. Francis R. Gouin, "Compost Use in the Horticultural Industries," *Green Industry Composting*, undated.
13. United States from National Research Council, op. cit. note 8; Europe from Matthews, *Global Atlas*, op. cit. note 4, and from Matthews, letter

to author, op. cit. note 4.

14. E. Witter and J.M. Lopez-Real, "The Potential of Sewage Sludge and Composting in a Nitrogen Recycling Strategy for Agriculture," *Biological Agriculture and Horticulture*, vol. 5 (1987).

15. Carl R. Bartone, "International Perspective on Water Resources Management and Wastewater Reuse—Appropriate Technologies," *Water Science Technology*, vol. 23 (1991).

16. Outbreaks from Hillel I. Shuval, "Wastewater Irrigation in Developing Countries: Health Effects and Technical Solutions," Summary of World Bank Technical Paper Number 51 (Washington, DC: World Bank, 1990).

17. Share of nutrients in municipal waste is a Worldwatch calculation based on data from OECD, op. cit. note 9, on U.S. waste data from Environmental Protection Agency (EPA), *Characterization of Municipal Solid Waste in the United States: 1995 Update*, Executive Summary (Washington, DC: March 1996), on nutrient value of municipal waste from XinTao He, Terry J. Logan, and Samuel J. Traina, "Physical and Chemical Characteristics of Selected U.S. Municipal Solid Waste Composts," *Journal of Environmental Quality*, May–June 1995, and on fertilizer use from U.N. Food and Agriculture Organization (FAO), *FAOSTAT Statistics Database*, <http://www.apps.fao.org>, Rome, viewed 16 May 1997. Countries selected were those for which complete data were available. Share of nutrients in human waste does not include the 33 percent of sludge produced in OECD countries that is already applied to land. Share is a Worldwatch calculation based on nutrient value of human waste from Witter and Lopez-Real, op. cit. note 15, on population data from U.S. Agency for International Development and U.S. Department of Commerce, *World Population Profile 1996* (Washington, DC: 1996), and on fertilizer use from FAO, op. cit. in this note.

18. Estimate of nutrient overapplication based on Dale Lueck, *Policies to Reduce Nitrate Pollution in the European Community and Possible Effects on Livestock Production* (Washington, DC: U.S. Department of Agriculture (USDA), Economic Research Service (ERS), September 1993), which reports nitrogen overapplication in Europe to be 57 percent greater than crop needs, on U.S. grain data from USDA, *Production, Supply, and Distribution*, electronic database, Washington, DC, updated October 1996, and on fertilizer application rates from USDA, ERS, *Agricultural Resources*, February 1993, which are used to calculate a U.S. fertilizer overapplicaton rate of 36 percent.

19. "Institutions Save by Composting Food Residuals," *Biocycle*, January 1997.

20. Paul Vossen and Ellen Rilla, "Trained Home Composters Reduce Solid Waste by 18%," *California Agriculture*, September–October 1996; costs from Ellen Rilla, "CE Offices Facilitate Community Composting Efforts," *California Agriculture*, September–October 1996.

21. Dave Baldwin, Community Recycling and Resource Recovery, Inc., Lamont, CA, discussion with author, 21 February 1997.

22. Stephen Grealy, "Supermarket Composting in California," *Biocycle*, July 1997; compost volume and area applied from Baldwin, op. cit. note 23; value of compost from Community Recycling and Resource Recovery, Inc., "Community Recycling Compost Typical Analysis," factsheet (Lamont, CA: undated).

NITROGEN FIXATION CONTINUES TO RISE
(pages 132–33)

1. This trend has been quantified in several papers in recent years. See, for example, Peter Vitousek et al., *Human Alteration of the Global Nitrogen Cycle: Causes and Consequences* (Washington, DC: Ecological Society of America, 1997), and Ann P. Kinzig and Robert H. Socolow, "Human Impacts on the Nitrogen Cycle," *Physics Today*, November 1994.

2. Vitousek et al., op. cit. note 1.

3. Vaclav Smil, *Cycles of Life: Civilization and the Biosphere* (New York: Scientific American, 1997).

4. Vitousek et al., op. cit. note 1.

5. Ibid.

6. Calculated from data in ibid.

7. Vitousek et al., op. cit. note 1.

8. Smil, op. cit. note 3.

9. Tripling of soybean production from U.S. Department of Agriculture, *Production, Supply, and Distribution*, electronic database, Washington, DC, updated December 1997.

10. Lester R. Brown, "Fertilizer Use Rising Again," in Lester R. Brown, Michael Renner, and Christopher Flavin, *Vital Signs 1997* (New York: W.W. Norton & Company, 1997).

11. Ibid.

12. Ibid.

13. Organisation for Economic Cooperation and Development, *Towards Sustainable Agricultural Production: Cleaner Technologies* (Paris: 1994).

14. Ibid.

15. Ibid.

16. Susanne M. Scheierling, *Overcoming Agricultural Pollution of Water: The Challenge of Integrating Agricultural and Environmental Policies in the European Union*, World Bank Technical Paper No. 269 (Washington, DC: World Bank, 1995).

17. Ibid.

18. Robert J. Diaz, "Causes and Effects of Coastal Hypoxia Worldwide: Putting the Louisiana Shelf Events in Perspective," < http://pelican. gmpo.gov/gulfweb/hypoxia/diaz.html, > viewed 22 July 1997.

19. Ibid.

20. Jonathan Tolman, "Poisonous Runoff from Farm Subsidies," *Wall Street Journal*, 8 September 1995.

21. Species diversity from David Wedin and David Tilman, "Influence of Nitrogen Loading and Species Composition on the Carbon Balance of Grasslands," *Science*, 6 December 1996.

22. Ibid.

23. Vitousek et al., op. cit. note 1, and C. Mlot, "Tallying Nitrogen's Increasing Impact," *Science News*, 15 February 1997.

24. Vitousek et al., op. cit. note 1.

25. John Harte, "Acid Rain," in Jack M. Hollander, *The Energy-Environment Connection* (Washington, DC: Island Press, 1992).

26. Ibid.

27. "Nitrogen Deposition Affects Carbon Sink," *Global Environmental Change Report*, 22 August 1997.

28. Ibid.

ACID RAIN THREATS VARY
(pages 134–35)

1. Data for Europe 1980–95 from the European Monitoring and Evaluation Programme, reported in Christer Agren, "Monitoring Figures Show Decline," *Acid News*, December 1997; data for Europe 2000–10 from Markus Amann et al., *Cost-Effective Control of Acidification and Ground-Level Ozone*, Third Interim Report to the European Commission (Laxenburg, Austria: International Institute for Applied Systems Analysis (IIASA), October 1997), and from Janusz Cofala, Rainer Kurz, and Markus Amann, *Application of the Current EU Air Emissions Standards to the Central and Eastern European Countries: An Integrated Assessment of the Environmental Effect*, Final Report to the European Environmental Agency (Laxenburg, Austria: IIASA, September 1997); U.S. data from U.S. Environmental Protection Agency (EPA), *National Air Pollutant Emission Trends Report, 1900–1996* (Washington, DC: U.S. Government Printing Office, 1997); data for Asia 1980 from Jane Dignon, "Historic SO_2 Emissions from Fossil Fuel Burning," submitted to *Atmospheric Environment*, 1998; data for Asia 1990–2010 from Robert Downing, Ramesh Ramankutty, and Jitendra J. Shah, *RAINS–Asia: An Assessment Model for Acid Deposition in Asia* (Washington, DC: World Bank, 1997).

2. John Harte, "Acid Rain," in Jack Hollander, ed., *The Energy-Environment Connection* (Washington, DC: Island Press, 1992).

3. Ibid.

4. Jack M. Hollander and Duncan Brown, "Air Pollution," in Hollander, op. cit. note 2.

5. Marc Levy, "European Acid Rain: The Power of Tote-Board Diplomacy," in Peter M. Haas et al., eds., *Institutions for the Earth* (Cambridge, MA: The MIT Press, 1993).

6. EPA, op. cit. note 1; "Green Taxes Proven Successful, Evaluation by Swedish EPA Says," *International Environment Reporter*, 16 April 1997.

7. Sultan Hameed and Jane Dignon, "Global Emissions of Nitrogen and Sulfur Oxides in Fossil Fuel Combustion, 1970–1986," *Journal of the Air and Waste Management Association*, February 1992.

8. Cofala, Kurz, and Amann, op. cit. note 1.

9. Neeloo Bhatti, David G. Streets, and Wesley K. Foell, "Acid Rain in Asia," *Environmental Management*, vol. 16, no. 4, 1992.

10. "Research Finds that China's SO2 Emissions Greatly Surpassed Japan's Boom Time Levels," *International Environment Reporter*, 1 October 1997.

11. Downing, Ramankutty, and Shah, op. cit. note 1.

12. Gywneth Howells, *Acid Rain and Acid Waters*, 2nd ed. (London: Ellis Horwood Limited, 1995).

13. Dianwu Zhao and Bozen Sun, "Air Pollution and Acid Rain in China," *Ambio*, vol. 15, no. 1, 1986; Wenxing Wang and Tao Wang, "On Acid Rain Formation in China," *Atmospheric Environment*,

vol. 30, no. 23, 1996.

14. Howells, op. cit. note 12.

15. Ibid.

16. Ibid.

17. National Acid Precipitation Assessment Program, *1990 Integrated Assessment Report* (Washington, DC: 1991); Environmental Resources Limited, *Acid Rain: A Review of the Phenomenon in the EEC and Europe*, Prepared for the Commission of the European Communities (New York: Unipub, 1983); U.N. Economic Commission for Europe, International Cooperative Programme on Assessment and Monitoring of Air Pollution Effects on Forests, *Executive Report 1997*, < http://www.dainet.de/bfh/icpfor/execrep.htm >, viewed 17 February 1998.

18. X.B. Xue and J.L. Schnoor, "Acid Deposition and Lake Chemistry in Southwest China," *Water, Air, and Soil Pollution*, vol. 75, pp. 61–78, 1994.

19. "Report Warns of Effects of Acid Rain from Eastern Asia on Japan's Ecosystem," *International Environment Reporter*, 30 April 1997; "Government Panel: Acid Rain Damaging Ecosystem," *The Daily Yomiuri*, 19 April 1997.

20. Cited in Downing, Ramankutty, and Shah, op cit. note 1.

21. World Bank, *Clear Water, Blue Skies: China's Environment in the New Century*, China 2020 Series (Washington, DC: 1997).

22. Harte, op. cit. note 2.

23. "Report Warns of Effects," op. cit. note 19.

24. Ram M. Shrestha, S.C. Bhattacharya, and Sunil Malla, "Energy Use and Sulfur Dioxide Emissions in Asia," *Journal of Environmental Management*, vol. 46, pp. 359–72, 1996.

25. Downing, Ramankutty, and Shah, op. cit. note 1.

26. Masaharu Yagishita, "Establishing an Acid Deposition Monitoring Network in East Asia," *Water, Air, and Soil Pollution*, vol. 85, 1995; "International Conference on Acid Rain Monitoring Network in East Asia to be Held in Tokyo," *Japan Economic Newswire*, 31 October 1997.

27. Peter Hadfield, "Raining Acid in Asia," *New Scientist*, 15 February 1997.

28. "Japan to Loan China $1.7 Billion to Promote Environment, Industry," *International Environment Reporter*, 17 September 1997.

29. Tom Korski, "Mainland to Crack Down on Acid Rain," *South China Morning Post*, 13 February 1998.

30. J.T. Houghton et al., eds., *Climate Change 1995: The Science of Climate Change*, Contribution of Working Group I to the Second Assessment Report of the Intergovernmental Panel on Climate Change (Cambridge, U.K.: Cambridge University Press, 1996).

31. Ibid.

PRIVATE CAPITAL FLOWS TO THIRD WORLD SLOW (pages 138–39)

1. World Bank, *Global Development Finance 1997: Volume 1* (Washington, DC: 1997). Numbers for 1996 are preliminary estimates. The World Bank classifies all low- and middle-income countries as developing, including all of Africa and Latin America, and selected countries in Asia and the Pacific, the Caribbean, Eastern Europe, and the Middle East. These numbers reflect net resource flows, including repayment of principal on loans. However, interest payments on loans and the repatriation of profits on foreign direct investment are not subtracted.

2. World Bank, op. cit. note 1; reasons for aid's decline from Organisation for Economic Co-operation and Development (OECD), *Development Cooperation: 1996 Report* (Paris: 1997).

3. World Bank, op. cit. note 1.

4. International Monetary Fund (IMF), *World Economic Outlook, Interim Assessment* (Washington, DC: December 1997). World Bank figures for 1997 were not available as this report went to press; IMF and World Bank estimates have been roughly comparable in recent years.

5. IMF, op. cit. note 4.

6. World Bank, op. cit. note 1.

7. Based on World Bank, *World Development Indicators on CD-ROM* (Washington, DC: 1997), and on World Bank, op. cit. note 1.

8. World Bank, op. cit. note 1.

9. Ibid.; total excludes some countries for which no data are given.

10. World Bank, op. cit. note 7.

11. World Bank, op. cit. note 1.

12. Ibid.

13. Ibid.

14. Ibid.

15. Ibid.; IMF, op. cit. note 4.

16. Michael P. Todaro, *Economic Development, Fifth Edition* (New York: Longman, 1994).

17. World Bank, op. cit. note 1.

18. George Soros, "Asia's Crisis Demands a Rethink of International Regulation," *Financial Times*, 31 December 1997; Henry Kissinger, "The Asian

Collapse: One Fix Does Not Fit All Economies," *Washington Post*, 9 February 1998.

19. IMF, *World Economic Outlook, October 1997* (Washington, DC: 1997).

20. Asian Development Bank, *Emerging Asia: Changes and Challenges* (Manila: 1997); World Resources Institute et al., *World Resources 1996–97* (New York: Oxford University Press, 1996).

21. OECD, *Economic Globalization and the Environment* (Paris: 1997).

22. Richard J. Barnet and John Cavanagh, *Global Dreams: Imperial Corporations and the New World Order* (New York: Simon and Schuster, 1994); Lester R. Brown, "The Future of Growth," in Lester R. Brown et al., *State of the World 1998* (New York: W. W. Norton & Company, 1998).

23. OECD, op. cit. note 21.

24. Hilary F. French, *Investing in the Future: Harnessing Private Capital Flows for Environmentally Sustainable Development*, Worldwatch Paper 139 (Washington, DC: Worldwatch Institute, February 1998).

TAXATION SHIFTING IN EUROPE
(pages 140–41)

1. Sweden description from P. Bohm, "Environment and Taxation: The Case of Sweden," in Organisation for Economic Co-operation and Development (OECD), *Environment and Taxation: The Cases of the Netherlands, Sweden and the United States* (Paris: 1994); Sweden quantity from Nordic Council of Ministers, *The Use of Economic Instruments in Nordic Environmental Policy* (Copenhagen: TemaNord, 1996); Denmark 1994 description and quantity from Mikael Skou Andersen, "The Green Tax Reform in Denmark: Shifting the Focus of Tax Liability," *Journal of Environmental Liability*, vol. 2, no. 2 (1994); Spain description from Thomas Schröder, "Spain: Improve Competitiveness through an ETR," *Wuppertal Bulletin on Ecological Tax Reform* (Wuppertal, Germany: Wuppertal Institute for Climate, Environment, and Energy), summer 1995; Spain quantity from Juan-José Escobar, Ministry of Economy and Finance, Madrid, letter to author, 29 January 1997; Denmark 1996 description and quantity from Ministry of Finance, *Energy Tax on Industry* (Copenhagen: 1995); Netherlands

description from Ministry of Housing, Spatial Planning, and Environment (VROM), *The Netherlands' Regulatory Tax on Energy: Questions and Answers* (The Hague: 1996); Netherlands quantity from Koos van der Vaart, Ministry of Finance, The Hague, discussion with author, 18 December 1995; United Kingdom description and quantity from "Landfill Tax Regime Takes Shape," *ENDS Report* (London: Environmental Data Services), November 1995; Finland description and quantity from OECD, *Environmental Taxes and Green Tax Reform* (Paris: 1997); total tax revenues for all countries from OECD, *Revenue Statistics of OECD Member Countries 1965–1996* (Paris: 1997).

2. Swedish Environmental Protection Agency (SEPA), *Environmental Taxes in Sweden: Economic Instruments of Environmental Policy* (Stockholm: 1997).

3. European Commission, Statistical Office of the European Communities (Eurostat), *European Economy* (Office for Official Publications of the European Communities, Luxembourg), no. 64 (1997).

4. OECD, *Revenue Statistics*, op. cit. note 1.

5. Thomas Sterner, *Environmental Tax Reform: The Swedish Experience* (Gothenburg, Sweden: Department of Economics, Gothenburg University, 1994).

6. Ibid.; Svante Axelsson, Swedish Nature Protection Society, Stockholm, discussion with author, 29 January 1998.

7. SEPA, op. cit. note 2.

8. Ibid.

9. European Commission, op. cit. note 3; European Commission, Eurostat, "EU Unemployment Falls to 10.6% in November," press release (Luxembourg: January 1998).

10. "Why Wages Aren't Growing," interview with Gary Burtless, *Challenge*, November-December 1995.

11. Figures for 1970 from Lorenz Jarass and Gustav M. Obermair, "More Jobs, Less Pollution: Tax Incentives and Statutory Levies," *The Natural Resources Tax Review*, November 1994; 1995 figures from Lorenz Jarass and Gustav M. Obermair, *More Jobs, Less Tax Evasion, Cleaner Environment: Options for Compensating Reductions in the Taxation of Labour—Taxation of Other Factors of Production*, commissioned by the European Commission (Wiesbaden, Germany: College of Wiesbaden, August 1997). Figure for Germany in 1970 is for the former

West Germany only.

12. Unemployment effects from C.R. Bean, P.R.G. Layard, and S.J. Nickell, "The Rise in Unemployment: A Multi-Country Study," *Economica*, vol. 53, S1–S22, cited in OECD, *The OECD Jobs Study: Taxation, Employment and Unemployment* (Paris: 1995).

13. Andersen, op. cit. note 1; Ministry of Finance, op. cit. note 1; OECD, *Environmental Taxes and Green Tax Reform*, op. cit. note 1; VROM, op. cit. note 1; Schröder, op. cit. note 1; "Landfill Tax Regime Takes Shape," op. cit. note 1.

14. Worldwatch estimate, based on Andersen, op. cit. note 1, on Ministry of Finance, op. cit. note 1, and on OECD, *Revenue Statistics*, op. cit. note 1.

15. European Environment Agency, *Environmental Taxes: Implementation and Environmental Effectiveness* (Copenhagen: 1996).

16. OECD, *Environmental Taxes in OECD Countries* (Paris: 1995).

17. Michel Potier, "China Charges for Pollution," *The OECD Observer*, February/March 1995; "NEPA to Impose 'Pollution Tax' on Industry to Curb Dramatic Increase in SOx Emissions," *International Environment Reporter*, 6 March 1996; Philippines from World Bank, *Five Years After Rio: Innovations in Environmental Policy*, Environmentally Sustainable Development Studies and Monograph Series no. 18 (Washington, DC: 1997).

18. For further discussion, see David Malin Roodman, *Getting the Signals Right: Tax Reform to Protect the Environment and the Economy*, Worldwatch Paper 134 (Washington, DC: Worldwatch Institute, May 1997).

19. M. Jeff Hamond, *Tax Waste, Not Work* (San Francisco, CA: Redefining Progress, 1997); John P. Weyant, Stanford University, Energy Modeling Forum, Stanford, CA, draft manuscript, June 1995.

20. Roodman, op. cit. note 18.

21. Ibid.

FOSSIL FUEL SUBSIDIES FALLING (pages 142–43)

1. Worldwatch estimates, converted to dollars using market exchange rates, using data for the former Soviet Union from Andrew Sunil Rajkumar, *Energy Subsidies*, Environment Department working paper (Washington, DC: World Bank, 1996), and data for other countries from World Bank, Environment Department, *Expanding the Measure of Wealth: Indicators of Environmentally Sustainable Development* (Washington, DC: 1997). The regional estimates allocate the $10 billion that the Rajkumar study estimates for countries not systematically analyzed based on their carbon emissions.

2. Christine Kerr and Leslie Citroen, *Household Expenditures on Infrastructure Services*, background paper for *World Development Report 1994* (Washington, DC: World Bank, undated).

3. Worldwatch estimate, based on Rajkumar, op. cit. note 1.

4. U.S. Congress, Office of Technology Assessment, *Energy Efficiency Technologies for Central and Eastern Europe* (Washington, DC: U.S. Government Printing Office (GPO), 1993).

5. E. Gurvich et al., "Greenhouse Gas Impacts of Russian Energy Subsidies," in Organisation for Economic Co-operation and Development (OECD), *Environmental Implications of Energy and Transport Subsidies* (Paris: in press).

6. Ibid.

7. Ibid.

8. World Bank, op. cit. note 1.

9. Thomas T. Vogel, Jr., "Venezuela to Drive Up Gasoline Prices," *Wall Street Journal*, 15 April 1996.

10. World Bank, op. cit. note 1.

11. Ibid.; pattern from David Malin Roodman, "Energy Productivities Vary Widely," in Lester R. Brown, Hal Kane, and David Malin Roodman, *Vital Signs 1994* (New York: W.W. Norton & Company, 1994).

12. World Bank, op. cit. note 1.

13. OECD, International Energy Agency, *Energy Policies of IEA Countries* (Paris: various years).

14. Ibid.

15. A.P.G. de Moor, *Perverse Incentives* (The Hague: Institute for Research on Public Expenditure, 1997).

16. For more discussion, see David Malin Roodman, *Paying the Piper: Subsidies, Politics, and the Environment*, Worldwatch Paper 133 (Washington, DC: Worldwatch Institute, December 1996).

17. Douglas Koplow, *Federal Energy Subsidies: Energy, Environmental, and Fiscal Impacts* (Washington, DC: Alliance to Save Energy, 1993).

18. U.S. Department of Energy, Energy Information Administration, *Annual Energy Review 1996* (Washington, DC: GPO, 1997).

19. Worldwatch estimates, based on OECD, op. cit.

note 13, on OECD, *Coal Prospects and Policies in IEA Countries—1987 Review* (Paris: 1988), and on OECD, *Coal Information* (Paris: various years), with costs converted to dollars using a 1996 exchange rate.

20. OECD, op. cit. note 13; OECD, *Coal Prospects and Policies*, op. cit. note 19; OECD, *Coal Information*, op. cit. note 19.

21. Worldwatch estimates, based on OECD, op. cit. note 13, on OECD, *Coal Prospects and Policies*, op. cit. note 19, and on OECD, *Coal Information*, op. cit. note 19.

22. World Bank, op. cit. note 1.

23. China from Ved P. Gandhi, Dale Gray, and Ronald McMorran, "A Comprehensive Approach to Domestic Resource Mobilization for Sustainable Development," in U.N. Department for Policy Coordination and Sustainable Development, *Finance for Sustainable Development: The Road Ahead*, Proceedings of the Fourth Group Meeting on Financial Issues of Agenda 21, Santiago, Chile, 1997 (New York: 1997).

PAPER RECYCLING CLIMBS HIGHER (pages 144–45)

1. Pulp and Paper International (PPI), *International Fact and Price Book 1997* (San Francisco, CA: Miller Freeman Inc., 1996).

2. Ibid. Wastepaper recovery rate was calculated by dividing the total volume recovered by apparent consumption of paper and paperboard—production plus imports minus exports.

3. U.N. Food and Agriculture Organization (FAO), *State of the World's Forests 1997* (Oxford, U.K.: 1997); recovery rate calculated by dividing FAO's projected recovered paper volume by projected paper and paperboard consumption.

4. Few studies have examined the relative proportions of pre- and post-consumer waste in recovered-paper statistics. The U.S. Environmental Protection Agency (EPA), which prefers to account for only post-consumer waste in its municipal solid waste statistics, relies on data developed in Franklin Associates, Ltd. *Evaluation of Proposed New Recycled Paper Standards and Definitions*, Report for the Recycling Advisory Council (Prairie Village, KS: Franklin Associates, Ltd., 27 January 1992). This study reported that post-consumer paper recovery represented 69.2 percent of total recovered paper in 1990 and projected that this

share would increase to 73.7 percent in 1995. In estimating, EPA deducts estimated volumes of recovered scrap and returned overissue newspapers from the total recovery volumes reported by the American Forest and Paper Association.

5. PPI, *North American Fact Book 1997* (San Francisco, CA: Miller Freeman, Inc. 1996); Nels Johnson and Daryl Ditz, "Challenges to Sustainability in the U.S. Forest Sector," in World Resources Institute, *Frontiers of Sustainability* (Washington, DC: Island Press, 1997).

6. L. Göttschuing et al., *Analysis of Waste Paper Recycling and Disposal Options in Germany* (London: International Institute for Environment and Development (IIED), December 1996); PPI, op. cit. note 1.

7. IIED, *Towards a Sustainable Paper Cycle* (London: 1996).

8. U.S. figure from Franklin Associates, Ltd., "Characterization of Municipal Solid Waste in the United States: 1996 Update," report prepared for EPA, Municipal and Industrial Solid Waste Division, Office of Solid Waste, June 1997; Europe from IIED, op. cit. note 7.

9. PPI, op. cit. note 5.

10. PPI, op. cit. note 1.

11. John Fiske, "Americans Recycle More Paper Despite Low Demand," *Christian Science Monitor*, 20 October 1997; American Forest and Paper Association, "50% Paper Recovery Goal," < http://www.afandpa.org/Recycling/Paper/ programs.html#Goal >, viewed 18 January 1998.

12. "Divided EU Agrees on Packaging Directive, Joint Ratification of Climate Change Treaty," *International Environment Reporter*, 12 January 1994; "Council Agrees on FCP Phase-out, Packaging Recycling, Hazardous Waste List," *International Environment Reporter*, 11 January 1995.

13. PPI, op. cit. note 1; Skogsindustrierna, Swedish Forest Industries Association Press Briefings (Stockholm: 17 October 1997).

14. PPI, op. cit. note 5; 1940s from Maureen Smith, *The U.S. Paper Industry and Sustainable Production* (Cambridge, MA: The MIT Press, 1997).

15. PPI, op. cit. note 5; PPI op. cit. note 1.

16. Sayuri Carbonnier, *Paper Recycling and the Waste Paper Business in Japan* (London: IIED, September 1996).

17. PPI, op. cit. note 1.

18. Ibid.

19. Ibid.
20. Gary L. Stanley, "1997 Industry Forecast, Paperboard, Imports, and Exports to Fuel 1997 Growth," *TAPPI Journal*, January 1997.
21. Ibid.
22. PPI, op. cit. note 5.
23. IIED, op. cit. note 7; PPI, op. cit. note 1.
24. PPI, op. cit. note 1.
25. "Asian Market to Hold Through 2010," *Paper Recycler*, October 1997.
26. "Outlook 1998, Pulp and Paper Markets are Expected to Weather Financial Turmoil in Southeast Asia," *Pulp and Paper*, January 1998.
27. Jerry Powell, "News Flash: Recovered Paper Prices Will Soon Rise," *Resource Recycling*, July 1997; "Fiscal Incentives Needed to Stimulate Collection of Waste Paper, Say Experts," *International Environment Reporter*, 15 October 1997.
28. Wood pulp from FAO, FAOSTAT electronic database, < http://apps.fao.org/ >, viewed 16 December 1997.
29. IIED, op. cit. note 7.
30. A recent summary of some of the points of debate can be found in the *Journal of Industrial Ecology*, special issue on the industrial ecology of paper and wood, vol. 1, no. 3, 1998.

CIGARETTE TAXES ON THE RISE
(pages 146–47)

1. Ruth Roemer, *Legislative Action to Combat the World Tobacco Epidemic*, 2nd ed. (Geneva: World Health Organization (WHO), 1993).
2. Kenneth E. Warner, "Tobacco Taxation and Economic Effects of Declining Consumption," in B. Durston and K. Jamrozik, eds., *Tobacco and Health 1990: The Global War*, Proceedings of the Seventh World Conference on Tobacco and Health (Perth: Health Department of Western Australia, 1991).
3. Roemer, op. cit. note 1.
4. David Sweanor, Senior Legal Counsel, Smoking and Health Action Foundation, Ottawa, ON, Canada, letter to author, 5 December 1997.
5. Ibid.
6. Ibid.
7. Ibid.
8. Tobacco Institute, *The Tax Burden of Tobacco*, Vol. 27 (Washington, DC: 1996).
9. Action on Smoking and Health, "ASH & Others: Boost Cigarette Taxes NOW," *ASH Review* (Washington, DC), September-October 1997.
10. Luk Joossens, "Taxes on Tobacco Products in the European Union: Taking Health into Account," *Further Comments on the Commission Report [COM (95) 285 final] on the Approximation of Taxes on Manufactured Tobacco* (Brussels: EU Liaison Office of the International Union Against Cancer (UICC), September 1996), citing R. Garran, "Setback for RYO (Roll Your Own): EU's Tobacco Tax Harmonisation," *Tobacco International*, December 1995.
11. Jeffrey E. Harris, "Prepared Statement Before the Senate Democratic Task Force on Tobacco, Sen. Kent Conrad (D-ND), Chairman," Dirksen Senate Office Building, Washington, DC, 21 October 1997, citing F.J. Chaloupka and M. Grossman, *Price, Tobacco Control Policies, and Youth Smoking*, Working Paper No. 5740 (Cambridge, MA: National Bureau of Economic Research, September 1996).
12. Joossens, op. cit. note 10.
13. Roemer, op. cit. note 1, citing S. Chapman and J. Richardson, "Tobacco Excise and Declining Tobacco Consumption: the Case of Papua New Guinea," *American Journal of Public Health*, May 1990.
14. WHO, *Tobacco or Health: A Global Status Report, Country Profiles by Region, 1997* (Geneva: 1997).
15. Ibid.
16. Murray Laugesen, Health New Zealand, Waiheke, Auckland, e-mail to author, 9 December 1997.
17. Joossens, op. cit. note 10.
18. Ibid.
19. Ibid.
20. Alison Motluk, "Canada Declares War on Tobacco," *New Scientist*, 14 December 1996.
21. "Canada Vs. Cigarettes: New Taxes, Bans on Ads," *New York Times*, 29 November 1996.
22. WHO, op. cit. note 14.
23. Rowena van der Merwe, Economics of Tobacco Control Project, School of Economics, University of Cape Town, South Africa, letter to author, 5 January 1998.
24. WHO, op. cit. note 14.
25. Van der Merwe, op. cit. note 23.
26. "Cigarette Smoking Before and After an Excise Tax Increase and an Antismoking Campaign— Massachusetts, 1990-96," *Morbidity and Mortality Weekly Report* (Centers for Disease Control and Prevention), 8 November 1996.
27. Ibid.
28. Ibid.

29. WHO, op. cit. note 14.
30. Rhonda Galbally, "Taxing Harm for Health," *World Health*, May–June 1997.
31. Ibid.
32. "Tobacco Tax Initiative: Oregon, 1996," *Morbidity and Mortality Weekly Report* (Centers for Disease Control and Prevention), 21 March 1997.
33. Ibid.
34. Judith MacKay, Asian Consultancy on Tobacco Control, Hong Kong, on the UICC-sponsored GLOBALink Tobacco Control conference, 24 February 1997.
35. Derek Yach, Policy Action Coordinator, Tobacco or Health Program, WHO, Geneva, e-mail to author, 27 October 1996.
36. Latvia from WHO, op. cit. note 14; Nepal and Peru from MacKay, op. cit. note 34.
37. MacKay, op. cit. note 34.
38. Luk Joossens and Martin Raw, "Tobacco and the European Common Agricultural Policy," *British Journal of Addiction*, vol. 86, no. 10, 1991.
39. WHO, op. cit. note 14.
40. Roemer, op. cit. note 1, citing the Advisory Committee on Health Education, *An Evaluation of the Effects of an Increase in the Price of Tobacco and a Proposal for the Tobacco Price Policy in Finland in 1985–87* (Helsinki: March 1985).

METALS EXPLORATION EXPLODES IN THE SOUTH

(pages 148–49)

1. Based on Metals Economics Group (MEG), *Strategic Report*, September/October 1992; MEG, "Latin America Tops Exploration Spending for the Fourth Year," press release (Halifax, NS: 16 October 1997). The calculations of this Canadian consultancy group are based on budgets reported by major mining companies that represent some 80 percent of worldwide exploration expenditures for precious, base, and other nonferrous hard metals. In 1997, this totaled $4.03 billion; an additional $1.07 billion was spent by smaller companies.
2. Based on MEG, *Strategic Report*, op. cit. note 1; MEG, *Strategic Report*, November/December 1991; MEG, *Strategic Report*, September/ October 1993; MEG, "Major Increase in Junior Spending," press release (Halifax, NS: 14 October 1994); MEG, "1996 Exploration Surges Upward," press release (Halifax, NS: 16 October 1996).
3. Gold and copper shares from MEG, *Strategic Report*, September/October 1997.
4. Falling prices from Jonathan Fuerbringer, "Spot Gold Price is Under $280 Briefly in London and New York," *New York Times*, 9 January 1998, from Gold Institute, *Annual Exploration Survey of U.S. Gold Producers* (Washington, DC: October 1997), and from U.S. Geological Survey (USGS), "Copper in October 1997," *Mineral Industry Surveys*, 3 February 1998.
5. Williams de Broë, "Can the Collapse Continue?" research report posted at < http://www.gold.org/Gedt/Speeches/Debr9712/Debroe.htm >, December 1997. According to this London-based stock brokerage, more than 50 percent of world gold production is economically unsustainable at a price of $300 per ounce of gold.
6. John Culjak, MEG, Halifax, NS, discussion with author, 9 January 1998; Paul Bateman, Executive Vice President, Gold Institute, Washington, DC, discussion with author, 9 January 1998.
7. MEG, press release, op. cit. note 1; Steve Kral, "Conference Explores African Mining Possibilities," *Mining Engineering*, August 1997; David R. Wilburn, USGS, "Annual Review 1996: Exploration," *Mining Engineering*, May 1997.
8. Developing countries from William C. Symonds et al., "All that Glitters is Not Bre-X," *Business Week*, 19 May 1997.
9. Economic incentives from James P. Dorian, "Mining—Changing Picture in Transitional Economies," *Mining Engineering*, January 1997.
10. Inter-American Development Bank/Institute for European-Latin Relations, *Foreign Direct Investment in Latin America in the 1990s* (Madrid: 1996).
11. MEG, "Latin America Tops Exploration," op. cit. note 1; MEG, November/December 1991, op. cit. note 2.
12. Peru from Tomas C. Wexler and Luis Marcelo De-Bernadis, "Peru: Mining in the Spotlight," *Supplement to Mining Journal*, 4 April 1997, and from Alfredo C. Gurmendi, "The Mineral Industry of Peru," in USGS, *Minerals Yearbook, Volume III—Area Reports: International* (Reston, VA: 1996); Chile from Pablo Velasco, Country Specialist, USGS, discussion with author, 26 January 1998.
13. Mining as share of exports from United Nations Conference on Trade and Development, *Handbook of International Trade and Development Statistics 1995* (New York: United Nations,

1997); Argentina's reforms from Symonds et al., op. cit. note 8; Ken Warn, "Argentina and Chile Clinch Mining Accord," *Financial Times*, 30 December 1997; Pablo Velasco, "The Mineral Industry of Argentina," in USGS, *Minerals Yearbook, Volume III—Area Reports: International* (Reston, VA: 1995).

14. "Argentine Mining Progress," *Supplement to Mining Journal*, 4 April 1997.

15. MEG, "Latin America Tops Exploration," op. cit. note 1.

16. Michael Spriggs, "Financing Projects in Africa," *Supplement to Mining Journal*, 31 January 1997.

17. Asia and Pacific region does not include Australia or New Zealand; Indonesian gold production from World Gold Council, "Gold Mining in the 1990s," Gold Information Sheet No. 3 (Geneva: 6 February 1997).

18. Kumara Rachamalla, "India Offers Increased Mining Opportunities for Foreign Companies," *Mining Engineering*, February 1997; Bruce Gilley, "Lost Glitter," *Far Eastern Economic Review*, 20 November 1997; "Asian Snapshots," *Mining Magazine*, March 1997.

19. Based on MEG, "Latin America Tops Exploration," op. cit. note 1; MEG, *Strategic Report*, op. cit. note 1.

20. "South African Gold: Panned," *The Economist*, 7 February 1998; Kral, op. cit. note 7; "Significant Events, Trends, and Issues," in USGS, *Mineral Commodity Summaries* (Reston, VA: 1997); Kenneth Gooding, "SA Mining Power 'More Concentrated'," *Financial Times*, 13 November 1997.

21. John Lutley, President, Gold Institute, Washington, DC, discussion with author, 17 December 1997.

22. James Brooke, "Mining Companies Increasingly Look Abroad," *New York Times*, 13 August 1996.

23. MEG, "1996 Exploration," op. cit. note 2; Geoff Crinean, MEG, Halifax, NS, discussion with author, 14 January 1998. Each of these 279 companies spends more than $3 million a year on metals exploration.

24. MEG, op. cit. note 3.

25. Culjak, op. cit. note 6; Bateman, op. cit. note 6.

26. Chin S. Kuo, "The Mineral Industry of Cambodia," in USGS, op. cit. note 12.

27. Asian Development Bank, *Emerging Asia: Changes and Challenges* (Manila: 1997); Olivier Bomsel, "The Political Economy of Mining Rents," in John E. Tilton, ed., *Mineral Wealth and Economic Development* (Washington, DC:

Resources For the Future, 1992).

28. John E. Young, *Mining the Earth*, Worldwatch Paper 109 (Washington, DC: Worldwatch Institute, July 1992); Brooke, op. cit. note 22.

29. Young, op. cit. note 28.

30. Production from Gold Fields Minerals Services cited in "World Gold Demand up 16 pct in 1997—GFMS," *Reuters*, 8 January 1998; waste is Worldwatch estimate based on ibid., and on John E. Young, "Gold Production at Record High," in Lester R. Brown, Hal Kane, and David Malin Roodman, *Vital Signs 1994* (New York: W.W. Norton & Company, 1994). Seven hundred and twenty-five million tons of gold mining waste could fill 3.3 million 218-ton, 13-meter-long dump trucks; these could form a 41,000-kilometer line, slightly more than the circumference of Earth.

31. Young, op. cit. note 30; "Mining in Latin America," *Mining Environmental Management*, September 1994.

32. Roger Moody, "The Lure of Gold—How Golden is the Future?" Panos Media Briefing No. 19 (London: Panos Institute, May 1996).

33. Ibid.

34. "Costa Rica Halts Exploration," *Mining Journal*, 21 March 1997.

35. Peter Busowski, "OPIC Raised Environmental Concerns about Indonesian Mine Dating Back to 1989, Data Show," *International Environment Reporter*, 21 August 1996; Robert Bryce, "Aid Cancelled for Gold Project in Indonesia," *New York Times*, 2 November 1995.

36. "Forest Gold," *The Economist*, 12 July 1997; Bart Jones, "Feisty Environmental Movement Defends Ecological Paradise," *Associated Press*, 18 August 1997.

37. "'Green' Groups Cheer Venezuelan Gold Ruling," *Journal of Commerce*, 13 November 1997.

38. Busowski, op. cit. note 35.

39. Minerals Information Team, USGS, "Recycling—Metals," *Minerals Information Summary* (Reston, VA: 1996); electricity savings based on Young, op. cit. note 28, and on Energy Information Administration, U.S. Department of Energy, *Monthly Energy Review*, December 1997. A ton of recycled aluminum takes about 15,700 kilowatt-hours less electricity to produce than a ton of primary aluminum. By recycling 3.3 million tons of aluminum, the United States saved 5.2 billion kilowatt-hours—about 0.5 percent of 1996 U.S. residential electricity use.

POLLUTION CONTROL MARKETS EXPAND (pages 150–51)

1. Figures for 1992 and 1997 from Environmental Business International (EBI), cited in Office of Technology Assessment (OTA), *Industry, Technology, and the Environment: Competitive Challenges and Business Opportunities* (Washington, DC: U.S. Government Printing Office, January 1994); 1994 figure from EBI, *The Global Environmental Market and United States Environmental Industry Competitiveness* (San Diego, CA: undated).
2. OTA, op. cit. note 1.
3. Aerospace industry comparison from OTA, op. cit. note 1; arms industry from Michael Renner, "Arms Production Falls," in Lester R. Brown, Michael Renner, and Christopher Flavin, *Vital Signs 1997* (New York: W.W. Norton &. Company, 1997).
4. EBI, op. cit. note 1.
5. EBI data reported in Regional Technology Strategies, Inc., *Exports, Competitiveness, and Synergy in Appalachian Industry Clusters. A Report to the Appalachian Regional Commission* (Chapel Hill, NC: February 1997).
6. U.S. Department of Energy study, cited in OTA, op. cit. note 1.
7. Gary Gardner, "Steel Recycling Rising," in Lester R. Brown, Nicholas Lenssen, and Hal Kane, *Vital Signs 1995* (New York: W.W. Norton & Company, 1995).
8. EBI, op. cit. note 1.
9. Ibid.
10. OTA, op. cit. note 1; *Environmental Business Journal* (published by EBI), April 1996.
11. Roger H. Bezdek, *Jobs and Economic Opportunities During the 1990s in the U.S. Created by Environmental Protection* (Oakton, VA: Management Information Services, Inc., June 1997).
12. OTA, *Development Assistance, Export Promotion, and Environmental Technology—Background Paper* (Washington, DC: U.S. Government Printing Office, August 1993); EBI, op. cit. note 1.
13. EBI, op. cit. note 1.
14. Ibid.
15. OTA, op. cit. note 1; "China Plans Expensive War on Pollution," *Journal of Commerce*, 9 September 1996.
16. "First ASEAN State of the Environment Report," cited in "Southeast Asia: Lack of Financing, Trained Personnel Hinder Region's Environmental Enforcement," *International Environment Reporter*, 15 October 1997.
17. EBI, op. cit. note 1.
18. Ibid.; "Environmental Infrastructure Market Could Reach $25 Billion by 2010, Official Says," *International Environment Reporter*, 18 September 1996.
19. EBI, op. cit. note 1.
20. "Commission to be Created for Promoting Foreign, Domestic Environmental Investments," *International Environment Reporter*, 5 March 1997.
21. "Poland: Environment Spending Will Have to Triple to Meet EU Standards, According to Report," *International Environment Reporter*, 15 October 1997.
22. Ibid.; "Denmark Provides Funds to Help Combat Pollution," Foreign Broadcast Information Service, Environment, 2 April 1996.
23. OTA, op. cit. note 1.
24. Worldwatch calculation based on EBI, op. cit. note 1.
25. Bezdek, op. cit. note 11. This includes direct and indirect multiplier effects.
26. "Tendenzen der umweltschutzinduzierten Beschäftigung in Deutschland," *DIW Wochenbericht* (Deutsches Institut für Wirtschaftsforschung, Berlin, Germany), no. 9/1997.

FEMALE EDUCATION GAINING GROUND (pages 154–55)

1. UNESCO, "Education for Women and Girls: An Ongoing Struggle for Equality," Press Kit on Education for All: Achieving the Goal (Paris: undated).
2. UNICEF, "Norway Gives $24 Million For Girls Education In Africa," press release (New York: 1 November 1996).
3. UNICEF, *The Progress of Nations 1995* (New York: 1995).
4. Ibid.
5. Ibid.
6. Ibid.
7. Ibid.
8. U.N. Population Fund (UNFPA), *Population Issues: Population Briefing Kit 1997* (New York: 1997).
9. UNICEF, op. cit. note 3.
10. Population Action International (PAI), "Closing The Gender Gap: Educating Girls," wall chart

(Washington, DC: 1993).

11 UNICEF, *The State of the World's Children 1996* (New York: Oxford University Press, 1996).

12. UNESCO, op. cit. note 1.

13. Ibid.

14. Barbara S. Mensch and Cynthia B. Lloyd, *Gender Differences in the Schooling Experiences of Adolescents in Low-Income Countries*, Working Paper No. 95 (New York: Population Council, 1997).

15. UNFPA, op. cit. note 8.

16. Sunita Kishor and Katherine Neitzel, *The Status of Women: Indicators for Twenty-Five Countries*, Demographic and Health Surveys Comparative Studies No. 21 (Calverton, MD: Macro International, December 1996).

17. UNICEF, *The Progress of Nations 1997* (New York: 1997).

18. Organisation for Economic Co-operation and Development (OECD), *Education at a Glance: OECD Indicators, 1997* (Paris: 1997).

19. Ibid.; U.S. Bureau of the Census, *Statistical Abstract of the United States: 1997* (Washington, DC: 1997).

20. OECD, op. cit. note 18.

21. Ibid.; American Veterinary Medical Association (AVMA), "Enrollment in Vet Medical Colleges, 1995-1996 and 1996-1997," *Journal of the American Veterinary Medical Association*, 15 November 1997; Nancy Clemente, AVMA, Center for Information Management, discussion with Brian Halweil of Worldwatch, 3 March 1998.

22. OECD, op. cit. note 18.

23. Ibid.

24. UNICEF, op. cit. note 11; UNFPA, op. cit. note 8.

25. PAI, op. cit. note 10.

26. UNICEF, op. cit. note 2.

27. UNICEF, op. cit. note 3.

28. UNICEF, op. cit. note 17.

29. Ibid.

30. Ibid.

31. UNICEF, op. cit. note 3.

32. Asian Development Bank, "ADB Approves US$45 Million Soft Loan to Pakistan for Primary Education For Girls," ADB news release no. 89 (Manila: 15 August 1996).

33. Ibid.

34. UNICEF, op. cit. note 2; UNESCO, op. cit. note 1.

SANITATION ACCESS LAGGING
(pages 156–57)

1. World Health Organization (WHO), Water Supply and Sanitation Collaborative Council, and UNICEF, *Water Supply and Sanitation Sector Monitoring Report, 1996* (New York: WHO, 1996). Data are based on a survey of 84 of 130 developing countries, not including Eastern Europe or Central Asia.

2. UNICEF, *Progress of Nations* (New York: 1995).

3. WHO, Water Supply and Sanitation Collaborative Council, and UNICEF, op. cit. note 1.

4. UNICEF, op. cit. note 2.

5. WHO, "Water and Sanitation," Fact Sheet No. 112 (Geneva: November 1996).

6. Ibid.

7. Barbara Crossette, "Unicef Tells How Half the World Lacks Even Basic Sanitation," *New York Times*, 23 July 1997.

8. Mark Hereward, Project Officer, Statistics and Monitoring, UNICEF, New York, e-mail to author, 21 November 1997.

9. WHO, Water Supply and Sanitation Collaborative Council, and UNICEF, op. cit. note 1.

10. K.M.A. Aziz et al., *Water Supply, Sanitation, and Hygiene Education: Report of a Health Impact Study in Mirzapur, Bangladesh*, Water and Sanitation Report Series Number 1, UNDP–World Bank Water and Sanitation Program (Washington, DC: World Bank, 1990).

11. WHO, op. cit. note 5.

12. UNICEF, op. cit. note 2.

13. WHO, Water Supply and Sanitation Collaborative Council, and UNICEF, op. cit. note 1.

14. Kenneth J. Cooper, "Battling Waterborne Ills In a Sea of 950 Million," *Washington Post*, 17 February 1997.

15. UNICEF, op. cit. note 2.

16. R.I. Glass, M. Libel, and A.D. Brandling-Bennett, "Epidemic Cholera in the Americas," *Science*, 12 June 1992.

17. WHO, Water Supply and Sanitation Collaborative Council, and UNICEF, op. cit. note 1.

18. Ibid.

19. Per capita cost from WHO, op. cit. note 5; real GDP from U.N. Development Programme, *Human Development Report 1996* (New York: Oxford University Press, 1996).

20. UNICEF, op. cit. note 2.

21. Ibid.

22. Crossette, op. cit. note 7.

23. Peter H. Gleick, ed., *Water in Crisis: Guide to the*

World's Fresh Water Resources (New York: Oxford University Press, 1993).

24. European access from ibid.; country data from "EBJ Numbers," *Environment Business Journal*, August 1995.

25. Gleick, op. cit. note 22; John Briscoe and Mike Garn, "Financing Agenda 21: Freshwater," prepared for the United Nations Commission on Sustainable Development (Washington, DC: World Bank, February 1994).

26. Grupo de Tecnologia Alternativa (GTA), "The SIRDO from Mexico 1979–1992" (Mexico City: GTA, undated); Josefina Mena Abraham, GTA, Mexico City, e-mail to author, 16 June 1997; Sidonie Chiapetta, National Wildlife Federation, e-mail to author, 18 June 1997.

27. WHO, Water Supply and Sanitation Collaborative Council, and UNICEF, op. cit. note 1.

28. Ibid.

29. Ibid.

SMALL ARMS PROLIFERATE
(pages 160–61)

1. Michael Klare, "Stemming the Lethal Trade in Small Arms and Light Weapons," *Issues in Science and Technology*, fall 1995.

2. Rachel Brett and Margaret McCallin, *Children: The Invisible Soldiers* (Växjö, Sweden: Rädda Barnen [Swedish Save the Children], 1996).

3. Natalie J. Goldring, "Bridging the Gap: Light and Major Conventional Weapons in Recent Conflicts," paper prepared for the annual meeting of the International Studies Association, Toronto, Ontario, 18–21 March 1997.

4. Christopher Smith, "Light Weapons and the International Arms Trade," in Christopher Smith, Peter Batchelor, and Jakkie Potgieter, *Small Arms Management and Peacekeeping in Southern Africa*, United Nations Institute for Disarmament Research (UNIDIR), Disarmament and Conflict Resolution Project (New York: United Nations, 1996); Swadesh Rana, *Small Arms and Intra-State Conflicts*, UNIDIR Research Paper No. 34 (New York: UNIDIR, 1995).

5. Jasjit Singh, "Introduction," in Jasjit Singh, ed., *Light Weapons and International Security* (Delhi: Indian Pugwash Society and British American Security Information Council, December 1995).

6. Bonn International Conversion Center (BICC), *Conversion Survey 1997: Global Disarmament and Disposal of Surplus Arms* (New York: Oxford University Press, 1997).

7. United Nations General Assembly, "Report of the Panel of Governmental Experts on Small Arms," A/52/298 (New York: 27 August 1997).

8. Ibid.

9. Prashant Dikshit, "Internal Conflict and Role of Light Weapons," in Singh, op. cit. note 5; United Nations, op. cit. note 7; "Counterfeit Weapons Flood World Arms Market," *The Press* (Christchurch, New Zealand), 3 July 1997.

10. Michael Renner, "'Small Arms' Are Easy to Get, Hard to Control," *Christian Science Monitor*, 2 December 1997.

11. BICC, op. cit. note 6.

12. John Mintz, "Amendment Could Bring Flood of Guns Into U.S.," *Washington Post*, 31 July 1997.

13. Michael T. Klare, "Light Weapons Diffusion and Global Violence in the Post-Cold War Era," in Singh, op. cit. note 5.

14. Goldring, op. cit. note 3.

15. Michael Renner, *Small Arms, Big Impact: The Next Challenge of Disarmament*, Worldwatch Paper 137 (Washington, DC: Worldwatch Institute, October 1997).

16. Jacklyn Cock, "A Sociological Account of Light Weapons Proliferation in Southern Africa," in Singh, op. cit. note 5.

17. Salvadorans killed since 1992 from Michael Klare and David Andersen, *A Scourge of Guns: The Diffusion of Small Arms and Light Weapons in Latin America* (Washington, DC: Arms Sales Monitoring Project, Federation of American Scientists, August 1996); people killed during the war from Ruth Leger Sivard, *World Military and Social Expenditures 1996* (Washington, DC: World Priorities, 1996).

18. Larry Rohter, "In U.S. Deportation Policy, A Pandora's Box," *New York Times*, 10 August 1997.

19. One of the earliest attempts to define the issue was Jeffrey Boutwell, Michael T. Klare, and Laura W. Reed, eds., *Lethal Commerce: The Global Trade in Small Arms and Light Weapons* (Cambridge, MA: Committee on International Security Studies, American Academy of Arts and Sciences, 1995).

20. Raymond Bonner, "After Land-Mine Triumph, A Crusade Against Small Arms," *New York Times*, 7 January 1998.

THE VITAL SIGNS SERIES

Some topics are included each year in Vital Signs; others, particularly those in Part Two, are included only in certain years. The following is a list of the topics covered thus far in the series, with the year or years each appeared indicated in parentheses.

Part One: KEY INDICATORS

FOOD TRENDS
Grain Production (1992–98)
Soybean Harvest (1992–98)
Meat Production (1992–98)
Fish Catch (1992–98)
Grain Stocks (1992–98)
Grain Used for Feed (1993, 1995–96)
Aquaculture (1994, 1996, 1998)

AGRICULTURAL RESOURCE
TRENDS
Grain Area (1992–93, 1996–97)
Fertilizer Use (1992–98)
Irrigation (1992, 1994, 1996–98)
Grain Yield (1994–95, 1998)

ENERGY TRENDS
Oil Production (1992–96, 1998)
Wind Power (1992–98)
Nuclear Power (1992–98)

Solar Cell Production (1992–98)
Natural Gas (1992, 1994–96, 1998)
Energy Efficiency (1992)
Geothermal Power (1993, 1997)
Coal Use (1993–96, 1998)
Hydroelectric Power (1993, 1998)
Carbon Use (1993)
Compact Fluorescent Lamps (1993–96, 1998)
Fossil Fuel Use (1997)

ATMOSPHERIC TRENDS
CFC Production (1992–96, 1998)
Global Temperature (1992–98)
Carbon Emissions (1992, 1994–98)

ECONOMIC TRENDS
Global Economy (1992–98)
Third World Debt (1992, 1993, 1994, 1995)
International Trade (1993–96, 1998)
Steel Production (1993, 1996)

Paper Production (1993, 1994, 1998)
Advertising Expenditures (1993)
Roundwood Production (1994, 1997)
Gold Production (1994)
Television Use (1995)
Storm Damages (1997–98)
U.N. Finances (1998)

TRANSPORTATION TRENDS
Bicycle Production (1992–98)
Automobile Production (1992–98)
Air Travel (1993)
Motorbike Production (1998)

ENVIRONMENTAL TRENDS
Pesticide Resistance (1994)
Sulfur and Nitrogen Emissions (1994–97)
Environmental Treaties (1995)
Nuclear Waste (1995)

COMMUNICATIONS TRENDS
Satellite Launches (1998)
Telephones (1998)
Internet Use (1998)

SOCIAL TRENDS
Population Growth (1992–98)
Cigarette Production (1992–98)
Infant Mortality (1992)
Child Mortality (1993)
Refugees (1993–98)
HIV/AIDS Incidence (1994–98)
Immunizations (1994)
Urbanization (1995–96, 1998)

MILITARY TRENDS
Military Expenditures (1992, 1998)
Nuclear Arsenal (1992, 1994–96)
Arms Trade (1994)
Peace Expenditures (1994–98)
Wars (1995, 1998)
Armed Forces (1997)

Part Two: SPECIAL FEATURES

ENVIRONMENTAL FEATURES
Bird Populations (1992, 1994)
Forest Loss (1992, 1994–98)
Soil Erosion (1992, 1995)
Steel Recycling (1992, 1995)
Nuclear Waste (1992)
Water Scarcity (1993)
Forest Damage from Air Pollution (1993)
Marine Mammal Populations (1993)
Paper Recycling (1994, 1998)
Coral Reefs (1994)

Energy Productivity (1994)
Amphibian Populations (1995)
Large Dams (1995)
Water Tables (1995)
Lead in Gasoline (1995)
Aquatic Species (1996)
Environmental Treaties (1996)
Ecosystem Conversion (1997)
Primate Populations (1997)
Ozone Layer (1997)
Subsidies for Environmental Harm (1997)

Tree Plantations (1998)
Vertebrate Loss (1998)
Organic Waste Reuse (1998)
Nitrogen Fixation (1998)
Acid Rain (1998)

AGRICULTURAL FEATURES
  Pesticide Control (1996)
  Organic Farming (1996)

ECONOMIC FEATURES
  Wheat/Oil Exchange Rate (1992, 1993)
  Trade in Arms and Grain (1992)
  Cigarette Taxes (1993, 1995, 1998)
  U.S. Seafood Prices (1993)
  Environmental Taxes (1996, 1998)
  Private Finance in Third World (1996, 1998)
  Storm Damages (1996)
  Aid for Sustainable Development (1997)
  Food Aid (1997)
  R&D Expenditures (1997)
  Urban Agriculture (1997)
  Electric Cars (1997)
  Arms Production (1997)
  Fossil Fuel Subsidies (1998)
  Metals Exploration (1998)
  Pollution Control Markets (1998)

SOCIAL FEATURES
  Income Distribution (1992, 1995, 1997)
  Maternal Mortality (1992, 1997)
  Access to Family Planning (1992)
  Literacy (1993)
  Fertility Rates (1993)
  Traffic Accidents (1994)
  Life Expectancy (1994)
  Women in Politics (1995)

Computer Production and Use (1995)
Breast and Prostate Cancer (1995)
Homelessness (1995)
Hunger (1995)
Access to Safe Water (1995)
Infectious Diseases (1996)
Landmines (1996)
Violence Against Women (1996)
Voter Turnouts (1996)
Aging Populations (1997)
Noncommunicable Diseases (1997)
Extinction of Languages (1997)
Female Education (1998)
Sanitation (1998)

MILITARY FEATURES
  Nuclear Arsenal (1993)
  U.N. Peacekeeping (1993)
  Small Arms (1998)

Now you can import all the tables and graphs from *Vital Signs 1998* and other recent Worldwatch publications into your spreadsheet program, presentation software, or word processor with the . . .

1998 WORLDWATCH DATABASE DISK

The Worldwatch Database Disk Subscription gives you current data from all Worldwatch publications, including the *State of the World* and *Vital Signs* annual book series, WORLD WATCH magazine, Worldwatch Papers, and Environmental Alert Series books.

Your subscription includes: a disk (IBM or Macintosh) with all current data and a FREE copy of *Vital Signs 1998*. In January 1999, you will receive a six-month update of the disk with a FREE copy of *State of the World 1999*. This disk will include updates of all long-term data series in *State of the World*, as well as new data from WORLD WATCH and all new Worldwatch Papers.

The disk covers trends from mid-century onward . . . much not readily available from other sources. All data are sourced, and are accurate, comprehensive, and up-to-date. Researchers, students, professors, reporters, and policy analysts use the disk to—

- ◆ *Design graphs to illustrate newspaper stories and policy reports*
- ◆ *Prepare overhead projections on trends for policy briefings, board meetings, and corporate presentations*
- ◆ *Create specific "what if?" scenarios for energy, population, or grain supply*
- ◆ *Overlay one trend onto another, to see how they relate*
- ◆ *Track long-term trends and discern new ones*

To order the 1998 Worldwatch Database Disk for just $89 plus $4 shipping and handling:
Phone: (202) 452-1999 (credit cards accepted: Mastercard, Visa or American Express)
Fax: (202) 296-7365; E-mail: wwpub@worldwatch.org; Website: http://www.worldwatch.org
Or send your request to:

1776 Massachusetts Ave., NW
Washington, DC 20036

The global trends documented in *Vital Signs 1998*—from spreading water scarcity to big increases in wind power—will play a large part in determining the quality of our lives and our children's lives in the next decade.

This seventh volume in the series from the Worldwatch Institute shows in graphic form the key trends that often escape the attention of the news media and world leaders—and are often ignored by economic experts as they plan for the future. Written by the staff of the award-winning Worldwatch Institute, this book lets readers track key indicators that show social, economic, and environmental progress, or the lack of it. This authoritative data has been distilled from thousands of documents obtained from government, industry, scientists, and international organizations into "vital signs" of our times.

Each year, *Vital Signs* presents emerging trends in more than one hundred clear and compelling charts, tables, and graphs, accompanied by concise, thoughtful analysis. Among the findings:

- 1997 was the hottest year since record keeping began in 1866.
- The amount of carbon dioxide in the atmosphere reached its highest point in 160,000 years.
- China accounts for half of world pork production and consumption.
- The Internet has more than doubled in size each year in the last decade, but more than 90 percent of Internet users are in industrial countries.
- Nearly 6 million people contracted HIV—the virus that causes AIDS—in 1997, a new record. More than 40 percent of these new infections occurred in women.
- Every week more than one million people are added to the world's urban centers.
- The amount of private capital flowing into the "emerging markets" of the developing world exploded in the early 1990s.

Whether you read *Vital Signs* for a preview of the next decade or to verify a particular trend, you will find it comprehensive and authoritative. *Vital Signs* is an excellent companion to Worldwatch's annual *State of the World*.

W. W. NORTON
NEW YORK · LONDON

ISBN 0-393-31762-5

9 780393 317626

$12.00 USA $16.99 CAN.

http://www.wwnorton.com